SOCIAL GAMES

FOR

RECREATION

EVELYNE BORST

and

ELMER D. MITCHELL

University of Michigan

Second Edition

THE RONALD PRESS COMPANY · **NEW YORK**

Library of Congress Catalog Card Number: 59-6110

PREFACE

With its streamlined presentation and its workable organization, this book should be helpful to any person planning a program of social games. It can be used either as a textbook for recreation and physical education students pursuing courses in social and active games, or as a reference book for recreation and playground directors, camp counselors, parents, teachers, scout and cub leaders, church workers, boys' and girls' club leaders, and social group workers.

The descriptions of the games note the materials that must be secured and prepared prior to conducting the game, the basic information for starting the game, and the rules and methods for playing it. The games are grouped according to their patterns or objectives. Each chapter opens with alphabetized lists of games according to type; a leader can readily determine by these lists what games he wants to use, and also save himself time and effort in planning. He will find games which appeal to both young people and adults, and games which are appropriate to use for either those who have had experience in playing social games or those who have not. Many of the games require little or no equipment and supplies.

Part I presents social games for indoors. To set the stage, the first chapter includes techniques for swinging into action; a list of steps essential to preparing and conducting games successfully; and some easy-to-follow illustrations and descriptions of starting formations, the maneuvering of groups from one formation to another, and the forming of teams.

The remaining chapters in Part I present various types of indoor games. The chapter on Defrosters describes games which help to thaw the players by giving everyone something to do to minimize self-consciousness and by affording ways for players to find partners and meet other members of the group in a friendly social setting.

The games in the chapter on Socializers further assist in warming the atmosphere. Everyone will enjoy playing these games which can be used with any group and for any occasion.

Games with a nature theme are gathered together in the chapter on Indoor Naturettes. Through these games a leader may increase a player's appreciation of the outdoors by stimulating interest in nature indoors.

Association, guessing, and memory form the core around which the patterns for the games in the chapter on Brain Teasers are fashioned. These games afford pleasant mental activity and appeal to adults as well as to youths.

The games in the chapter on Sense Alerters, in addition to being fun to play, offer the players opportunities to evaluate their degree of awareness to sensory impressions.

With the players' senses sharpened, the games in the chapter on Mystifiers appeal to the Sherlock Holmes instinct for detecting clues and discovering how tricks are performed. In these games a bit of intrigue between the performer of the trick and an accomplice keeps the observer's wits on edge. The number tricksters give the players some revealing answers about their age, month of birth, and the amount of change they have with them.

The chapter on Creative Fun Makers offers games providing an outlet for self-expression. The player can put his imagination into action through such means as pantomime, dramatization, group-tale, and creative drawing and costuming. These games are a fun-way to creative expression; they do not demand artistic perfection.

Part II contains detailed helps for arranging and conducting parties. Ten special theme parties, with appropriate games, are described. In addition, Part II delineates numerous games for rotative parties and explains how to run off a party of this type.

Part III is devoted to outdoor social games. One chapter shows how to plan and direct a program of games to arouse the enthusiasm of picnickers; included are hide-and-seek games, contests, relays, and races. In another chapter, the objective of the games is to get individuals to use their eyes and ears outdoors—an entrée to an appreciation of the beauty and wonders of nature by actual experience. Through playing these games the participants learn to identify many birds, animals, trees, and flowers.

In general, the book emphasizes the social, mental, and creative aspects of games. Its ultimate aim is to help the leader achieve his

goal of getting everyone into activities which afford fun, companion-
ship, and relaxation.

The authors wish to express their gratitude to Edith E. Brown,
who undertook much of the research in connection with the games
for the theme parties.

Evelyne Borst
Elmer D. Mitchell

January, 1959

CONTENTS

Part I

INDOOR SOCIAL GAMES

Part II

PARTIES

Part III

OUTDOOR SOCIAL GAMES

PART I

INDOOR SOCIAL GAMES

INDOOR SOCIAL GAMES

CHAPTER 1

SWINGING

INTO ACTION

While the leader of social games knows that everyone possesses social impulses which motivate an individual's desire to be with others, he is aware, also, that getting every member of a group to participate and find the experience enriching is a major assignment.

As individuals in a group vary in Intelligence Quotients (IQ's), they, likewise, differ in their Social Quotients (SQ's). The SQ of an individual is of utmost importance to the leader of social games, for it expresses the ratio of a person's social experience (SE) to his chronological age (CA): $SQ = SE/CA$. It is the gradation in SQ's among the members of the group that affects their desires to participate in social activities. Depending upon a person's previous experience, his opportunities to develop social attitudes, and his adjustability to others, he may participate readily, hesitantly, or grudgingly.

It is this combination of individuals with varying SQ's that the leader of social recreation inherits when he directs a program of games. The leader's responsibility is to create a friendly atmosphere, so that everyone wants to participate and will find the experience enjoyable.

Starting, guiding, and stopping are three essential techniques which the driver of an automobile needs to master. Surprisingly, starting, guiding, and stopping are three techniques essential also for successful leadership in social recreation. Good acceleration into the activities, skillfully guiding the players from one activity

3

to another, and halting the games while everyone still enjoys them, are techniques which the leader of social recreation needs to know and employ.

ESSENTIALS FOR LEADERSHIP

In planning, starting, and guiding group activities, the leader of social games must be aware of the essentials required to conduct the program successfully. A leader should:

1. Learn to know groups of games instead of individual ones, through their objects or patterns, to save considerable planning time.

2. Select appropriate activities. He should consider the group's interests and social experience, the players' attire, the play area, the availability of equipment or supplies, and the objective that is to be achieved through playing the games.

3. Appoint committees or assistants whenever they are needed.

4. Discuss the plans with the committees or assistants, obtain suggestions and comments, and assure that each individual understands his responsibilities.

5. Understand the rules of the games before presenting them.

6. Assemble and check the supplies and equipment needed to play the games. In games requiring players to write and in situations where tables are not available for a writing surface, he should provide a magazine, sheet of cardboard, or card for each person. All equipment should be ready, but not kept where the members of the group can handle them prior to the games.

7. Prepare in advance any material that needs to be used in playing the games: lists, diagrams, or other items. When duplicate lists are needed for playing the game, a copy should be made on a blackboard or large sheet of paper so that the lists are clearly legible to all players. Individual copies for the players should be made in advance. Or the players can prepare their own lists if the leader dictates them.

8. Have the starting and goal lines drawn for relays or other activities requiring markings. If it is not possible to draw them in advance, the leader should ask someone from the group to draw them. The leader should not attempt to draw lines, control the group, and teach a game at the same time.

9. Use some signal to secure the players' attention and to start and halt activities when necessary. Such signals are a raised hand, a chord on a piano, a whistle, or a verbal direction.

10. Get the players into the basic formation or group needed to start the game.

11. State simply and clearly the directions for playing a game.

12. Use illustrations when they are helpful in teaching a game.

13. Ask the members of a committee, assistants, or persons in the group to demonstrate how a game is played when this will help teach the activity. The leader should be sure that all participants know how to play a game, and it may be necessary at times to practice prior to the demonstration.

14. Ask for questions to clear up any uncertainty about playing the game.

15. After the game is started, keep suggestions regarding playing procedure at a minimum.

16. Move from the first activity to the next one while the players still enjoy playing the first game. However, the leader should not hurry from one game to another before the players get a chance to understand and enjoy the first game.

17. Have flexibility in the program. More activities should be planned than are needed, so that there are substitutes ready to use. The leader should be prepared to adjust and insert a substitute activity if the one planned seems inappropriate.

18. Bring the program to a close while enjoyment is at a peak.

PSYCHOLOGICAL EFFECTS OF GAME FORMATIONS

The leader's ability to maneuver the players skillfully into formations and groups is especially important. In his use of formations he must also be aware that while formations are the framework for playing games, they have psychological effects on the players. Some of these effects are as follows.

Standing or sitting in a *circle* has a unifying effect on the players by giving them a feeling of belonging and being a part of the group. The circle allows players to see the other members of the group and to gain a more friendly spirit toward one another. Being with others in a circle gives a player assurance and imparts a feeling of shared interest and enthusiasm. In addition the circle is a defrosting device, for it helps players to forget themselves as they participate in the activities with the other members of the group.

The action of *assembling, scattering,* and *reassembling* has a defrosting effect, for it minimizes self-consciousness by keeping everyone busy. Players assemble in a group to obtain instructions for proceeding with the game and securing necessary supplies. Then everyone is off hunting objects hidden before the game, securing other players' signatures, seeking names of items pinned on the backs of the players' clothing, or procuring other designated items.

Through their searching the players meet the other members of the group readily and easily by having to approach them as they seek designated items or persons. When the leader reassembles the group to check the players' findings, he sees the players in a much more friendly mood.

Standing in a *line* creates in individuals a feeling of "action," for the line frequently is the springboard for activity. For example, the players line up, count off, and then "go" to a particular area for action. The line is, also, a symbol of racing. With the players toeing a line and awaiting the "go" signal, a competitive spirit is aroused. Even in games in which teams form two lines and face one another or in the hollow square formation consisting of four lines, the members of each team are geared to "go" whether the game requires physical or mental exertion.

Standing in *files*, one player behind the other, symbolizes relays—group competition. In most individuals it arouses the desire to have their team excel, to be first to complete a designated activity.

Having an understanding of the psychological effects of various formations on the players will be helpful to the leader of social recreation in using the following illustrations and descriptions of the basic formations for playing games, the ways of achieving formations, and the techniques for forming groups. The leader will observe that the three basic formations from which most of the other formations originate are the line, file, and circle.

Techniques for moving into basic formations, changing directions in circle formations, and forming teams or groups of players are illustrated and described on the following pages.

Techniques for Maneuvering Groups

I. FORMING LINES, FILES, AND CIRCLES

A. Forming one line

GOAL

Or, ask players to stand side by side behind a starting line, facing a goal.

1. From a scattered group.

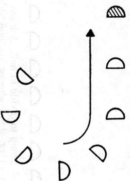

Ask players to stand side by side in a line, facing leader.

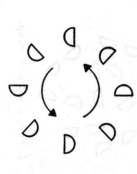

2. From a single circle, players moving counterclockwise.

Designate one person to break from circle and lead group to one side of area.

When all players are in single file behind designated person, ask them to make a quarter turn to their left, facing leader.

7

B. Forming two lines

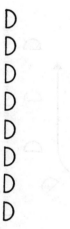

1. From a scattered group.

Ask group to divide in half. Ask one half to sit or stand abreast on one side of area; ask other half to sit or stand abreast on other side facing the first group.

2. From a line. Ask players to count off by twos. Then designate two persons to head up files.

2 1 2 1 2 1 2 1 2 1 Etc.

Ask players to line up in single files behind designated (head) person.

1's   2's

Ask each head to lead his file to one side of area. The players now sit or stand abreast, one line facing the other.

8

C. Forming a hollow square

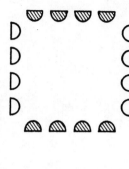

Ask each head to lead his file to a designated side of a square formed by drawn lines or by chairs.

The players at each side now face their opposites.

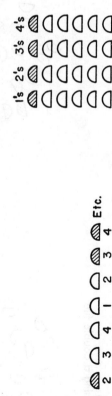

Ask players to line up in single files behind designated (head) persons.

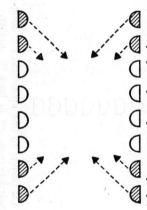

Ask the required number of players—in this case, two—at each end of both lines to leave their lines and form the sides of a square.

1. From one line. Ask players to count off by fours. Then designate four persons to head up files.

2. From two lines.

D. Forming a single file

1. From a scattered group. Designate one person to head up the file.

Ask players to line up behind the designated person, one in back of another.

E. Forming a double file

1. From a scattered group, by choosing partners.

Ask the players to choose partners. Designate one couple to head up the file.

Request the couples to line up behind the designated couple, one in back of another.

Ask the first player in each file to lead the players to the middle of the room. As boy meets girl the two become partners and proceed down the middle of the room until each person has a partner.

Ask the boys to stand on one side of the room, the girls on the opposite side, in single files.

2. From a scattered group, by separating boys and girls.

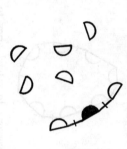

Ask everyone to join hands and form circle, all facing center.

Extend arms to clasp hands of two nearest players.

F. Forming a single circle

1. From a scattered group, with leader initiating action.

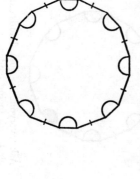

Ask the group, hands still clasped, to make a circle, all facing center.

Ask everyone to extend arms to clasp hands of nearest players.

2. From a scattered group, with players initiating action.

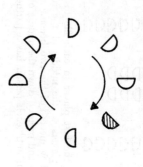

Group, moving clockwise (or counter-clockwise), completes circle when starter comes up behind player who was last in line.

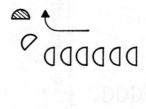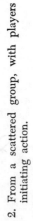

Ask starter to move to his right (or left) to circumscribe a circle around area. Ask players to follow starter.

3. From a file. Designate player at head of file as starter.

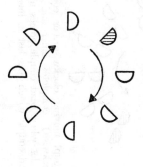

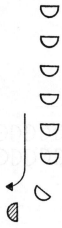

4. From a line, players facing the leader. Ask players to form a file by making quarter turns to their left (or right). Designate first player as starter.

Ask starter to move to his right (or left) to circumscribe a circle in clockwise (or counterclockwise) direction. Ask players to follow starter.

Group, moving clockwise (or counter-clockwise), completes circle when starter comes up behind player who was last in line.

G. Forming a double circle

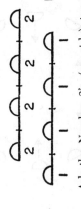

1. From a line, players facing leader. Ask players to count off, beginning with player at leader's right, by twos (or arrange line with boys and girls alternating).

Ask the Number 2's (or girls) to step forward and join hands. Then ask the Number 1's (or boys) to join hands.

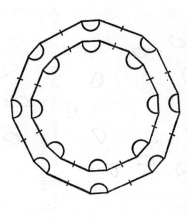

Ask the end players of the Number 2's (or girls) to move toward each other to form inner circle, and the end players of the Number 1's (or boys) to move around them to form outer circle. The Number 1's will have to extend arms a greater distance.

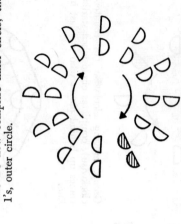

The 2's now comprise inner circle; the 1's, outer circle.

Group, moving clockwise (or counter-clockwise), completes inner and outer circles when head couple comes up behind couple which was last in line.

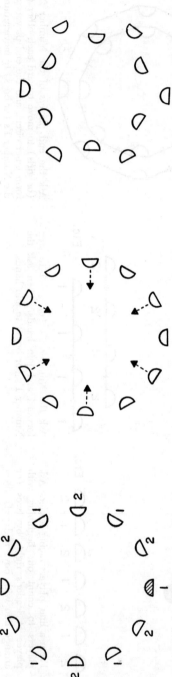

2. From a single circle, players facing center. Beginning with designated person, ask players to count off by twos (or arrange circle with boys and girls alternating).

Ask Number 2's (or girls) to take two steps forward. The Number 1's (or boys) remain in place.

3. From a double file. Designate persons at head of file as starters (head couple).

Ask head couple to move to their right (or left) to circumscribe circle around area. Ask couples to follow head couple.

14

II. CHANGING DIRECTION IN CIRCLES

A. In a single circle

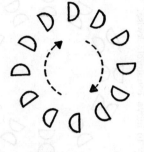

1. From facing center, to face to proceed clockwise.

Ask each player to make quarter turn to his *left*.

Players, now one behind another, are ready to move in clockwise direction.

2. From facing center, to face to proceed counterclockwise.

Ask each player to make a quarter turn to his *right*.

Players, now one behind another, are ready to move in counterclockwise direction.

B. In a double circle

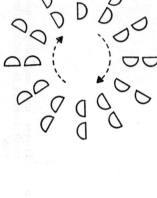

Couples are now one behind another, ready to move in clockwise direction.

Couples are then one behind another, ready to move counterclockwise.

Players in inner circle are now facing partners in outer circle.

Ask players to make quarter turn to their *left* so that each is beside a partner.

Ask players to make quarter turn to their *right* so that each is beside a partner.

Ask players in inner circle to turn around (about face).

1. From facing center, to face to proceed *clockwise*.

2. From facing center, to face to proceed *counterclockwise*.

3. From facing center, to face partner.

16

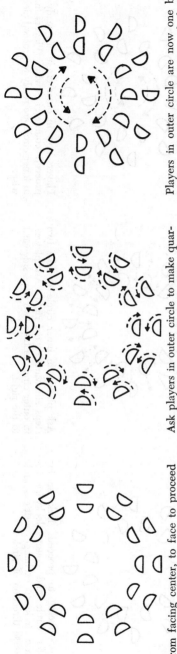

Players in outer circle are now one behind another, ready to move in clockwise direction. Players in inner circle are ready to proceed counterclockwise.

Players are now facing center. Each player in outer circle is directly behind a player in inner circle.

Ask players in outer circle to make quarter turn to their *left*. Ask players in inner circle to make quarter turn to their *right*.

Ask players to make a quarter turn to their *right*.

4. From facing center, to face to proceed clockwise in outer circle, counterclockwise in inner circle.

5. From facing to proceed *clockwise*, to face center.

17

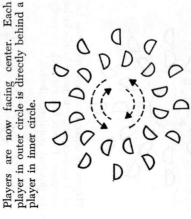

Players are now facing center. Each player in outer circle is directly behind a player in inner circle.

Players now in outer circle are ready to proceed counterclockwise. Players now in inner circle are ready to proceed clockwise.

Ask players to make a quarter turn to their *left*.

Ask players in inner circle to take two steps sideward to the right. Ask players in outer circle to take two steps sideward to the right.

6. From facing to proceed *counterclockwise*, to face center.

7. From facing to proceed clockwise in outer circle and counterclockwise in inner circle, to exchange positions and reverse direction of circles.

III. ASSEMBLING, SCATTERING, REASSEMBLING

Assembling: Assemble the individual players (or groups of players) in a particular area. Give them instructions and supplies if needed.

Scattering: Ask the individual players (or groups of players) to move anywhere or to a designated area to secure specified items or information, find persons meeting certain descriptions, or perform a specified activity.

Reassembling: At the end of an allotted time, reassemble the players (or groups of players) to obtain the results of their findings.

Or, with groups, have the groups remain in their designated areas, with players facing the leader. Ask each recorder to read his group's answers and determine the winning group. Or have each group in turn present its skit while the other groups attempt to guess the meaning.

IV. FORMING TEAMS

A. For any type of game

1. By players standing in a line.

Ask players to count off, beginning with designated player at either end. For two teams, ask players to count by twos. The Number 1's then comprise Team 1; the Number 2's, Team 2.

For three teams, ask players to count by threes. The Number 1's then comprise Team 1; the Number 2's, Team 2; the Number 3's, Team 3.

2. By players standing in a single circle, facing center.

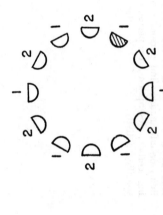

Ask players to count off by twos, beginning with designated player.

Ask Number 2's to turn around (about face). Ask Number 1's to remain facing center. The Number 1's then comprise Team 1; the Number 2's, Team 2.

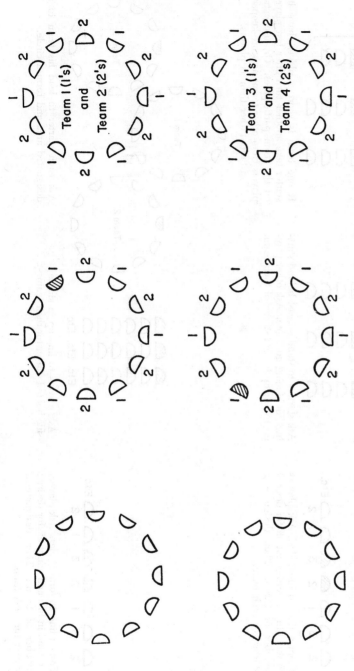

Team 1 (1's)
and
Team 2 (2's)

Team 3 (1's)
and
Team 4 (2's)

Ask Number 2's in each circle to turn around (about face). Ask Number 1's to remain facing center. The Number 1's comprise Teams 1 and 3; the Number 2's, Teams 2 and 4.

Ask players in each circle to count off by twos, beginning with designated player.

3. By players standing in two single circles, facing center.

21

B. For standard relays

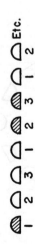

1. From a line, to form files. Ask players to stand in line and count off for desired number of teams. Then designate a starter for each team.

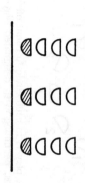

Ask starters to stand abreast behind starting line, facing goal line. Ask other players to line up behind starter of their team.

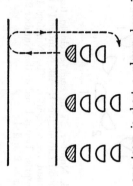

If one team is short a player, have its starter take another turn after last player on the team participates. *Or,* use extra players from other teams as score-keepers or assistants rather than as players.

2. From a line, to form circles. Ask players to stand in line and count off for desired number of teams. Then designate a starter for each team.

Ask players to line up in single file behind starter for their team.

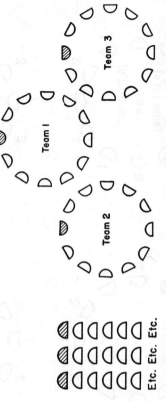

Ask each starter to lead his team to a designated area and form a circle.

C. For shuttle relays

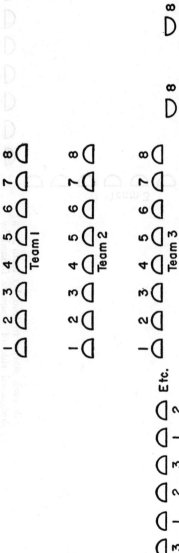

Team 1
1 2 3 4 5 6 7 8

Team 2
1 2 3 4 5 6 7 8

Team 3
1 2 3 4 5 6 7 8

Etc.
1 2 3

1. From a line. Ask players to stand in line and count off for desired number of teams.

Ask each team to stand in line and count off consecutively.

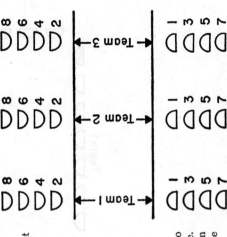

8 6 4 2 ← Team 3 → 1 3 5 7

8 6 4 2 ← Team 2 → 1 3 5 7

8 6 4 2 ← Team 1 → 1 3 5 7

Ask odd-number players on each team to stand in single file behind one goal line. Ask even-number players on each team to stand in single file behind the opposite goal line.

23

D. Four teams

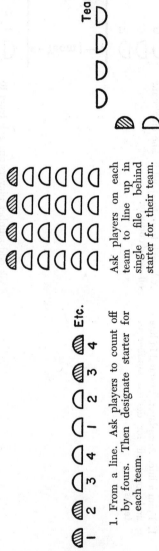

1. From a line. Ask players to count off by fours. Then designate starter for each team.

Ask players on each team to line up in single file behind starter for their team.

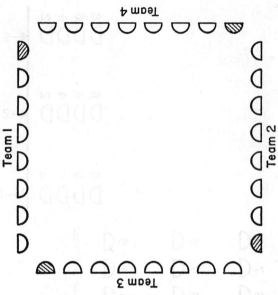

Ask each starter to lead his team to a designated side of a square formed by drawn lines or by chairs.

24

V. FORMING GROUPS BY MATCHING

A. Matching colors

Determine how many groups are desired and how many persons will comprise a group. Prepare as many sets of different-colored 3 × 5-inch slips of paper as there are groups—for example, for four groups of eight persons, prepare four different-colored sets of slips, eight to each set.

Issue a colored slip to everyone. Ask each person to seek all the players holding the same color as he. When the individuals meet, they form a group.

B. Matching numbers

Determine how many groups are desired and how many persons will comprise a group. Select a number to designate each group. Label as many sets of 3 × 5-inch slips of paper as there are groups—for example, for five groups of six persons, label six slips of 1's for Group 1, six 2's for Group 2, six 3's for Group 3, and so on.

Issue a number slip to each player. Ask each person to seek all of the players holding the same number as he. When the individuals meet, they form a group.

C. Matching names

Determine how many groups are desired and how many persons will comprise a group. Choose a category for each group (literature, art, drama, dance, moving pictures, radio, television). Prepare as many sets of slips bearing the names of well-known individuals in the selected category or categories as there are groups. For example, for four groups of five persons and using two categories, music and literature, write *Chopin* on one set of five slips, *Brahms* on another set, *Hawthorne* on a third set, and *Dickens* on a fourth.

Issue a name slip to everyone. Ask each person to seek all of the players holding the same name as he. When the individuals meet, they form a group.

25

D. Matching sounds

1. Bird or animal calls.

Determine how many groups are desired and how many persons will comprise a group. Prepare a list of birds or animals with distinctive calls. Prepare as many sets of slips bearing the name of the bird or animal as there are groups. For example, for four groups of six persons, and using two birds and two animals, write *crow* on one set of six slips, *cardinal* on another set, *dog* on a third set, and *cat* on a fourth.

Issue a bird or animal slip to each player. Ask everyone to utter the call of the creature on his slip. When all of the birds of a feather or animals of a fur find one another they form a group.

2. Hums.

Determine how many groups are desired and how many persons will comprise a group. Prepare a list of well-known songs. Prepare as many sets of slips bearing the names of selected songs as there are groups. For example for four groups of five persons and using four songs write "Yankee Doodle" on one set of five slips, "My Old Kentucky Home" on another set, "Smiles" on a third set, and "Tea for Two" on a fourth.

Issue a song slip to each person. Ask each to hum the tune of the song on his slip. When all humming the same tune find one another, they form a group.

26

E. Matching actions

Determine how many groups are desired and how many persons will comprise a group. Prepare a list of individuals whose actions are readily recognizable and easy to pantomime (pianist, trombonist, traffic policeman, golfer). Prepare as many sets of slips bearing these selected individuals as there are groups. For example, for four groups of six players, write "pianist" on one set of six slips, "trombonist" on a second set, "traffic policeman" on a third, and "golfer", on a fourth.

Distribute a labeled slip to each person. Ask everyone to pantomime the action of the individual on his slip. When all pantomiming the same action recognize one another, they form a group.

F. Matching items

Determine how many groups are desired and how many persons will comprise a group. Secure several kinds of items, enough of each for members in a group. For example, for four groups of five players, have at hand five safety pins, five table tennis balls, five pennies, and five paper clips.

Distribute one item to each player. Ask everyone to search for the persons having the same item as he. All the persons possessing the same item form a group.

27

Instead of repeating the techniques for forming and maneuvering groups throughout the book, the illustrated methods are combined in the first chapter for ready reference.

REWARDS FOR "LOSERS"

It seems incongruous to spend time getting players into groups to play a game and then after a brief period of participation to eliminate them one at a time from the activity because they fail to give a "correct" response or performance. Yet in many social games this is the outcome, and the players return to their chairs as observers and remain there until the conclusion of the game.

Being penalized for giving an incorrect response or some other failure and having to sit out the game is not fun and causes embarrassment. A game which puts a shy individual on the side lines is returning the person to the same self-conscious shell from which he may have momentarily emerged.

Instead of seeing how many individuals sit on the side lines, the aim of the social recreation leader should be keeping the players participating. The leader will find some suggestions for maintaining participation in many of the games in this book. For example, in Ghost, the game which for generations has quickly removed its players from participation, the disappearing act no longer takes place, for the person who becomes a ghost has a point scored against him but continues to participate with the mortals.

Another example is the game Listen and Hustle, in which the music stops and everyone including "it" hustles for a circle drawn on the floor. There is one less place than there are players, but instead of eliminating the person who fails to get a place, this player is allowed to remain in the game and assume the role of "it," who leads the group around the room until the music stops again. If after three attempts "it" fails to secure a place, he may select someone to take his place while he joins the group, rather than be embarrassed by continuing to remain displaced.

Playing the role of "it" for great lengths of time is embarrassing to some individuals. To eliminate this possibility, the number of times "it" remains in the role should be set before the game is begun. For example, in Great Hobby, if after three attempts "it" fails to induce a player to laugh, he is permitted to select another person to take his place while he joins the group.

Another device for making social games enjoyable—as well as for keeping players in the game—is to credit them for trying. For example, in Aunt Nellie's Cat, in which two players of opposing teams vie to be first to supply an adjective beginning with a designated letter and describing the cat, the first player to respond correctly scores three points, but the opposing player scores one point for trying instead of the usual zero.

Through social awareness and organizational devices, the leader of social recreation enhances the enjoyment of all individuals in his groups. This, however, does not mean that he stretches the duration of activities beyond their capacity for affording fun. While it may sound strange, many social activities end in boredom—because the leader does not know when to conclude the games. One of the secrets of many a celebrated cook is to serve the diner just less than enough so that he will always want more. Likewise, the leader of social games should not continue until the players are sated. He stops while enjoyment is in high gear, and while the players still want to play.

In the activities which follow, the word "leader" always refers to the person conducting the games and not to any particular player. The player in a group who exerts leadership in initiating or continuing an activity is designated by a title such as captain, "it," starter, or head player.

CHAPTER 2

DEFROSTERS

CONTENTS

Preparing individuals for social recreation requires using techniques to induce the members of a group to put their self-consciousness in a remote corner and to meet and talk with others. The Defrosters included in this chapter help to remove the frigid atmosphere that often hovers over a group before activities begin, and they provide a device to encourage individuals to participate.

One of the best methods for helping an individual to feel at ease is to give him something to do and to have everyone else, also, engage in the activity so that the person does not feel he is soloing. Having other members of the group perform at the same time gives him the encouragement and security that make it fun to participate.

Games useful in defrosting a group follow certain major patterns. The players are requested to

Talk with others (Chatterboxers)
Secure signatures of others (Sign-Ups)
Obtain lists of items from others (Item Spotters)
Elicit a response from others (Responders)
Locate a partner (Partner Finders)

The activities are alphabetized at the beginning of the chapter under these five headings for ready reference. For some of the activities a record player or piano and accompanist are helpful, although the leader, lacking these, can conduct the games almost as well using a radio. A minimum of simple supplies and equipment are needed for Defrosters. Items such as chairs, coins, buttons or beans, paper clips, rulers, pins, bars of soap, paper bags, crayons, and paper and pencils are easily obtained.

CHATTERBOXERS

Mysterious Couple

Select a couple, either the same or opposite sex, for the mysterious twosome. Do not disclose the pair's identity to the group. Announce that there is a mysterious couple in the group that the players are to identify.

On signal the players start asking every couple seen together if they are the mysterious twosome. To add to the difficulty of becoming identified, the pair need appear together only occasionally. When someone finds the mysterious twosome together, he wins the game. He announces their names to the group.

Spare a Quarter? Give a quarter to one of the couples. Everyone tries to identify the couple. The first person to address the couple when the pair is together with the words, "Can you spare a quarter?" wins the coin.

Gertie and Jake. One of the sought pair is Gertie Gugler; the other, Jake Jerker. Gertie and Jake do not appear together at any time. The first person who discovers either Gertie or Jake wins the game. To win, the player must say, "I found Gertie" or "I found Jake." Continue the game until both of them are found or for a designated time. For large groups, have several Gerties and Jakes.

Dimes in the Crowd

Without the knowledge of the participating players, select three individuals and give each a dime. Announce that each of three persons in the group holds a dime. The dime-holder will give the coin to the seventh person who shakes his hand and identifies him by calling out, "Seven coming up."

On signal, the players move around the room and busily engage in shaking hands in the desire to find the dime-holders. Each of the money-holders, upon shaking hands with the seventh person, gives the dime to the lucky handshaker who identifies the dime-holder by calling out, "Seven coming up." The game continues until the group finds the three dime-holders. If the budget allows, appoint more dime-holders, especially if the group is large.

Get Acquainted Excursion

Arrange chairs to resemble the seating arrangement in the coach of a train (double file). Have two chairs for each seat on each side of the aisle. Couples occupy the chairs. Each couple pretends to have met on the train.

Ask the members of each couple to introduce themselves. Since the object of the mixer is to get individuals to converse with one another, a starter for stimulating conversation might include: "Why do you enjoy traveling? What trip have you enjoyed tremendously? What are your hobbies?"

At frequent intervals call a station. Designate which member of the couple is to move forward when the station is called: the player near the aisle or the player seated near the imaginary windows of the coach. If couples are of the opposite sex, the boys move forward one seat. After each has a place, conversation begins with a new partner.

Stop and Talk

Ask the players to form a double circle—girls in the inner one, boys in the outer. Girls face in a counterclockwise direction; boys, clockwise.

On signal or to music the girls promenade in a counterclockwise direction; the boys, clockwise. At intervals give a signal or stop the music for the group to halt. Circles face one another. Every person introduces himself to the person he faces. Each time the group halts announce a different topic of conversation for the players to discuss: favorite television program or star, favorite composers, popular authors, a vacation to the moon, and other topics which are appropriate for the group.

On signal or resumption of the music, play continues. At each halt, the players find a new person with whom to converse.

Famous Characters

Provide a pin and a slip of 2 × 2-inch paper containing the name of a famous person for each player. As each person arrives, pin one of the slips on his back, but do not let him know the name of the famous character he represents.

On signal, players move around the room to observe the names appearing on each other's slips. They converse with one another as if they were talking with the persons named on the slips. As the conversation continues, each tries to pick up clues from the others in order to establish his identity. Continue the game until several persons have discovered who they are.

Walking Slogans. On each slip of paper write an advertising slogan of a well-known product. Players move about and converse with each other and make comments about the slogans until several have guessed the names of the products they are advertising.

Introductions

Players sit in a circle. Distribute to everyone a sheet of paper 8½ × 11 inches and a pencil or, preferably, a black crayon. Ask each person to print his name on the paper in large, bold letters so that every player in the circle can read it. Collect the pencils or crayons after the players finish printing their names. Request the players to hold the papers so that everyone can read them.

Have each player in turn introduce himself to the person on his right. Call on one of the players to start the introductions. He turns to the player on his right and says, "My name is George Brown." The individual responds with "How do you do, George Brown? My name is Marion Smith." The player to her right says, "How do you do, George Brown, Marion Smith. My name is Flora Perrin."

Play continues with each person repeating the names of the preceding persons and then giving his own name. To help the players repeat the names, let them refer to the name card which everyone holds in front of him, so that no player suffers embarrassment from failing to remember the names as the list grows longer.

Suggestion: If the group is large have several circles of players, for the game slows down if individuals have too many names to repeat.

Farmer Jones' Hen

The players sit in a circle. Distribute to each player a sheet of 8½ × 11-inch paper and a pencil. Ask each player to print his name in large letters on the paper. Request each to hold his name so that everyone can read it.

Start the game by asking one of the players to say to the person on his right, "Farmer Jones has a fine red cackling hen." The person responds with the question, "Who says that she cackles?" The first individual replies, "James [player's first name] says that the hen cackles." The player to his right remarks, "James says and John says [adding his own name] that the hen cackles." In turn each person on the right repeats the first names of the preceding players, adds his own name, and repeats the clause, "that the hen cackles."

To help the players remember the names, permit them to refer to the name card which everyone holds in front of him.

Suggestion: For large groups of players, have several circles, for the game slows down if the individuals have too many names to repeat.

Paper Bag Handshake

Give everyone a paper bag large enough to fit over a hand. Everyone places a paper bag over one of his hands.

Each player proceeds to shake hands with as many persons as he can within a given time. He may shake hands with the bagged hand only.

Silly Doings

Prepare one list of silly-sounding imaginary places the players are to visit, and another one giving some ridiculous activities they are to perform while they are there. Select two assistants and give each one of the lists. Ask the other players to sit in a circle. Request one assistant to move around the circle and whisper to each person the name of one of the imaginary places. The second assistant whispers to everyone a ridiculous activity.

Ask each person, in turn, to give his own name and tell where he is and what he is doing. A reply might be, "My name is Tom Butler. I'm on the Coconut Islands sliding on banana peels." Or, "I'm Joe Rodgers. I'm on Cloud Seven, polishing moonbeams."

Odd or Even

Give everyone twelve small buttons or similar objects.

On signal, every person holding a chosen number of buttons concealed in one of his hands approaches another member of the group and says, "Odd?" or "Even?" If, for example, the approaching player holds seven buttons in his extended hand and the person he queries responds, "Odd," the guesser receives the seven buttons. If the guesser is wrong, he gives the approaching player seven buttons. At the end of a given time the person with most buttons wins the game. Call a halt to the game before too many players are out of buttons.

Yes or No

Give everyone ten navy beans or substitute items.

Have the players move around the room and ask questions of one another. The questions should be phrased in such a manner that the one questioned has no other reply except "Yes" or "No." Whenever a questioner is answered "Yes" or "No," he wins a navy bean from his "opponent." If the opponent can answer in some other manner than "Yes" or "No," the questioner moves on to another player. At the end of a specified time, the person with the largest collection of beans wins the game.

Forbidden Pronouns

Have a watch or clock available, and give each player ten navy beans or a substitute.

Everyone approaches someone, and two together engage in discussion for thirty seconds. If at any time during their half-minute conversation either of the players uses any of the taboo pronouns—"I, you, we, me, or us"—he gives the other person one of his beans.

At the end of thirty seconds, give a signal. Everyone finds another person with whom to talk. The winner is the player with the largest number of beans after five minutes of timed conversations.

Four of a Kind

Have a 2 × 4-inch slip of paper for everyone. Group the slips in sets of fours. On each set write the name of a different song that the players are apt to know. Distribute a slip to each person.

Ask everyone to seek the three other persons who have a slip bearing the name of the same song. The first foursome to get together presents itself to the leader and wins the game.

Allow the others to continue to find the members of their groups. When most of the foursomes are together, call the game to a halt. Present the winning foursome and announce the name of its song. Ask the entire group to join in either humming or singing the song.

Suggestion: The use of popular dance steps is a good variation for teenage groups.

SIGN-UPS

Autographs

Give each player a sheet of paper 8½ × 11 inches and a pencil.

On signal, the players hustle to get the signatures of as many persons as they can within a designated time. Call time and ask the players to count the signatures on their lists. The player with the longest list reads it. Verify the list by having him read each name. Ask every person whose name is read to raise his hand and call out, "I'm alive."

Count the number of persons who respond and check with the total number on the list. The person with the longest correct list of autographs wins the game.

Left-Handed Mixer. Secure signatures written with the left hand. Play the same as Autographs.

Lotto Mixer

For each person who is to participate have prepared sheets of paper with twenty-five ½-inch squares marked off. Put five squares in each row. As each person arrives, give him a pencil and a sheet of paper containing twenty-five squares.

Ask everyone to introduce himself to twenty-five persons, who in turn introduce themselves. Each player writes in one of the squares on his sheet the name of the person with whom he has exchanged introductions. Players may use a name only once unless another person actually has the same name.

After most of the players have completed filling in the squares, assemble the players and have each in turn read one name from his sheet. As a name is read, the person bearing the name raises his hand, and any of the players who finds the name on his sheet checks the square in which it appears. The first person to have five checks in a vertical, horizontal, or diagonal row calls out, "Glad to have met you."

Check the list, and if it is correct, announce the winner. If it is incorrect, continue the game until another player has five checks in a row.

Your Initials, Please?

Give everyone a sheet of paper, 8½ × 11 inches, and a pencil. Ask the players to write down on the left-hand side of the paper a predetermined word associated with the season, theme of the party, or a special occasion.

On signal, the players search for persons whose first or last names begin with one of the letters in a selected word, for example, "birthdays." When a player finds a person whose first or last name begins with one of the letters, he asks him to sign his name to the right of the letter. Although the person signs both his first and last name, he writes them in the order in which they are needed:

> B — Belding, Cora
> I — Inga Sanders
> R — Ross, Edith
> T — Thompson, Arthur
> H — Heimick, Helen
> D — Doris Zirkel
> A — Anna Anderson
> Y — Yates, William
> S — Stella Jennings

The first player to find the persons whose first or last names begin with the letters in the selected word reports to the leader. Call a halt to the game and assemble the players. Read the name appearing next to each letter, and ask the person whose name is read to raise his hand. Place a check mark after each correct name. If the complete list is correct, the player wins the game. If his list is not correct, call on the person with the next highest number of names.

In the event that no one's first or last name begins with one of the letters in the selected word, everyone may write next to the missing letter, "Miss Nobody." The player with the most complete correct list wins the game.

Chief's Orders

Give everyone a pencil and a sheet of paper on which the following or similar requests appear. Allow a space to the right for the players' signatures.

1. Find a person wearing green and introduce him to someone wearing blue. Get both signatures. _____
2. Find someone whose hobby is golf. _____
3. Find two individuals with brown eyes. _____
4. Find an individual who drives an automobile the name of which begins with the letter *C*. _____
5. Find a person who has black curly hair and one who has brown curly hair. _____
6. Find two persons who are left-handed. _____
7. Find two persons having the number nine in their addresses. _____
8. Talk with anyone in the group and list the name of his favorite flower. _____
9. Talk with anyone and list his favorite television program. _____
10. Talk with anyone and list his favorite movie idol. _____

On signal, everyone moves around the room and seeks the persons fulfilling the listed requirements. Each person who fulfills the need signs his name on the right-hand side of the sheet next to the request.

The first player to follow completely the chief's requests brings his sheet of paper to the leader. Call a halt to the game. Verify the winner's answer by calling upon the players whose signatures he has secured. If his answers are correct, he is the speediest searcher and wins the game. If not, call in the next list having the most signatures and check.

Suggestion: The leader of games can be imaginative by including items that are appropriate for special occasions, for holidays, as well as for certain subjects—history, music, nature, and others. In addition he may wish to use items that follow the theme of the occasion.

ITEM SPOTTERS

Best Dater

Have a slip of paper 2×2 inches for everyone. On each slip write a fictitious telephone number. Keep a record of the numbers and use it to check the winner's list. Pin a slip on the back of each member of the group who stands or sits in a circle. Give everyone a sheet of paper 8½ × 11 inches and a pencil.

On signal everyone scurries to list as many telephone numbers as he can read from the slips pinned on the backs of the other players' clothing. Players may twist and turn to prevent others from reading the numbers on their backs, but they may not back against objects or persons, lie on their backs, or do anything to make it impossible to read the numbers.

At the end of a designated time, call a halt to the game. Assemble the players and ask them to count the numbers they have spotted and recorded. The person with the longest list reads the numbers he has acquired. Check the numbers against the ones on the original list. If his list is correct he wins the title, the Best Dater. In case of error check the next highest for accuracy.

Speedy Shopper. On each slip of paper write the name of an item found in one of the chosen stores: grocery, drug, sporting goods, department, gift, hobby shop, and others. Play the same as Best Dater.

Gathering Titles. On each slip of paper write the name of a book, movie, song, television or radio program, or others. Play the same as Best Dater.

On the Go. On each slip of paper write the name of a city, state, country, river, or a famous place to see. Play the same as Best Dater.

Find the Celebrities. On each slip of paper write the name of a famous person: composer; explorer; scientist; author; artist; movie, stage, radio, or television star; and others. Play the same as Best Dater.

Gathering Monikers

Give each player a pencil, a 3 × 5-inch and an 8½ × 11-inch slip of paper, and a pin. Ask him to write his name on the 3 × 5-inch slip. Ask each player to pin the name-slip to the clothing on his left shoulder.

On signal, the players move anywhere in the room in an attempt to write on their 8½ × 11-inch sheets of paper the names of as many persons as possible.

After a designated time, call a halt to the game. Assemble the players and ask them to count the number of names on their lists. Ask the person with the longest list to read the names. To verify the list request each individual whose name is read to stand and say, for example, "I am Zula Ludwick." If the list checks correctly, the person who gathered the most monikers wins the game. If his list is not correct, call on the person with the next highest number of monikers.

RESPONDERS

Bumpety-Bump-Bump

Players sit or stand in a large circle. For every ten players in the group select one to be "it." (For thirty players there are three "its.") The "its" stand in the center of the circle. Give the players a chance to learn the names of the persons on their right and left.

On signal, each of the "its" approaches anyone in the circle, points to him, and says, "Right [or left] bumpety-bump-bump." Before "it" finishes the last word, "bump," the player must respond with the name of the person on his right or left.

If the player gives the correct response, "it" moves on to try to catch someone else. If the player fails to respond correctly, he changes places with "it." Whenever an "it" gets a place, give him the opportunity to learn the names of the persons on his right and left. If after a reasonable number of tries an "it" fails to secure a place, select another person to take his place.

Hicky-Hikey-Hokey-Pokey. "It" approaches a player and says, "Right [or left] hicky-hikey-hokey-pokey." Before "it" finishes the last word, "pokey," the player must respond with the name of the person on his right or left.

Who Are Your Neighbors? "It" approaches one of the players in the circle and says, "Who are your neighbors?" and immediately starts to count to five. Before "it" reaches "five," the player must respond by giving the names of the neighbors on his right and left. If he fails, he changes places with "it." If he succeeds, "it" approaches someone else.

PARTNER FINDERS

Famous Meet Famous

On one slip of 3 × 5-inch paper write the name of a famous person and the character the player is to seek. For example, "You are Eleanor Roosevelt. Find Winston Churchill." On a corresponding slip, reverse the order of the characters, for example, "You are Winston Churchill. Find Eleanor Roosevelt." Have a set for each couple.

On signal, each player tries to find the person whose famous name appears on his slip. The first couple to discover each other wins the game, and these two famous individuals are partners. Continue until everyone has a partner.

Suggestion: Try names of famous composers, actors, actresses, authors, poets, artists, historical figures, or any other category of individuals suitable for the group and appropriate for the occasion.

Topnotchers

Prepare two sets of 2 × 2-inch slips of paper, one for the girls, one for the boys. Write the name of a well-known individual from literature, art, music, drama, the dance, movies, radio, or television on the girls' set of slips and duplicate the names on the boys' slips. Give a slip to each girl and a duplicate one to every boy.

On signal, each player seeks the person holding the same name as he. When they find one another they are partners.

Artists' Creations. On one set of papers write the name of a composer, author, painter, or poet. On the other set write the name of one of the composer's selections, the author's publications, the painter's masterpieces, or the poet's verses. Distribute one set to the girls and the other set to the boys.

On signal, the players set out to match the names of the artists with the titles of their creative endeavors. When the composer and selection, the author and publication, the painter and masterpiece, or the poet and poem meet, the two players are partners.

State and Capitals

Write the name of a state on a 2 × 2-inch slip of paper. On another slip write the name of its capital. Have a slip for everyone. Distribute the slips among the players.

On signal, the players try to match the state with its capital. The first couple to match up correctly wins. Play continues until everyone has a partner.

Matching Flowers

Write the name of a flower on a slip of paper. On a duplicate slip write the same name. Have a slip for everyone.

On signal everyone tries to match his flower. The first couple to match the name of a flower wins the game. Play continues until everyone matches the name of his flower and has a partner.

Matching Birds. Write the name of a bird on each pair of slips. Play the same as Matching Flowers.

Matching Vegetables. Write the name of a vegetable on each pair of slips. Play the same as Matching Flowers.

Matching Trees. Write the name of a tree on each pair of slips. Play the same as Matching Flowers.

Matching Animals. Write the name of an animal on each pair of slips. Play the same as Matching Flowers.

Split Proverbs

Write proverbs on slips of paper of the same size and cut each slip in half. Have enough halves for each person and distribute them.

On signal everyone seeks the person having the other half of his proverb. One person may have the half "When in Rome"; the person he seeks has the other half, "do as the Romans do." The first couple to find one another wins, and the two are partners. Continue until everyone has a partner.

Prepare the slips from the following list of proverbs:

All that glitters is not gold.
A stitch in time saves nine.
A fool and his money are soon parted.
Every cloud has a silver lining.
It never rains but it pours.
Make hay while the sun shines.
A watched pot never boils.
A barking dog never bites.
Never look a gift horse in the mouth.
A rolling stone gathers no moss.
Better late than never.
Birds of a feather flock together.
A bird in the hand is worth two in the bush.
Never put off 'til tomorrow what can be done today.
It's a long lane that has no turning.
A place for everything and everything in its place.
Lie down with the dogs, get up with the fleas.
It's better to have loved and lost, than never to have loved at all.
Drunken days all have their tomorrows.
What's good for the goose is good for the gander.
He laughs best who laughs last.
There are two sides to every question.
Out of sight, out of mind.
As you make your bed, so you must lie in it.
Too many cooks spoil the broth.
Rome wasn't built in a day.
Where there's a will, there's a way.
You cannot have your cake and eat it.
Absence makes the heart grow fonder.
The early bird catches the worm.
Everything comes to him who waits.
Laugh and the world laughs with you; weep and you weep alone.
Idleness is the mother of evil.
An empty barrel makes the most noise.

All's well that ends well.
A new broom sweeps clean.
When in Rome, do as the Romans do.
It's an ill wind that blows nobody good.
It takes a thief to catch a thief.
God helps those who help themselves.
The pot calls the kettle black.
It's the shovel that laughs at the poker.
People in glass houses shouldn't throw stones.
Silence gives consent.
Well done or not at all.
A person is known by the company he keeps.
A word to the wise is sufficient.
Forewarned is forearmed.
One good turn deserves another.
In the kingdom of the blind, the one-eyed are kings.
All good things must come to an end.
Everyone knows best where his shoe pinches him.
Well done is better than well said.
Contentment is better than riches.
Health is better than wealth.
A friend in need is a friend indeed.
Faint heart never won fair lady.
To the victor belongs the spoils.
All's fair in love and war.
The proof of the pudding is in the eating.
Who counts without his host counts twice.
One cannot please all the world and his wife.
He who dances pays the fiddler.
He who smashes the window pays the glazier.
Evil to him who evil thinks.
No pay, no piper.
Two wrongs do not make a right.
The pen is mightier than the sword.
Brevity is the soul of wit.
Curiosity killed the cat.
Necessity is the mother of invention.
Variety is the spice of life.
He who excuses himself accuses himself.
It takes two to make a quarrel.
When a man is wrapped up in himself, the package is small.
Keep your eyes wide open before marriage, half shut afterward.
Speech is silver, silence is golden.
Take care of the pennies, the dollars will take care of themselves.
Who steals my purse steals trash.
There's many a slip 'twixt the cup and the lip.
Early to bed and early to rise makes a man healthy, wealthy, and wise.
Discretion is the better part of valor.
Nothing ventured, nothing gained.
Handsome is as handsome does.
They can because they think they can.
A penny saved is a penny earned.

Willful waste makes woeful want.
Honesty is the best policy.
Strike while the iron is hot.
A bad penny always comes back.
Enough is as good as a feast.
You may bring a horse to water, but you can't make him drink.
Marry in haste, repent at leisure.
Beggars should not be choosers.
Like father, like son.
Once does not make a habit.
Sorrow treads upon the heels of mirth.
Hitch your wagon to a star.
A cloudy morning often changes to a fine day.
Behind bad luck comes good luck.
To see an old friend is as agreeable as a good meal.

Split Affinities

Write an affinity on a slip of paper and cut each slip in half. Give everyone half an affinity.

On signal, each player seeks the person having the other half of the slip. When they meet they are partners. Continue until everyone in the group has a partner.

Prepare the slips from the following list of affinities:

Bread and butter	Nut and bolt
Salt and pepper	Gas and oil
Knife and fork	Cap and gown
Potatoes and meat	Car and driver
Ham and eggs	Stocks and bonds
Pork and beans	Army and Navy
Ice cream and cake	Stars and Stripes
Pen and ink	Crackers and cheese
Paper and pencil	Lock and key
Day and night	Cream and sugar
Light and dark	Brother and sister
Fair and warmer	Soap and water
Thunder and lightning	Comb and brush
Cup and saucer	Macaroni and cheese
Bow and arrow	Li'l Abner and Daisy Mae
Horse and wagon	Anthony and Cleopatra
House and lot	Jack and Jill
Coat and hat	Adam and Eve
Collar and tie	Cain and Abel
Shoes and stockings	David and Goliath
Romeo and Juliet	Jonah and the whale
Liver and bacon	Pat and Mike
Bat and ball	Rod and reel
Hit and run	Sword and shield
Mother and father	Saddle and bridle
Dog and cat	Bag and baggage
Hammer and nail	Needle and thread

Split Old Sayings

Write an old saying on a slip of paper and cut it in half. Distribute half an old saying to each player.

On signal, everyone seeks the person having the other half of his old saying. When a player finds the other half, he has found his partner. Continue until everyone has a partner.

Prepare the slips from the following list of old sayings:

Strong as an ox	Spry as a spring chicken
Fat as a pig	Funny as a monkey
Hard as a rock	Tall as a giraffe
Clear as crystal	Slippery as an eel
Thin as a rail	Still as a mouse
Cold as ice	Swift as a hare
Dead as a doornail	Bright as the sun
Light as a feather	Tight as a drum
Sly as a fox	Quick as lightning
Pretty as a picture	Poor as a church mouse
Black as coal	Mad as a March hare
Sharp as a razor	Fair as a flower
Sour as a lemon	Ugly as sin
White as snow	Flat as a pancake
Green as grass	Red as a beet
Yellow as gold	Crazy as a loon
Neat as a pin	Brown as a nut
Cross as sticks	Blind as a bat
Brave as a lion	Mean as a miser
Slow as molasses in January	Full as a tick
Dry as a bone	Plump as a partridge
Sweet as honey	Clean as a whistle
Hot as fire	Hard as flint
Huge as an elephant	Fine as a fiddle
Bitter as gall	Stiff as a poker
Heavy as lead	Calm as a clock
Soft as velvet	Busy as a bee
Tough as shoe leather	Pure as a lily
Deep as the ocean	Proud as a peacock

Split Advertisements

Cut well-known advertisements from newspapers or magazines or write widely advertised slogans on a piece of paper and cut in half. Distribute a half to each player.

Each person seeks the missing half. When halves match, these two persons are partners.

Split Poetry

Write one or two lines of a well-known poem, jingle, or rhyme on a slip of paper. Write the next line or two on another slip of paper. Distribute the slips among the group.

Everyone tries to match his line or two with the missing portion. When he succeeds he has found his partner.

Find the Missing Piece

From cardboard, cut out circles about 4 inches in diameter. Have one circle for each couple which is to participate. Cut each circle at a different angle into two pieces. Distribute the pieces among the group.

Each player tries to find the missing and matching part of his circle. When he succeeds he has located his partner.

Holiday Cut-Ups. Use appropriate symbols for holiday occasions and cut these in half: *Valentine's Day*—hearts, valentines; *Christmas* —bells, stockings, trees, cards, Santa Clauses, snowmen; *Easter*— eggs, bunnies, baskets. Play the same way as Find the Missing Piece.

Fur and Feather Partners

On duplicate slips of paper write the name of an animal or bird having a characteristic call with which most of the group is familiar. Names might include: donkey, horse, cow, pig, dog, cat, duck, turkey, rooster, hen, wolf, lion, whippoorwill, bobwhite, bobolink, or others. Give a slip to each person. Be sure that there are two slips in circulation for each animal and bird.

On signal, everyone begins searching for his partner. Whether it is an animal or bird, each player must give the characteristic call of the creature on his slip in his effort to find his partner in fur or feathers.

Any player who does not know the characteristic call or has not the inclination toward sounding like a bird or animal may respond, "Lost—one animal," or "Lost—one bird," depending upon what name is on his slip. The lost creatures seek each other until the bird or animal of a kind finds its partner.

Humming Tunes

On duplicate slips write the name of a tune with which everyone in the group is familiar. Give a slip to each person.

On signal each player hums his own tune and sets out to find the person humming the same tune. When the two locate each other they are partners.

Pantomime Partners

On duplicate slips of paper write the name of a character who can readily be impersonated in pantomime. Distribute the slips among the group.

Each person pantomimes the significant actions of the assigned character and looks for the person who is pantomiming the same or similar actions. These two are partners.

Characters having pronounced gestures which are desirable in pantomiming include the following:

orchestra director	traffic policeman
trombone player	automobile driver
harpist	ballet dancer
golf player	gardener
baseball pitcher	shoe shiner
baseball batter	skater
pianist	tennis player
auctioneer	swimmer

Cinderella's Slipper

Separate the boys and girls. Have the boys in a group alone at one end of the playing area. Ask each girl to remove one shoe and place it in a corner.

On signal the boys rush to the pile of shoes, and everyone takes one. As soon as a boy gets a shoe, he searches for the Cinderella who wears the matching shoe. When he finds the girl, the two are partners.

Partner Sleuth

Give every girl a 3 × 5-inch card and a pencil. Allow everyone a few minutes in which to write a brief description of herself: color of hair, eyes, shoes, clothing, or other identifying features. Place the cards in a box. Mix the cards and give one to each boy. Ask the boys to read the description on their cards.

On signal, every boy seeks the girl meeting the description. When he finds her, she is his partner.

Numbered Partners

Have two sets of 2 × 2-inch slips of paper, one for the boys, the other for the girls. Number each set according to the number of the individuals who will participate. Give a slip from one set to every girl; and from the second, distribute a duplicate number to each boy.

On signal the players move around the area and try to find the member of the opposite sex who holds the same number. When boy meets girl, they are partners.

Find the Girl

Write each girl's name on a 3 × 5-inch slip of paper. Fold it and place the slip in a box. Ask the boys to form a single line on one side of the room. Pass the box down the line and in turn have each boy take a slip.

On signal, each boy seeks the girl whose name he has drawn. When the two meet, they are partners.

Is It the Same?

Have a chair for each boy and place it in a circle. Ask the boys to stand at one end of the room. Have each girl stand behind one of the chairs. Give each girl a slip containing a number. Write duplicates of the numbers on slips for the boys. Give a slip to every boy.

On signal, the boys rush to the circle to sit in a chair. Each boy checks with the girl behind him to see if his number is the same as hers. If they are identical, the two are partners. If not, the boys move from chair to chair until everyone has a partner.

Two of a Kind

Secure two of each of the following items: rulers, paper clips, pencils, clothespins, bars of soap, canned goods, magazines, books, crayons, and gloves. Distribute the items among the players.

On signal, each player seeks the person having the same item as he. When the two players meet, they are partners.

Partners Meet

The boys form a file on one side of the room; the girls, on the opposite side. Both files face the rear of the room. Provide march music—record player, pianist and piano, or a radio.

As soon as the music starts, both groups march to the rear of the room and turn at the corner. As each couple meets, the two players are partners and march double file up the center of the room. Stop the music when each person has a partner.

Opposites

Form a double circle—the girls in the inner circle facing in a clockwise direction, the boys in the outer circle facing in a counterclockwise direction. Use march music—record player, piano and pianist, or a radio.

With the start of the music the boys and girls march around in opposite directions. Halt the music. The girl and boy opposite one another are partners.

Hook a Partner

Players are in couples and stand anywhere within a designated area. One individual, "it," stands in the center of the group.

"It" issues a series of requests: shake hands, stoop, stand on one foot, join hands, wave the right hand, or others. At any time he may say, "Hook a partner." Each person must seek a new partner while "it," also, tries to obtain one. Partners lock elbows. The person without a partner is "it" and stands in the center of the area and issues his directions to the group. If after three attempts "it" fails to secure a partner, he selects someone to take his place and he joins the group.

CHAPTER 3

SOCIALIZERS

CONTENTS

In order that a contagion of enthusiasm and friendliness prevail in the social recreation atmosphere, a leader of social games needs a great deal more than technical achievement and a winning smile. To achieve a good group-leader relationship, the director of games must be sincerely pleasant and possess genuine enthusiasm. These attributes are essential in creating a receptive group spirit.

In addition to creating a friendly atmosphere, the leader of social recreation must maintain it. The socializers in this chapter will help to keep enthusiasm and the desire to participate at a high pitch. They readily fall into distinct groupings or patterns which the leader can check at a glance through the use of the chapter index. If he wants activities to induce participants to laugh, he should choose from the laugh inducers. If he desires to move his group around, the mixers will help. In the mixers players shift their places and "it," who has no "place," tries to secure one. Those activities which require participants to search for designated items, are brought together under the heading "hide and seekers."

Relays are good socializers, too. Since the relay fun makers described here require each person on a team to complete a certain antic quickly and correctly to put the group in the winning class, everyone eagerly awaits his turn. Through his interest in participating he finds himself an enthusiastic team member.

Supplies and equipment for playing the socializers are of the simplest variety and can be assembled quickly. To conduct *all* the activities, a leader needs objects such as pencils, paper, cardboard, chalk, and twine; paper bags, balloons, balls, toothpicks, spoons, playing cards, handkerchiefs or cloths; wastebaskets, brooms, chairs, old magazines, and milk cartons; unbreakable or paper plates and cups; and a few staples such as potatoes and raisins. Some of the activities require no equipment. All of the socializers can be conducted in a comparatively small space.

LAUGH INDUCERS

Crossed Wires

Players sit or stand in a group.

Ask everyone to follow these simple but fun-invoking directions.

51

"With your right hand take a hold of your left ear. Now, with your left hand take a hold of your nose."

When everyone has assumed or at least has tried to assume this position, ask the players to change: "With your left hand take a hold of your right ear. With your right hand, your nose."

Pat and Rub. Ask the players to rub their stomachs with their right hands and to pat the tops of their heads with their left. With the signal, "Change," have them rub their stomachs with their left hands and pat the tops of their heads with the right.

Ha, Ha, Ha

Players sit in a circle.

Ask one player to turn to the person on his right and say, "Ha." The second player turns to the person on his right, adds a "ha," thus saying, "Ha, ha." In turn each person in the circle repeats the previous "ha's" and adds his own.

All "ha-ha-ing" is done without laughing. Anyone who laughs must scowl during the balance of the game. The person or persons maintaining a sober face the longest wins the feat. Any player becoming confused with the number of "ha's" he must repeat remains in the game, but he must scowl during the balance of the activity.

Hold the Word

The players sit in a circle. Give each person a slip of 2 × 2-inch paper and a pencil.

Ask each person to write down the name of some object, fold the paper, and pass it around the circle. On signal, passing stops, and everyone keeps the paper he has in his possession.

Have one of the players ask his right-hand neighbor a question. The neighbor must answer the question with the word written on his paper. In turn each person asks the player on his right a question which he must answer with the word he holds.

Toss and Laugh

Secure a man's handkerchief or a piece of cloth about that size. Players sit in a circle. One player, "it," stands in the center.

"It" tosses the handkerchief into the air. While the handkerchief is in midair, the players must laugh. As soon as the handkerchief strikes the floor, laughs must turn to frowns. Anyone who laughs when he should frown or frowns when he should laugh takes the tosser's place.

If "it" catches several players giving the wrong response, he selects one of them to toss the handkerchief. The others remain in

"It" approaches someone in the circle and seriously says, "I have a great hobby." The player replies, "What is it?" "It" performs some silly action—sings, pretends to play an instrument, dances with himself or others—in his attempt to get the player to laugh. If "it" succeeds, he exchanges places with the person. If he fails, he tries another player. When "it" fails to invoke laughter after three tries, he selects someone to take his place.

Famous Tillie. "It" approaches a player and repeats the following as often as he wishes in his effort to get him to laugh:

> The rising young contralto, Tillie Humperdink, approaches the platform,
> While the maestro awaits (player bows) and adjusts his set of ear plugs.

If "it" succeeds, he exchanges places with the person. If he fails, he tries another person. When "it" fails to induce laughter after three attempts, he selects someone to take his place.

Tongue Twisters

Write a tongue twister on a 3×5-inch slip of paper for each player. Distribute the papers among the group.

In turn, ask each player to read his tongue twister as quickly as he can. Use the following list of well-known tongue twisters:

> She sells sea shells by the seashore.
> Three gay geese on three green hills,
>   Gray were the geese and green were the hills.
> Peter Piper picked a peck of pickled peppers;
>   A peck of pickled peppers Peter Piper picked.
>   If Peter Piper picked a peck of pickled peppers,
>   Where is the peck of pickled peppers Peter Piper picked?
> Amidst the mists with angry boasts
>   He thrusts his fists against the posts
>   And still insists he sees the ghosts.
> Sarah sits by six sick city slickers.
> Three throbbing thumping thrush thoroughly thwarting thirty thrashers.
> Round the rough and rugged rock the ragged rascal rudely ran.
> How much wood would a woodchuck chuck
>   If a woodchuck would chuck wood?
> Nine nimble noblemen nibbling nuts.
> Eve eating eagerly elegant Easter eggs.
> Robert Rowley rolled a round ball round.
> One obstinate old ostrich ordering ordinary oranges.
> Fresh flesh of fresh fried fish.
> Four fat fellows fanning flickering flames.
> Sister Susie's swiftly sewing sixty shirts for soldiers.
> Seven serious staunch soldiers setting sail south suddenly.

the game, and "it" joins the circle. If after three tosses "
no one, he selects someone to take his place.

Bounce and Laugh. Secure a ball that can be bounc
player, "it," stands in the center of the circle. Have "it" b
ball. While he is bouncing the ball, all players laugh. W
stops bouncing the ball, laughs turn to frowns. Play the bala
the game the same as Toss and Laugh.

Laugh on Request

Secure a handkerchief or piece of cloth. Players form a ci
and count off by fours. One player is "it" and stands in the cen
of the circle.

"It" tosses a handkerchief up into the air and at the same tim
calls a number, for example, "Four." All of the Fours start laughing
and continue until the handkerchief touches the floor. Then everyone stops laughing. Anyone who continues to laugh exchanges
places with "it." If everyone controls his laughter, "it" tosses the
handkerchief again. If after three tosses, "it" fails to catch someone
giving the wrong response, he chooses someone to take his place.

Special Laughs. Before tossing the handkerchief and calling a
number, "it" designates the kind of laugh with which the players
must respond: baby's, man's, child's giggle, fat man's or Santa
Claus' chuckle, woman's high-pitched, or others. The game continues the same as Laugh on Request.

Handouts

Players sit in a circle. One player, "it," stands in the center.

"It" approaches each person in turn and asks him what item he
wishes to give in equipping the newlyweds' kitchen. Each person
names one item: measuring spoons, teakettle, toaster, freezer, or
others. "It" then approaches anyone in the group and asks him some
questions. The player's only answer is the name of the item he contributed. For example, "What's your favorite hobby?" If the player
gave the measuring spoons, he replies, "Measuring spoons." "What
kind of job do you have?" "Measuring spoons."

"It" asks the various questions in the attempt to get the person
to laugh. If the player laughs, he exchanges places with "it." If
"it" is unsuccessful in getting a laugh, he moves on to someone else.
After three unsuccessful tries, "it" may select another person to take
his place.

Great Hobby ∨

Players sit in a circle. One player, "it," stands in the center.

Two tiny timid toads trying to trot to Tarrytown.
Ten tiny titmice tipping ten tall tamarack trees.
Sarah in a shawl shoveled soft snow softly.
Six thick thistle sticks.
She is a thistle sifter. She has a sieve of sifted thistles and a sieve of
    unsifted thistles, for she is a thistle sifter.
Quizzical Quiz, kiss me quick.
David Daldrom dreamt he drove a dragon.
    Did David Daldrom dream he drove a dragon?
    If David Daldrom dreamt he drove a dragon,
    Where's the dragon David Daldrom dreamt he drove?
Oliver Ogilvie ogled an olive and oyster.
    Did Oliver Ogilvie ogle an olive and oyster?
    If Oliver Ogilvie ogled an olive and oyster,
    Where is the olive and oyster Oliver Ogilvie ogled?
Theophilus Thistle thrust three thousand thistles through the thick of his
    thumb.
Slim Sam Slick sawed six slim, sleek, slightly aslant, slender saplings.
A big black bug bit a big black bear.
Shall shy Sadie shiver sadly in the shadowy silence?

Mixed Responses

Secure two small boxes. Players sit in a circle. Give each person
a pencil and two slips of 3 × 5-inch paper.

Ask each person to write a question on one slip and the answer
on the other one. Gather the questions in one box, and the answers
in the other. Mix the questions, pass the box, and allow each person
to take a question. Then mix the answers, pass them, and ask everyone to take one. If a player happens to get his own set, he puts
them back and selects another question and answer.

Have everyone read his mixed question and answer in turn.

Grinners and Grouches

Have the players count off by twos to form two teams. Ask the
teams to stand or sit facing one another about 6 feet apart. The
players in Team 1 are the Grinners; Team 2, the Grouches.

Call out the name of one of the teams—Grinners or Grouches.
When the Grinners are called they immediately start to laugh, and
the Grouches scowl. With their silly laughter the Grinners try to
make the Grouches laugh. Any member of the Grouches who smiles
or laughs joins the opposing team.

When the Grouches are called, they exhibit their grumpiness by
using exaggerated facial expressions. Since the Grinners must maintain sober faces, anyone who smiles or laughs joins the Grouches.

At the end of a designated time, the team with the most players
wins.

MIXERS

Moving Day

Have a chair (house) for every player except one designated as "it." Place the chairs in four rows, far enough apart so that a player can walk easily between them. Everyone occupies a chair except "it," who stands between two rows.

On signal, "it" walks between the rows. Immediately the players begin changing places. "It" is on the lookout, and he keeps trying to get a house. If he succeeds, the houseless player is "it." If "it" fails to get a place, he keeps on trying.

When the houses stay too well occupied, "it" calls, "Moving day." Everyone must find a new place, and "it" hustles to get a house. The person without a place is "it." If "it" fails after a reasonable length of time to secure a house, he selects someone else to take his place.

Fruit Basket

Players stand or sit in a circle. Select an "it" who stands in the center. Assign the name of a fruit to each person.

"It" calls the names of two fruits (he cannot call the one assigned to him), and the two players assigned the names exchange places. "It" tries to secure one of the places. If he succeeds, the person without a place is "it." If he fails, he calls the names of two other fruits. At any time that "it" wishes he may call out, "Fruit basket is upset," and everyone must seek another place while "it" scurries to get one. After "it" tries three times to secure a place and fails, he selects someone to take his place.

Suggestions: Instead of assigning individuals the names of fruits, ask the players to count off by fours. Call the ones, grapefruit; the twos, grapes; the threes, pears; and the fours, peaches. "It" calls the names of any two groups, and they exchange places while he tries to secure one. "Fruit basket is upset" is the cue for everyone to change places.

In assigning names or numbers when only two persons are to exchange places, "it" cannot call his own name or number. If he does, the activity fails, for "it" merely takes the place of the person having the same number as he. The other person is automatically "it."

When more than two persons have the same name or number, "it" can call his own, because there are several persons who change places while "it" tries to secure one.

Flower Garden. Assign the names of flowers to each person. Play with either two players changing places at a time with "it" trying to secure one of the places, or with two groups. The cue word for everyone to find a place is "bouquet."

Vegetable Patch. Assign the names of vegetables and play the same as Fruit Basket. The cue words for everyone to find another place are "off to market."

Wild Flowers. Assign the names of wild flowers and play the same as Fruit Basket. The cue words for everyone to find another place are "woodland wonders."

Animals on the Loose. Assign the names of animals and play the same as Fruit Basket. The cue words for everyone to find another place are "animals on the loose."

Birds Migrate. Assign the names of birds and play the same as Fruit Basket. The cue words for everyone to find another place are "birds migrate."

Walking Trees. Assign the names of trees and play the same as Fruit Basket. The cue words for everyone to find another place are "walking trees."

Department Store. Assign the names of items found in a department store. The cue words for everyone to find a new place are "bargain day!"

Postman. Assign everyone the name of a city. "It," the postman, says, "I have a letter from St. Louis to Detroit." The players having the names of the cities exchange places while "it" tries to obtain one. The cue words for everyone to find a new place are "special delivery."

Numbers Change

Players stand in a circle. Ask them to number off consecutively. Select one person for "it," and have him stand in the center of the circle. Have the players rearrange themselves in the circle so that the numbers are mixed.

"It" calls any two numbers except his own. Immediately the two individuals whose numbers he calls try to exchange places while "it" tries to obtain one of them. When "it" succeeds, the person without a place is "it." If "it" fails, he calls two other numbers and tries again to secure a place. When "it" fails after three tries, he selects someone else to take his place.

Suggestions: Instead of using the circle formation, have the players stand in a single line and face "it," who stands in front of the group. He calls any two numbers, and the players exchange places while "it" tries to obtain one of them.

For groups who know one another's names, "it" calls the names of two players. They exchange places while "it" tries to get one.

Circle Change

Within the playing area draw a chalk circle on the floor for each participant except one who is designated as "it." Have each person stand in a circle. "It" stands in the center of the play area.

"It" calls, "Circle change," and everyone must change to another circle. "It" scurries forth to get a place. If he succeeds, the player without a place is "it." If after three tries, "it" fails to secure a place, he selects another player to take his place.

Couple Change. A couple stands in each circle. "It," a selected couple, stands in the center of the area. One member of the couple is the spokesman and calls, "Couple change," and everyone must change to another circle. The twosome in the center tries to secure a circle. If this twosome succeeds, the couple without a circle is "it." If the couple who is "it" fails to secure a place within three attempts, the twosome selects another couple to take its place.

Stagecoach

Players sit in a circle. One player, "it," stands in the center. Assign each player the name of some item or person associated with an imaginary trip in a stagecoach.

"It" tells the thrilling story of a stagecoach trip. As he mentions any of the specified words, the player assigned the word stands, turns completely around, and sits down. "It" may mention any of the words as frequently as he chooses.

At any time he may say, "The stagecoach upset!" With this tragic news everyone jumps to his feet and dashes for another place in the circle. "It," also, seeks a place. The player without a seat tells the next tale. If "it" fails after two attempts to obtain a place, he selects another person to take his place.

Some words which might be assigned to players taking a trip in a stagecoach follow:

horses	spoke
harness	axle
bridle	nut
bit	lantern
tongue	door
whip	road
stagecoach	ruts
driver	blanket
driver's seat	rifle
wheel	cane

elderly gentleman	desperado
lady	lariat
young girl	six shooter
cowboy	sound of gun fire
suitcases	scream
bag of mail	upset
payroll bag	

Suggestion: Have "it" walk around the room as he tells the story. When he mentions an item or person in the tale, the player assigned the word gets up from the circle and follows "it." He can conclude his story at any time by saying, "The stagecoach upset!" Seated players rise and everyone dashes for a place while "it," also, tries to secure one. The player without a place is "it" and weaves the next tale.

Forced Landing. Assign players words or persons associated with an airplane:

propeller	stabilizer
wing	landing lights
radio	landing gear
fuselage	pilot
engine	passenger
rudder	hostess

The cue for trying to secure a place is "forced landing." Play the same as Stagecoach.

Train Wreck. Assign players the words or persons associated with a train:

engine	door
coach	seat
dining car	air conditioning
wheel	conductor
brakes	porter
lights	engineer
window	passenger

The cue remark for trying to secure a place is, "The train left the track." Play the same as Stagecoach.

Farm Crops. Assign each player the name of a farm crop: corn, wheat, oats, potatoes, peas, beets, beans, and others. The cue word for trying to secure a place is "Sold!" Play the same as Stagecoach.

Fumble. Assign a word or person associated with football:

coach	goal line
referee	side line
head linesman	halfback
band	fullback
drum major	quarterback

right end	drop kick
left end	place kick
headgear	forward pass
referee's whistle	touchdown
gun	time out
kickoff	substitute
punt	

The cue word for trying to secure a place is "Fumble."

Depending upon the group or occasion, use words and persons associated with various other sports. Play the same as Stagecoach.

Stop for Lunch. Assign a word or person associated with an automobile:

seat	fuel
hood	autronic eye
radiator	tinted glass
door	back-up lights
engine	taillights
speedometer	air conditioner
steering wheel	automatic transmission
tires	power steering
bolt	power brakes
accelerator	radio
starter	heater-defroster
fender	driver
headlights	passenger

The cue remark for trying to secure a place is "Stop for lunch." Play the same as Stagecoach.

Listen and Hustle

With chalk, mark a circle on the floor or place a cardboard disk, 9 inches in diameter, on the floor for each person except one designated as "it." Players form a single file behind "it," who stands on one side of the area of circles or disks. Use a record player or some other device for music.

"It" walks around the room, and the others follow him. At intervals stop the music. "It" and the other players dash for a circle. The person who does not secure a place is "it" for the next round of the game. If "it" is unable to secure a place after three attempts, allow him to select a player to take his place.

After each hurry to secure a circle the players resume the starting formation with "it" at the head of the file. Resume the music and continue.

Suggestion: If the chalk marks are erased during the scurry of securing a circle, have someone re-mark the circles.

Musical Chairs

Arrange chairs in a circle, seats toward the center. Have three less than the number of players, and have all players except three sit on the chairs facing the center. The three players without chairs are "it" and stand in the center. Secure a record player or other device for music.

With the start of the music everyone except the trio rises from his chair and marches around the circle in front of the chairs. At intervals stop the music. Everyone including "it" dashes for an empty chair. Any three players left standing go to the center of the circle and become "it."

Resume the game. If after three chances the threesome or any member of it does not get a place, allow each unsuccessful seat seeker to select someone to take his place.

Spoons

HIDE AND SEEKERS

Treasures Galore

From sheets of paper of four different colors—blue, yellow, orange, and green—cut disks the size of a quarter. On each of the blue disks write $1,000; on the yellow, $500; orange, $100; green, $10. Before the game hide the valuable disks. Have the players form a line formation and count off by twos. Ones form a team; Twos, another. Ask each team to select a Chief Banker.

On signal, the money seekers are off to find the treasures. Whenever a player finds a bit of wealth, he takes it to his team's Chief Banker. After a designated time call a halt to the hunt and request the Chief Bankers to come forth in front of the assembled players. Each counts his team's accumulated wealth and announces the amount. The team acquiring the largest treasure wins the search.

Ready to Move!

On each of four sets of six 2 × 2-inch slips write the following: decorating, electricity, water, floor covering, light fixtures, and draperies. Before the game place the slips around the room in plain view, so that the players do not have to open drawers or move objects to find them. On cardboard of four different colors—green, brown, orange, blue—draw the outline of a large key and then cut out each one. Place a string through the end of each key. Have the players form four groups and select one player in each group to play the role of the Key Bearer. Give each Key Bearer one of the colored keys, which he wears around his neck.

On signal the teams begin looking for the six items needed to complete their home. When a player finds a slip bearing the name of an item, he takes it to the Key Bearer. Players may not pick up more than one slip of a kind. If they find an item which they already possess, they replace it and are careful not to reveal the contents of the slip to the other groups.

As soon as a team succeeds in finding the six items (decorating, electricity, water, floor covering, light fixtures, and draperies) needed to make it possible to move into the house, the Key Bearer and his group rush to the leader, who checks to see that the slips are correct. If the house is ready for occupants, the Key Bearer enthusiastically states, "Ready to move!" First team to finish scores ten points; second, five; third, three; and the fourth, one for trying.

Color Counts

Secure sheets of colored paper—yellow, brown, blue, green, and black. Cut the sheets into small squares. Have enough pieces so that everyone has an opportunity to find some of the colored slips, which are placed around the room in open view before the players gather to play the game.

On signal, the players search for the colored pieces. Color really counts: each yellow slip has a value of five points; each brown, the value of four; blue, three; green, two; and black, one.

After a designated time, call a halt to the searching. Ask each player to check his colored slips and total his score. The person with the highest score wins the hunt.

Beany Hunt

Secure navy beans and paper bags, enough for everyone in the group. Before the players gather to play the game, hide navy beans in various places in the room. Call the group together. Give each person a small paper bag.

On signal, each person hunts for the beans. Any beans that he finds he puts in his sack. After a designated time call the hunt to a halt. Everyone counts his beans, and the person finding the largest number wins the search.

Proverbs in Pieces

Write well-known proverbs on slips of paper of the same size and cut each slip into two pieces. Prepare enough proverbs so that everyone has a chance to find some of the slips. Place the slips in plain view in various places in the room. Be sure that the players do not have to remove items, open drawers, or perform other feats in order to find them.

On signal, the players hurry to obtain as many pieces of proverbs as possible within a designated time. Since the point of the game is to obtain the largest number of complete proverbs, the scene is a trading mart, as the players hurriedly exchange slips to get the entire proverb.

At the end of the specified time call the game to a halt. The player with the most complete proverbs wins the search. Ask the winner to read his collection. To make checking easy have a list of the proverbs which were hidden in the room.

For a list of proverbs which can be used, see pages 42–44.

Affinities in Pieces. Write affinities (see list on page 44) on slips of paper and cut them into two pieces. Play the game the same as Proverbs in Pieces.

Old Sayings in Pieces. Write an old saying (see list on page 45) on slips of paper and cut them in half. Play the game the same as Proverbs in Pieces.

Scavenger Scurry

Give each person a pencil and a list of items that he is to locate and bring within a designated time to the starting scene. If the group is large, write the items on a blackboard or large sheet of paper, and ask the players to copy the items on a sheet of paper. Lists may include any item available in the immediate vicinity. Articles may not be purchased. It is wise to prepare persons in the area for scavengers who may call at their door with strange requests.

Have the players form groups of four. Name a designated time in which the players must return to the place of departure. Any players returning late are complimented for trying but are out of the competition. However, ask them to assist in checking the wares of the other scavengers.

Using no form of transportation other than their feet, the scavengers set off to find the requested items on their lists. After the designated time allowed for scavenging, everyone assembles at the starting scene. Each group displays its loot. Check which group has found all of the listed items or most of them. The group having found all or the largest number of items wins the hunt.

Suggestions: Have the groups secure items which need not be returned. This solves many problems. Some of the items which the scavengers seek might include: bus transfer, last year's calendar, dog biscuit, paper clip, safety pin, radish, 3-inch nail, envelope bearing the postmark of New York, two-pound candy box, wrapper from a loaf of whole-wheat bread, piece of celery, pinch of bird seed, or cereal box-top.

Lootless Scavenging. Sometimes it is more practical for the scavengers to hunt for specified items and record their findings on a sheet of paper instead of bringing items back. The lists for these games are endless, for they can be varied to meet any situation, place, occasion, and group.

A possible list includes the following with space to the right of each item for the player to record his findings:

1. Address of a colonial house with green shutters_____.
2. Date that a nearby church was erected _____.
3. Number of windows in a house on a given corner _____.
4. Number of trees on a designated side of a street _____.
5. Direction a nearby service station faces _____.
6. Find five houses having a different color trim, and give the colors and the addresses _____.
7. List ten items displayed in a designated store _____

8. Find five different makes of foreign automobiles in a particular area, and list their names and the addresses where they were found _____

9. Names and ages of children residing on the north, south, east, or west side of a designated street _____

10. Number of doors on a specified school building _____.

RELAY FUN MAKERS

Old Sayings Hustle

The players form two teams and sit facing one another about 10 feet apart. Place a carton at both ends of the two teams (four cartons). Put a clean cloth, about the size of a handkerchief, in the two cartons at one end of the teams.

Assign to each player on Team 1 the last word of various old sayings, for example, "crystal," from "Clear as crystal," for one player; "razor," from "Sharp as a razor," for the next player. Assign the same words to the players on Team 2. The players having the same word sit opposite one another. Keep a list of the assigned old sayings.

Call out the first part of an old saying, for example, "Clear as _____." Each of the two players assigned the word "crystal" races to the box containing the cloth. Each takes the one from his team's carton, hustles to deposit it in the empty container at the other end of his team, and returns to his seat.

The player reaching his seat first scores one point for his team; the team first to score eleven points wins the game. To keep the players alert do not call the old sayings in the same order in which they were assigned.

See page 45 for a list of old sayings.

Affinities' Rush. Play the same as Old Sayings Hustle except assign the last word of an affinity to each player, for example, "butter," from "Bread and butter," or "eggs," from "Ham and eggs." See page 44 for a list of affinities.

Musical Dash. Play the same as Old Sayings Hustle except assign the name of a well-known song to each player. Give the list of assigned songs to a pianist. As he starts playing a song, the two players who are assigned its name dash to their respective cartons, take the cloth, transfer it to the opposite container, and dash for their seats. The first one seated at his own place scores a point; the team scoring eleven points first wins the game.

Plate Stack

Players form teams and stand in single files. Give the last player on each team six paper plates.

On signal, the last player on each team passes the plates, one at a time, up the file to the player ahead of him. Passing continues until the first player obtains the plates. He stacks them on the floor. First team to have the six plates stacked scores five points; second, four points; third, three; all others, one for trying.

The first player from each row takes the plates and goes to the end of the team while everyone moves forward one place. Play continues until everyone has a chance to stack the plates. The team with the highest score wins the game.

Sir Walter Raleigh

Secure two pieces of cardboard 12 inches square for each team. Keep extra pieces of cardboard in reserve, for they receive hard wear and abusive handling. Draw a starting line, and 15 feet from it mark a parallel line. Players are in couples and stand in files behind the starting line. Give two pieces of cardboard to the gentleman of the first couple on each team. He places the two pieces of cardboard on the floor at the starting line, and the girl stands on them.

On signal, the gentleman of each pair moves one cardboard forward, and the girl steps on it. He quickly picks up the back cardboard and places it in front for the girl to step on it. Sir Walter Raleigh and his lady proceed in this fashion to the goal. When they cross the goal the gentleman picks up the cardboards and, locking arms, the pair hurries back to the starting line. Giving the cardboards to the next gentleman in line, the couple goes to the end of the team.

Play continues until one team is first to have all of its members participate and complete the action.

Tie and Untie

Players form four teams and sit in a hollow square (see page 9). Give the first player of each team a strip of colored cloth 24 inches long and 4 inches wide.

On signal, the first player ties the cloth with a loose knot around the left arm of the second player. The second unties it with his right hand and then ties it on the arm of the third player.

Tying and untying continues until the last player unties the cloth. He gets up and hurries to the starter, ties the cloth on his left arm, and returns to the end of his team. The head player quickly unties the cloth and immediately raises his hand, holding the cloth to indicate his team has finished. First team to complete the action wins.

Raisin Relay

Players form four teams and sit in a hollow square (see page 9). Give each player a toothpick. Present the first player of each team with a paper plate containing a raisin for every member. Place a waste container in front of the first player of each team.

On signal, the first player of each team spears a raisin with his toothpick and places it in his mouth. He then passes the raisins to the second player who takes one with his toothpick and sends the plate on to the third person. Passing continues until the last player takes a raisin. He then puts his toothpick on the plate and sends the plate up the line.

Each player puts his toothpick on the plate. When the head player gets the plate he puts his toothpick on it, tosses the plate and toothpicks in the container, and immediately raises his hand to indicate his team has finished. First team to complete the action wins the game.

Card Pass

Players form four teams and sit in a hollow square (see page 9). Give the first player on each team four playing cards or pieces of cardboard of the same size.

On signal, the first player sticks a card between each of the five fingers of the second player's left hand. Immediately the second player transfers and places the cards, one at a time, between the fingers of the third player's left hand. Play continues until the last player has the cards. He removes them one at a time from his left hand and takes the cards to the starter. First team to complete the action wins the game.

Happy Holiday. Use cardboard symbols that are appropriate for a particular holiday, for example, for Christmas: bells, trees, Santas, snowmen; for Easter: bunnies, eggs, baskets; for Halloween: cats, witches, pumpkins. The first player places the symbols between the fingers of the second player. In turn each player removes the cardboards, one at a time, and places them between the fingers of the next individual. When the last player removes the holiday symbols from his fingers, he takes them to the head player. As soon as the starter has them, he shouts, "Happy holiday!" The first team to express the team's best wishes wins the relay.

Clothespin Fingers

Players form four teams and sit in a hollow square (see page 9). Give the first player of each team five clothespins.

On signal, the first player places a clothespin on the end of each finger of the second player's left hand so that they constitute an extension of the fingers. As soon as player Number 2 has five pins on his hand, he takes them off, one at a time, and then puts them on the fingers of the third player's left hand. When the last person in the line removes the pins from his fingers, he brings the pins to the starter. First team to finish wins the activity.

Bottoms Up

Players sit in a hollow square (see page 9). Place a chair on the floor, legs up, in the front and center of each team. On the floor in front of each chair put four milk cartons whose tops have been cut off evenly.

On signal, the first player from each team gets up and runs to the chair, picks up the cartons one at a time, places one on each leg of the chair, and hustles to the end of his team. While he places the cartons on the legs of the chair, everyone moves up one place so that the last space is vacant.

As soon as the starter sits, the second player hurries to the chair, removes the cartons, one at a time from the legs of the chair, places them on the floor ahead of the chair, hurries to the end of his team, and sits. Play continues with the members of each team alternately placing the cartons on the legs of the chair and removing them. The first team to have its members complete the action wins the game.

Pillowcase Change

Secure an old pillow and pillowcase for each team. Have the players stand in a circle, alternately facing in and out, thus forming two teams (see page 20). Give a pillow and case to the first player on each team.

On signal, the first player on each team puts the case on the pillow and passes it to the second player. He removes the case and passes it and the pillow to the third person who again replaces the case. Players continue alternately to put on the case and to take it off until the last player completes the action. He raises the pillow overhead to indicate his team has finished. First team to raise its pillow wins the game.

String Wind

Secure a ball of soft twine (used in gardening for tying up plants) for each team. Players stand in a circle, alternately facing in and out, thus forming two teams (see page 20). Give a ball of twine to the first player on each team.

On signal, the starter for each team takes hold of the end of the twine and unwinds enough to pass the ball to the person on his right. Players continue to unwind the twine and pass it to the person on the right. When the last player has the ball he unwinds about 12 inches, but then he immediately starts winding the twine on the ball and passes it to the player on his left. In turn each player winds the twine on the ball and passes it to the person on the left until the starter completes winding the twine. First team to have all of the twine back in a ball wins the game.

Speedy Sweep

Draw a starting line on one side of the room. Fifteen feet from it draw a goal line. Players form teams and stand in single files behind the starting line and face the goal. Give a broom and a piece of 8½ × 11-inch paper to the head player on each team. He places the paper on the floor directly behind the starting line.

On signal, the first player of each team starts sweeping his paper to the goal line. As soon as he crosses the goal, he picks up the paper and hastens back to his team. At the starting line he gives the broom and paper to the second player on the team and goes to the end of his group. Play continues until everyone participates and the head player is back in his place. He shouts "Speedy sweep" to indicate his team has finished. The first team to finish wins the activity.

Balloon Sweep

Secure a carton, a broom, and a balloon for each team. Have additional balloons in case of blowouts. Place a carton on the goal directly in line with each team, which stands in a single file at the starting line 15 feet from it. Give a broom and balloon to the starter on each team. He places the balloon on the floor at the starting line.

On signal, the starter for each team sweeps the balloon to the carton, circles it, and continues sweeping the balloon to the starting line. As soon as he crosses the line, he hands the broom to the second player who places the balloon directly behind the line and starts sweeping. The player who completed his turn goes to the end of his team.

The first team to complete the action and have its players in their original positions wins the game.

Balloon Bat

Draw a starting line, and 15 feet from it indicate a goal line. Players form teams and stand in single files at the starting line. Give a balloon to the first player on each team. Have spare balloons in case of blowouts.

On signal, player Number 1 bats the balloon to the goal and then back to the starting line. He may use both hands in propelling the balloon. If at any time the balloon falls to the floor, he stops, picks it up, and continues to bat it.

As soon as he reaches the starting line, he gives the balloon to the second player and goes to the end of his team. The second player proceeds to bat the balloon to and from the goal. Play continues until one team is first to finish and wins the game.

Balloon Kick. In turn each player kicks the balloon to and from the goal. The first team to have its members complete the action wins.

Balloon Butt. In turn each player gets down on all fours and starts butting the balloon with his head toward the goal. After reaching the goal he must butt the balloon back to the starting line. The first team to have its members complete the action wins the relay.

Egg Pass

Have players stand in a circle alternately facing in and out, thus forming two teams (see page 20). Give everyone a tablespoon. Present a rubber or hard-boiled egg to the starter for each team. Request the starters to place the eggs on their spoons.

On signal, the starter of each team transfers the egg to the spoon of the player on his right. If the egg falls in the transfer, the player picks it up, places it on his spoon, and passes it again. Passing continues until the last player has the egg. He shouts, "The egg is here!" The first team to complete the action wins the game.

Potato and Spoon Pass

Have players stand in a circle, alternately facing in and out, thus forming two teams (see page 20). Indicate one person on each team as starter. Give each starter a tablespoon and a potato to place on the tablespoon.

On signal the starter of each team passes the tablespoon holding the potato to the player on his right. In turn each player passes the spoon containing the potato to the person on the right. When the last player holds the spoon bearing the potato, he starts passing it to the player on his left. Passing to the person on the left continues until the starter again holds the spoon containing the potato. The first team to have its players complete passing the spoon and potato around the circle to the right and left wins the game.

If the potato falls from the spoon any time during the passing, the player responsible picks it up, places it on the spoon, and resumes passing.

Bag Burst

Draw a starting line, and 20 feet from it indicate a goal line. Forming teams, the players stand in single files behind the starting line. Place a chair at the goal in line with each team. On it put a pile of paper bags, one for each member of the team and some spares; next to the chair place a wastebasket.

On signal, the first player of every team hurries to the chair, takes a bag, blows it up, bursts it with his hands, tosses it in the wastebasket, and returns to the starting line. As he crosses the starting line he touches the extended hand of the second player as the signal to go. The first player goes to the end of his team. If a player only deflates a bag instead of bursting it, he must try again.

Players continue the relay until one team is first to finish. When the starter is back in place he raises his hands and shouts, "The best bag bursters!"

Sit Fast!

Draw a starting line, and 15 feet from it indicate a goal line. Players form teams and stand in single files behind the starting line. On the goal place a folding chair in line with each team.

On signal, the first player of each team hustles forward to the chair, sets the chair up, sits on it, raises his feet off the floor, taps them together, stands, folds the chair, lays it on the floor, hurries back to the starting line, touches the extended hand of the second player, and goes to the end of his team. The second player and the other members perform the same sequence of actions. Play continues until one team is first to finish. The members of the winning group are acclaimed the "best folders and unfolders."

Seats for the Ladies

Draw a starting line, and 15 feet from it draw a goal line. Players in pairs—a boy and a girl—form two teams and stand behind the starting line. Give the boy of the first couple of each team a folding chair.

On signal, the first pair of each team hurries to the goal line. The boy sets up the chair; the girl sits on it, raises her feet from the floor, and then stands. Immediately the boy folds the chair, picks it up, and the couple hurries to the starting line. Giving the chair to the second couple, the twosome goes to the end of the line. Play continues until one team is first to finish and wins the game.

Chair Sit and Pass

Players form teams and stand in single files. Give the first player of each team a folding chair.

On signal he sits on the chair, lifts his feet off the ground, stands, and gives the chair to the next player, who repeats the action. In this way the chair is passed down the file to the end player. When the last player has completed the action, he folds the chair, and passes it to the player ahead of him. In turn each player passes the chair to the person ahead of him until the first player again has the chair. The team first to finish wins the game.

Captain's Seat

Players form teams and stand in single files. The first player of each team is called the Captain. Give each Captain a folding chair.

On signal, the Captain passes the chair to the second player. In turn each member passes it to the next one until the chair reaches the last player, who immediately starts the chair on its way up the line. When the Captain again has the chair, he sets it up, sits on it, and shouts, "I have the Captain's seat." The first team to have its Captain sitting on his chair wins the game.

Handle with Care!

Players stand in a circle, alternately facing in and out, thus forming two teams (see page 20). Give the first player of each team a small plate, cup, tumbler, and a spoon. (Be sure the china and tumbler are unbreakable or are odd pieces that will not be missed if they are broken.)

On signal, the first player of each team passes the items one at a time to the second person, who immediately passes the items to the next individual. The items may be passed in any sequence, but they must be passed one at a time. Passing continues until the last player has the four items. He passes them back one at a time. In turn each player assists in sending the items to the starter. When the head player again has the four items, he taps the side of the tumbler with the spoon to indicate his team has finished. The first team to "sound off" wins the game.

Alphabet Card Relay

Players form two teams and sit facing one another about 12 feet apart. Place a set of alphabet cards face down on a chair at one end of each team. On the other end of each team place an empty chair.

On signal the first player of each team hustles to the alphabet cards, fingers through them, and selects the letter A. Leaving the cards in a pile face down, he hurries and takes the letter to the vacant chair on the opposite end of his team. He places the card against the back of the chair so that the letter is visible to the players. Then he rushes back to his place, sits down, and touches the extended hand of the second player who hustles to the cards and selects the letter B, which he takes to the opposite chair and places ahead of the letter A.

Play continues until the entire alphabet is placed on the opposite chair and the letter Z is the last card visible to the players. The team finishing first in transferring the alphabet in its correct order from one chair to the other wins the game.

Since there are twenty-six letters to transfer from one chair to another, several persons may have more than one turn. As soon as the last player on a team gets a letter which is not Z, the first player again goes into action. Play continues with each person taking a turn until one individual secures Z, the last letter of the alphabet.

See "Words on Foot," page 132, for directions for making the alphabet cards.

Selecting Cards

Players form two teams and sit in lines facing one another about 10 feet apart. Give the first player of each team a deck of cards.

On signal, the first player fingers through the cards and selects the two of spades and lays it on the floor in front of him. He then hands the deck to the second player who takes out the three of spades. In turn each player selects the next highest card until the ace is secured. First team to complete the run of spades wins the round. If everyone has a turn and the run is incomplete, the first player goes into action as soon as the last participant brings the deck of cards to him. Play continues until the ace, the last card needed to complete the run of spades, is selected from the deck.

Continue the game by having the teams select the clubs, diamonds, and hearts in the same way. The members of the team winning the most rounds are the "fastest card selectors."

Roll and Unroll

Secure four old magazines (same page size) and four pieces of cloth 24 inches long and 2 inches wide. Players form teams and sit in a hollow square (see page 9). Give the first player of each team a magazine and a piece of cloth.

On signal, the first player of each team rolls the magazine, places the cloth around it, ties a bow, and passes it to the second player, who unties the bow, removes the cloth, and unrolls the magazine. He passes the magazine and cloth to the third person, who again rolls the magazine, and decorates it with a cloth bow.

Players continue to roll and unroll the magazine. When the last player completes the action, he brings the magazine and cloth to the starter, who stands and holds up the magazine to indicate his team has finished. First team to finish rolling and unrolling the magazine wins the game.

Pass It

Players form teams and sit in single files.

On signal, the last player taps the person ahead of him on the back. In turn each player passes the tap as soon as he feels it. When the first player on the team feels the tap, he stands and shouts, "We passed it!"

How Do You Do?

Players form teams and stand in single files.

On signal, the first player turns to the second person, shakes his hand, and says, "How do you do?" The second player turns, shakes hands with the third player, and greets him.

Each player in turn follows the action. When the second to last player shakes hands with the last person on the team, the two individuals shout, "How do you do, everyone!" The first team to complete the action and have the twosome extend their greetings wins the game.

INDOOR
NATURETTES

CONTENTS

* See Chapter II for description
** See Chapter III for description

Bringing elements of the outdoors indoors is a unique feature of Naturettes. Actually, through the use of very simple supplies—such as pictures of birds, trees, wild and garden flowers, and animals, and paper, pencils, some plant cuttings, and arranging materials—the outdoors imaginatively comes indoors in most of the games. With a little variation in a few games the leader might increase the players' sphere of nature appreciation by stimulating interest in fish, reptiles, insects, rocks, and minerals and by making them aware of the wonders of the sky, mountains, lakes, rivers, and oceans.

In presenting the activities the leader will discover that many of them are lead-up games which assist the players in acquiring a zest for outdoor recreation. The games provide fun, and they are also a device for learning a great deal about the outdoors. The leader and participants who are not experts in outdoor recreation will not find themselves at a loss, for the supplementary information offered for many of the games gives them a footing for enjoying the games.

To help the leader select activities appropriate for his occasion a list of them divided into several categories precedes this chapter. If the leader desires, he can select some activities from each of the various categories and conduct a series of balanced programs of games having nature for their theme.

DE-ICERS

Nature's Families

Prepare as many 3 × 5-inch slips of paper as there are players. On each slip write the name of a wildflower, a bird, and a tree. For example, on one slip write "Great Trillium, White-Breasted Nuthatch, Red Maple." Then on each of two other slips write the names of other members of the same families: "Nodding Trillium, Red-Breasted Nuthatch, Silver Maple"; and "Painted Trillium, Brown-Headed Nuthatch, Black Maple." Prepare the rest of the slips also in sets of three.

Assemble the players and give each person a slip.

On signal, each player seeks the other two individuals who hold slips bearing the names of a flower, bird, and tree in the same families as his. The first threesome to find one another wins the game, if the wildflowers, birds, and trees on the three slips are actually related. Sometimes in the excitement of searching the families acquire new members. Check the findings before announcing the winners.

Allow the other players to find the members of their families. Ask the winners to assist in checking the slips of the other individuals.

Other members of nature's families to use on the slips for the search include:

Wildflowers	*Birds*	*Trees*
Woodland Jack-in-the-Pulpit	Wood Thrush	Black Ash
Swamp Jack-in-the-Pulpit	Hermit Thrush	Blue Ash
Northern Jack-in-the-Pulpit	Olive-Backed Thrush	White Ash
Blue-Flag Iris	Hairy Woodpecker	Eastern White Oak
Vernal Iris	Downy Woodpecker	Bur Oak
Crested Iris	Red-Headed Woodpecker	Northern Red Oak
Wood Lily	Western Tanager	White Elm
Turk's-Cap Lily	Scarlet Tanager	Cork Elm
Midland Lily	Summer Tanager	Slippery Elm
Cardinal Lobelia	House Wren	Paper Birch
Great Blue Lobelia	Short-Billed Marsh Wren	Gray Birch
Lime Lobelia	Carolina Wren	River Birch
Broad-Leaf Golden Aster	Red-Eyed Vireo	Black Willow
New England Aster	Warbling Vireo	Sandbar Willow
White Wood Aster	Philadelphia Vireo	Missouri Willow
Green-Eyed Ladies' Tresses	Black-Capped Chickadee	Scarlet Hawthorn
Grass-Leaf Ladies' Tresses	Carolina Chickadee	Grove Hawthorn
Autumn Ladies' Tresses	Brown-Capped Chickadee	Flat-Topped Hawthorn

Colorful Relatives. Write the name of a garden flower and its family's name on a slip for each player. Make sets of three slips for each family. For example, on one slip write, "Alpine Aster—Compositae (Daisy)." On each of two other slips write the names of two other relatives in the family: "Michaelmas Daisy—Compositae (Daisy)" and "Double Sunflower—Compositae (Daisy)." Each person seeks the two other players with slips having the same family name. Play the same as Nature's Families.

Some other relatives and families to write on the slips are:

March Marigold—Ranunculaceae (Buttercup)
Common American Columbine—Ranunculaceae (Buttercup)
Fern-Leaved Peony—Ranunculaceae (Buttercup)

Golden-tuft—Cruciferae (Mustard)
Wall Rock-cress—Cruciferae (Mustard)
Alpine Wallflower—Cruciferae (Mustard)

Lily-of-the-valley—Liliaceae (Lily)
Poker Plant—Liliaceae (Lily)
Tiger Lily—Liliaceae (Lily)

Sweet William—Caryophyllaceae (Pink)
Carnation—Caryophyllaceae (Pink)
Cottage Pink—Caryophyllaceae (Pink)

Bleeding Heart—Fumariaceae (Fumitory)
Fern-Leaved Fumitory—Fumariaceae (Fumitory)
Noble Fumitory—Fumariaceae (Fumitory)

Blackberry Lily—Iridaceae (Iris)
Crested Dwarf Iris—Iridaceae (Iris)
Tall Bearded Iris—Iridaceae (Iris)

Creeping Phlox—Polemoniaceae (Phlox)
Jacob's Ladder—Polemoniaceae (Phlox)
Wild Sweet William—Polemoniaceae (Phlox)

Cowslip—Primulaceae (Primrose)
English Primrose—Primulaceae (Primrose)
Polyanthus—Primulaceae (Primrose)

Blue Sage—Labiatae (Mint)
False Dragonhead—Labiatae (Mint)
Large-Flowered Catmint—Labiatae (Mint)

Plant Meet Plant. Write the name of a house plant on all three slips of each set. Each person seeks the other two persons having the same plant name as his on their slips of paper. Play the same as Nature's Families.

Some plant names to write on the slips include:

African Violet	Dracaena	Asparagus Fern
Century Plant	Fuchsia	English Ivy
Rhododendron	Gloxinia	Begonia (Rex)
Caladium	Screw Pine	Azalea
Spider Plant	Coleus	Sansevieria
Croton	Picka-back	Cyclamen

WARM-UPS

Animal Symbolism

Prepare ahead of time a list of animals and the word most likely to symbolize each animal. Have a blackboard and chalk or a large sheet of paper and crayons. Players form teams and sit in single files. Give a piece of chalk to the first player of each team.

Call out a word symbolizing an animal, for example, "slyness." The first player of each team hurries to the blackboard and writes the name of the animal he associates with the symbol; in this case it should be "fox." The first player to write the name of the correct animal scores three points for his team. All others score one point for trying. The players return to their places and give the chalk to the second players on the teams.

Play continues until everyone has a chance to compete. The team with the highest score at the conclusion of the game wins.

Other words associated with animals include:

Fleetness—Deer	Stealthiness—Panther
Industry—Beaver	Fidelity—Dog
Hunger—Wolf	Majesty—Lion, Moose
Gentleness—Sheep	Strength—Ox
Easter—Rabbit	Coldness—Polar Bear
Stillness—Mouse	Spring—Woodchuck
Thirst—Camel	Tallness—Giraffe

Flower Symbolism. Use the words associated with various flowers and play the game the same way as Animal Symbolism. Words associated with flowers include:

Purity—Lily	Farewell—Sweet Pea
Easter—Lily	Mother's Day—Carnation
Modesty—Violet	Virtue—Lily
Remembrance—Forget-me-not	Peace—Poppy
Hay Fever—Ragweed	Contentment—Morning Glory
He loves me, he loves me not—Daisy	Cheerfulness—Chrysanthemum
Spring—Pussy Willow	Christmas—Holly, Poinsettia
Innocence—Pansy, Daisy	Sympathy—Rose
Love—Rose	Courage—Carnation

Bird Symbolism. Use the words associated with various birds and play the game the same way as Animal Symbolism. Words associated with birds include:

Happiness—Lark	Wisdom—Owl
Spring—Bluebird	Courage—Eagle
Cheer—Robin	United States—Eagle
Summer—Swallow	Craziness—Loon
Persistence—Woodpecker	Gracefulness—Swan

Nature's Names

Have a blackboard and chalk or a large sheet of paper and crayons. Players form teams and sit in single files. Give a piece of chalk to the first player on each team.

State the name of a flower, tree, bird, or animal, for example,

"Purple Martin." The first player of each team hurries to the blackboard and writes the name of the bird. The first person to finish writing it legibly and correctly scores five points for his team; second, four points; third, three; all others, one for trying.

As soon as the first players return to their places announce the name of another creature or object, and the second player of each team goes into action.

Continue until every member of the team has a chance to compete. The team with the highest score at the conclusion of the game wins.

Bird Watcher

Use a set of colored pictures of birds, large enough for players to see at a distance. Write the name of each bird on a separate 3 × 5-inch card. Make a set of the cards for each team. Players form four teams and sit in single files. Ask each group to number off consecutively. Place a table 10 feet ahead of each team and on each table put a set of cards face down.

Hold one of the pictures of the birds so that everyone can see it. On signal, the first player from each team dashes to his team's table and selects the name of the bird shown in the picture. The first individual to return to his place, sit, and exhibit the correct name of the bird scores three points for his team. All others score one point for trying.

Hold another picture, and on signal the second player of each team goes into action. Play continues until everyone has a chance to compete. The team with the highest score at the conclusion of the game wins.

In case no player returns to his place with the correct name, each player scores one point for trying.

Find the Flower. Using pictures and names of wildflowers or garden flowers, play in the same way as Bird Watcher.

Find the Fruit and Vegetable. Using pictures and names of fruits and vegetables, play in the same way as Bird Watcher.

Find the Animal. Using pictures and names of animals, play in the same way as Bird Watcher.

Find the Tree. Using the pictures and names of trees, play in the same way as Bird Watcher.

Pot the Cutting

Request each person in advance to bring a healthy cutting from a house plant. On a newspaper-covered table about 15 feet ahead of each team place a clay flower pot, a cutting, and a small stone or piece of broken flower pot for each member of the team. In addition, place a sufficient amount of potting soil and a supply of cleansing tissues on the table. On the floor to the right of the table put a carton or wastebasket. Players form teams and stand in single files behind a starting line.

On signal, the first player of each team hurries to the table, places the stone or piece of flower pot over the hole of the flower pot to prevent losing the soil, puts in soil, sets the cutting in place, adds more soil if needed, and packs the soil around the bottom portion of the cutting. After wiping his hands with some cleansing tissues which he deposits in the wastebasket, the player picks up the potted cutting, hurries back to his team, touches the hand of the second player, and goes to the end of the line.

Play continues until one team wins the game by being first to have all its members finish potting their cuttings. Allow the other teams time to pot their cuttings. Everyone keeps the cutting he potted.

QUIZZERS

Star Gazing

On sheets of paper (one for each team) draw the following constellations in their position in the sky: Great Bear (Big Dipper), Little Bear (Little Dipper), Cassiopeia (Queen), Cephus (King), and the Dragon. Label the constellations. Players form teams of five and stand in single files behind a starting line. Fifteen feet from the starting line place a table in front of each team. Put a copy of the constellations on each table. Give the first player of each team a green crayon.

On signal, the first player of each team rushes to the table, locates a constellation on the sheet, and encircles it and its name with his crayon. He hurries back to the team, gives the crayon to the second player, and goes to the end of the line. The second player hurries to the drawing and encircles another constellation.

Play continues until one team is first to have its members encircle the five constellations. Check the drawing, and if the five names of the constellations are correctly encircled, announce the winner.

Which Tree?

Players sit around the room. Select an "it" and ask him to leave the room.

In the absence of "it," the players select the name of a tree.

Recall "it," who tries to guess the name of the tree through a series of questions to which the players must respond with a statement about the tree. The individual supplying the statement that enables "it" to guess the right tree exchanges places with "it."

If "it" is unable to guess the name of the tree after a reasonable attempt, announce the name of the tree. "It" leaves the room again while the players select the name of another tree. If after two attempts "it" fails to guess correctly, he chooses someone to take his place and joins the group.

If the tree selected is a hickory, a series of questions and answers might include:

"It": Is the tree an evergreen or deciduous (loses all or most of its leaves annually)?
Player: It is deciduous.
"It": What kind of bark does it have?
Player: The bark is rough or shaggy.
"It": Are the leaves simple (consisting of one continuous blade) or compound (consisting of several leaflets)?
Player: They are compound, having between five to nine leaflets.
"It": Are the leaflets arranged alternately on the stem or opposite one another?
Player: The leaflets are opposite.
"It": Is it popular with any particular bird or animal?
Player: It is a favorite of squirrels.
"It": What is the appearance of the nuts it bears?
Player: They have a tough hard shell.
"It": Is it the hickory?
Player: Yes.

Which Bird? Have "it" query the players about the name of a bird which the group selects for him to guess. Play the same as Which Tree?

Which Flower? Have "it" query the players about the name of a wildflower or garden flower which the group selects for him to guess. Play the same as Which Tree?

Trees in Brief

Cut a slip of paper for each player. On each slip write the first and last letter of the names of several trees. Indicate the number of letters which the players are to add to complete each name by using the same number of dashes. For example, for Walnut write "W – – – – t." Give each player a list and a pencil.

Within a given time each player is to complete as many names as he can by filling in the correct letters. Call time and ask the individual with the most names filled in to read the names of the trees. If his list is correct, he wins the game.

Some suggestions for the list are:

	Answers
M – – – e	Maple
B – x E – – – r	Box Elder
H – – – – – y	Hickory
A – – – n	Aspen
B – – – h	Beech
O – k	Oak
R – d M – – – – – – y	Red Mulberry
L – – – – t	Locust
B – – – – – – d	Basswood
M – – – – – – n A – h	Mountain Ash
H – – – – – – n	Hawthorn
W – – – – w	Willow
S – – – – – – – s	Sassafras
S – – – – – – e	Sycamore
B – – – – – – – t	Butternut
C – – – – e T – – e	Coffee Tree
P – – e	Pine
H – – – – – k	Hemlock
S – – – – e	Spruce
B – – – – m	Balsam
C – – – r	Cedar

Wildflowers in Brief. Use the names of wildflowers. Play the same as Trees in Brief. Some suggestions for the list are:

	Answers
B – – – – – – – – r	Bellflower
B – – – k e – – d S – – – n	Black-eyed-Susan
B – – – – – – – t	Bloodroot
B – – – – – – l	Bluebell
C – – – – – – – e	Columbine
M – – – h M – – – – – – d	Marsh Marigold
V – – – – t	Violet
H – – – – – – a	Hepatica
I – – – – n P – – e	Indian Pipe
J – – k – – – – – P – – – – t	Jack-in-the-Pulpit
S – – – – – – – – – – e	Skunkcabbage
T – – – – – – m	Trillium

Birds in Brief. Use the names of birds. Play the game the same way as Trees in Brief. Some suggestions for the list are:

	Answers
C – – – – – – e	Chickadee
H – – – – – – – – – d	Hummingbird
B – – – – – – d	Bluebird
F – – – – – r	Flicker
P – – – – r	Plover
B – – – – – – e	Bobwhite
W – – – – – – – – – – – l	Whippoorwill

	Answers
B – – – – – – k	Bobolink
C – – – – – – l	Cardinal
W – – n	Wren
C – – – e	Crane
B – – e J – y	Blue Jay
S – – – – – – – r	Sandpiper
C – – w	Crow

Tree Facts

Prepare a series of questions and statements describing trees and their uses.

Read one of the questions or statements and follow it with the first letter of the correct answer. For example, "Name a sweet smelling tree beginning with the letter *B*" might be answered by "Balsam." The player who is first to call out a correct name scores one point. In case of a tie each person scores one point. The player with the most points at the end of a designated time wins the game. A sample of other statements and questions to use follows:

	Answers
Name a fire-by-friction wood beginning with *Y*.	Yucca
Give me a use for white cedar beginning with *P*.	Posts
Give me a use for hemlock bark beginning with *T*.	Tanning
Name a heavy hardwood beginning with *I*.	Ironwood
Name a commercial use for elm beginning with *H*.	Handles
Name something obtained from maple beginning with S.	Sugar
Give me a use for birch bark beginning with *B*.	Baskets
Why is dogwood so popular? *F*	Flowers

Scouting for Birds

Mount on cardboard a set of colored pictures of birds. Be sure the pictures are large enough for a group of players to see. Write the name of the bird on the back of each picture. Players sit in a circle.

Hold up one of the pictures. The player who is first to name the bird gets the picture. As soon as a player thinks he knows the bird, he shouts the name. The player with the most cards at the end of a designated time wins the game.

Suggestion: Instead of playing the game on an individual basis have the players form two teams sitting opposite one another. Stand or sit at one end of the teams.

Hold up a picture of a bird and ask the first player on Team 1 to identify it. If he succeeds, he scores a point for his team. Then give the first player on Team 2 a chance to identify the next picture. Continue with teams alternately having a chance to identify the pictures.

If a member of a team fails to identify a bird, the player on the opposing team has a turn. Continue alternating teams until one player is successful in naming the bird. If everyone fails, announce the name of the bird, select another picture, and continue the game.

Scouting for Wildflowers. Use pictures of wildflowers and play the same way as Scouting for Birds.

Scouting for Garden Flowers. Use pictures of garden flowers and play the same way as Scouting for Birds.

Scouting for Animals. Use pictures of animals and play the same way as Scouting for Birds.

Scouting for Vegetables and Fruits. Use pictures of vegetables and fruits and play the same way as Scouting for Birds.

Scouting for Trees. Use pictures of trees and play the same way as Scouting for Birds.

Seasonal Associations

Players form groups of four. Give one player of each group a pencil and a sheet of 8½ × 11-inch paper.

On signal, the recorder of each group is to list during a specified time the occurrences or objects the members of his group associate with the four seasons of the year: spring, summer, autumn, and winter.

At the end of a designated time call a halt and ask the recorder of each group to read the players' list. For each plausible association the group scores one point. The group scoring the most points wins the game.

Possible associations with the four seasons might include:

Spring	Summer	Autumn	Winter
new clothes	trips	bright colored	snow
Easter	swimming	foliage	sleds
green grass	boating	harvest time	skis
budding trees	golf	football	ice
and shrubs	tennis	return to school	snow creations
flowers	picnics	falling leaves	Christmas
birds in the nest	outdoor cooking	burning leaves	New Year's
new car	camping	migrating birds	skating
Spring fever	Independence	and water-	leafless trees
baseball	Day	fowl	birds at the
children on skates	vacation	Hallowe'en	feeder
and bicycles	sunburn	Thanksgiving	beauty of snow
	heat	pumpkins	and sleet on
	beautiful flowers	turkeys	trees and
	the neighbors'		shrubs
	radio and		human migrations
	television		to warmer
			climates

Birds Are Here!

Players form teams and sit in single files. Give the first player of each team a pencil and a sheet of 8½ × 11-inch paper. Have a bird guidebook to check answers.

On signal, the first player of each team writes the name of a bird, for example, "Cardinal," on the top of the paper. Immediately he passes the paper and pencil to the second person who adds the name of another bird, perhaps "Blue Jay."

In turn each player writes the name of a different bird. Each name may be used only once. When the last player writes the name of a bird, he passes the slip and pencil to the player ahead of him. Passing continues until the head player has the paper and pencil. He stands and shouts, "Birds are here!" First team to finish with a correct list of birds wins the game.

Growing Garden. Play the same as Birds Are Here! but have each player write the name of a garden flower. When the head player again has the slip he stands and shouts, "Growing garden."

Actual Animal Antics

Players form teams and sit in single files. Give the first player of each team a pencil and a sheet of 8½ × 11-inch paper.

On signal, the first player of each team writes the name of an animal on the top of the paper. He passes the paper to the second player, who must write an activity which the animal performs. For example, if the first player writes "dog," the other players in turn might add one such typical activity as "barks," "runs," "jumps," "eats," "yawns," "plays."

When the last player has written an activity which the animal is capable of performing, he takes the paper and pencil to the head player, who holds up the list and shouts, "Actual animal antics." The first team to present a correct list wins the game. In case of error the team having the longest correct list of animal antics wins the game.

Names of Leaves

Prepare identical sets of ten pictures of leaves (or mounted leaves), each leaf numbered. Players form groups of six. Give each group a set of pictures or mounted leaves, a sheet of 8½ × 11-inch paper, and a pencil.

Within a designated time the players try to identify the leaves. One of the players in each group writes on the sheet of paper the number appearing on the picture and next to it he records the name of the leaf.

Call time and ask the recorder of the group identifying the most leaves to read the list and present the pictures of the leaves. If the group identified the leaves correctly, it wins the game.

Crazy Mixed-Up Trees

Players sit at tables. Give each player a paper and a pencil.

Call out the words appearing in the word columns and request everyone to list these words on his paper. Within a designated time the players are to transpose the letters in each word to attempt to form the name of the tree listed below.

Word	Tree	Word	Tree
Mile	Lime	Cheap	Peach
Panes	Aspen	Melon	Lemon
Clouts	Locust	Lamp	Palm
Ample	Maple	Lump	Plum
Has	Ash	Mug	Gum

Call a halt to the transposing and ask the person with the longest list to read the names of the trees he discovered. The person having the longest correct list of trees wins the game.

Tree Riddles

Give each player a pencil and a copy of the riddles listed below or write the riddles on a blackboard or large sheet of paper and have each player copy them on a sheet of 8½ × 11-inch paper.

	Answers
1. What tree always sighs and languishes?	1. Pine
2. What tree is it that is made of stone?	2. Lime
3. What tree grows nearest the sea?	3. Beech
4. What tree always has a partner?	4. Pear
5. What tree is pulled from the water with a hook?	5. Bass (wood)
6. What tree is often found in bottles?	6. Cork
7. What tree is often used to describe a desirable position?	7. Plum
8. What tree is older than most other trees?	8. Elder
9. What tree is always found after a fire?	9. Ash
10. What tree do ladies wear around their necks?	10. Fir (fur)
11. What tree wages war on crops?	11. Locust
12. What is the neatest tree that grows?	12. Spruce
13. What tree is often found in people's mouths?	13. Gum
14. What tree runs over the meadows and pastures?	14. Yew
15. What tree does everyone carry in his hand?	15. Palm
16. What tree is an awful grouch?	16. Crab
17. What tree is particularly useful in snow and rain?	17. Rubber
18. What tree is worn in the Orient?	18. Sandal (wood)
19. What tree grieves more than any other?	19. Weeping Willow
20. What tree describes a pretty girl?	20. Peach
21. What tree is used in kissing?	21. Tulip

Within a designated time everyone is to answer each riddle with the name of a tree. He writes the answer to the right of each riddle. Call time and ask the player who has answered all or most of the riddles to read his answers. If they are correct, he wins the game.

Flower Riddles. Play the same as Tree Riddles, using the following riddles about flowers.

Answers

1. What flower do ladies tread under foot? — 1. Lady's Slipper
2. What flower is most used by cooks? — 2. Buttercup
3. What flower tells how a man may get rich quick? — 3. Marigold
4. What flower indicates late afternoon? — 4. Four-o'clock
5. What flower tells what father says when he wants someone to run an errand? — 5. Johnny Jump-up
6. A parting remark to a friend? — 6. Forget-me-not
7. What flower do some people go far to avoid? — 7. Ragweed
8. What flower do people get up early to enjoy? — 8. Morning Glory
9. What flower do men often handle? — 9. Lady Finger
10. What flower often hangs on the laundry line? — 10. Dutchman's Breeches
11. What flower reminds one of church? — 11. Jack-in-the-Pulpit
12. What flower goes with the easy chair and the paper? — 12. Dutchman's Pipe
13. What flower describes a beautiful specimen of an animal? — 13. Dandelion
14. What flower is both pleasant and unpleasant to the taste? — 14. Bittersweet
15. What flower reminds one of winter weather? — 15. Snowdrops
16. What flower tells what George Washington was to his country? — 16. Poppy
17. What flower reminds one of birds in a group? — 17. Phlox (flocks)
18. What flower suggests neat lines? — 18. Primrose (prim rows)
19. What flower suggests a feline bite? — 19. Catnip (cat nip)
20. What flower is a boy's delight in winter? — 20. Snowball

Guess My Name

Prepare eight statements similar to the following about particular birds, trees, or animals.

I AM A BIRD

8   I am bigger than a chickadee and smaller than a blackbird.
7   I go south in the fall and north in the spring.
6   In fact, I go north very early in the spring.
5   I make my nest in holes in trees, as well as in rails.
4   I love the old apple orchards and sunny fields.
3   I am often called the messenger of spring.
2   My breast is red.
1   My back is blue
        Answer: I am a bluebird.

Players form two lines which sit facing one another about 10 feet apart. One line is Team 1; the other, Team 2. Ask each team to number off consecutively, beginning at the same end until each person has a number. Thus members of each team having the same number will be opposite one another.

Read the first statement and ask the first player on each team (Number 1's) to try to guess the name of the bird. If neither player guesses correctly, read the second statement, and so on. The figure to the left of each statement indicates the scoring value. If either of the players names the bird on the initial statement, he scores eight points for his team; on the second description, he scores seven; and so on. If Number 1's are unable to name the bird after all the statements have been read, announce its name. To the next two players (Number 2's) read another series of statements about a bird, tree, or animal.

Play until each pair of players has a chance to guess the name of a bird, tree, or animal, or for a designated time. The team with the highest score wins the game.

The following descriptions may be used in playing the game. Similar ones may be created to fit particular groups and locations.

I AM A TREE

8   My leaves are small and flat.
7   My wood is light and soft.
6   The Indians used my wood for drum frames, my bark for wigwams.
5   I grow best in low damp woods, on lake shores, and in swamps.
4   My wood does not decay quickly in the ground.
3   Log cabins and rustic furniture are often made from my logs.
2   I stay green the year around.
1   I am often grown for hedges in the yards.
        Answer: I am a white cedar.

I AM A BIRD

8   I am smaller than a crow and larger than a wren.
7   Insects and worms I eagerly seek.
6   I climb tree trunks nimbly and well.
5   My four-toed feet cling fast to the bark of trees.
4   I make my nest in holes in stumps and trees.
3   My coat is of glossy black with a glint of green.
2   My head is red.
1   I hammer and peck on trees with my bill.
        Answer: I am a red-headed woodpecker.

I AM A MAMMAL

8   I live in the forest.
7   I have front teeth that are good for gnawing.
6   My fur is soft and a reddish gray in color.
5   My tail is bushy.

4   I often bury my food in the ground.
3   I am smaller than a cat.
2   I climb trees.
1   I eat nuts.
Answer: I am a fox squirrel.

I AM A MAMMAL

8   I live in dens along fence-rows and forest margins.
7   I sleep during the coldest part of the winter.
6   I am a respectable citizen if left alone.
5   I belong to the weasel family.
4   I eat mice, June bugs, and grasshoppers.
3   I cannot run very rapidly.
2   My defense is my odor.
1   My fur is black with white stripes.
Answer: I am a skunk.

I AM A MAMMAL

8   I belong to the gnawing family.
7   I eat aspen bark and lily pads.
6   I can swim and dive well.
5   My fur is a beautiful brown and highly prized.
4   I am as large as a fox or perhaps larger.
3   If startled while swimming, I often slap my tail on the water.
2   I build my house of sticks or burrow into the bank of a lake or stream.
1   I cut down trees, dam up streams, and dig canals.
Answer: I am a beaver.

I AM A MAMMAL

8   I am a little larger than a mink.
7   My fur is very valuable because it makes beautiful ladies' wraps.
6   I am very easy to trap.
5   My ears are larger than those of a mink.
4   My tail is bushier than that of a mink.
3   I belong to the weasel family.
2   I was once common in the Great Lakes Region.
1   I climb trees and catch red squirrels.
Answer: I am a pine marten.

I AM A BIRD

8   I am a little smaller than a robin.
7   I nest in trees and bushes and fly south in the winter.
6   I am shy and live in the woodlands.
5   Most of my relatives live in the tropics.
4   I feed upon flowers, fruit, and insects.
3   My song resembles that of the robin.
2   I am much more brightly colored than my wife.
1   I am bright scarlet with black wings and tail.
Answer: I am a scarlet tanager.

I AM A BIRD

8   I am about the size of a house sparrow.
7   I play through early summer without a care.

6 I feed mostly on seeds.
5 I rise and fall in flight, as if I were riding over waves.
4 I build my nest in late June and July in trees and bushes.
3 I line my nest with thistledown.
2 My flight song is a cheerful per-chic-o-ree.
1 I am yellow with black crown, wings, and tail.
              Answer: I am a goldfinch.

I AM A TREE

8 I grow with hemlock and sugar maple.
7 My bark is dark and rough when I am old, but smooth in my youth.
6 My trunk is straight and tall and was once used much for shipmasts.
5 My wood is soft and easily worked.
4 My branches resemble plumes at a distance.
3 My leaves are needle-like, soft, and flexible.
2 I hold my needles all winter.
1 My needles grow in bundles of five.
              Answer: I am a white pine.

I AM A TREE

8 I live in the North.
7 I am often used for fuel.
6 My twigs are slender, flexible, and dark in color.
5 I do not usually live to be very old.
4 I lose my leaves in winter.
3 My wood is used for spools and clothespins.
2 My bark is white and peels off in thin layers.
1 The Indians used my bark to make canoes.
              Answer: I am a paper birch.

I AM A TREE

8 I grow to be very old.
7 My wood is hard and is used for making furniture.
6 My leaves hang on my branches long after they die in the autumn.
5 When you cut off a twig, my pith is star-shaped.
4 My buds are clustered at the end of my twigs.
3 My bark is scaly, ridged, and gray in color.
2 My seeds are called acorns.
1 My leaves have rounded lobes.
              Answer: I am a white oak.

I AM A TREE

8 I grow very large and live in Canada and the United States.
7 I like moist soil best but grow almost anywhere.
6 My bark is gray and furrowed.
5 My flowers are small and bloom very early in the spring.
4 My seeds are winged and are ripe before summer.
3 My leaves are lop-sided at the base with one-half rounded and the other
       half wedge-shaped.
2 My wood is strong and tough and does not split easily.
1 I am often planted along streets.
              Answer: I am an elm.

I AM A TREE

8 My leaves are slender and soft.
7 My leaves grow in tufts on little stalks.
6 My trunk is straight and tall.
5 My seeds are winged and grow in small cones.
4 I grow in northern sphagnum swamps.
3 My wood snaps and crackles when I burn.
2 I am heavy and make good fence posts.
1 I drop my leaves in winter.
Answer: I am a tamarack.

Hidden Trees

Prepare sheets of paper containing sentences in which the names of trees are concealed, such as those listed below. Players sit at tables. Give each player one copy of the prepared sheets and a pencil.

On signal, everyone seeks to discover the hidden trees in the sentences. Each tree that he finds he underscores; for example, in the sentence, "Bring me a long str*ap, ple*ase," he discovers the word "apple."

After a designated time call a halt to the game. The player having the longest correct list of discovered trees wins the game.

The following sentences have the names of trees concealed in them:

	Answers
1. The *pin* extended under the skin.	1. Pine
2. A bumble *bee ch*ased him about the lawn.	2. Beech
3. The wind came up *so a k*ite was flown.	3. Oak
4. The *map le*d us to a lonely swamp.	4. Maple
5. Does chap*el m*ake you sleepy, too?	5. Elm
6. The ball boun*ced ar*tistically down the field.	6. Cedar
7. The *plum*es waved in the air.	7. Plum
8. I *will owe* you the balance.	8. Willow
9. We found the ow*l in dense* swamp brush.	9. Linden
10. Nan*cy press*ed Randolph's suit neatly.	10. Cypress
11. The airplane ap*pear*ed out of the clouds.	11. Pear
12. Beautiful *arch*es adorned the walls.	12. Larch
13. He must lea*p each* hurdle in turn.	13. Peach
14. He went *as h*urriedly as possible.	14. Ash
15. The teacher h*eld er*asers to clear the blackboard.	15. Elder

Hidden Birds. Play the same as Hidden Trees except conceal the names of birds in the sentences. For example:

	Answers
1. It takes a brave bandit to *rob in* daylight.	1. Robin
2. *Do doc*tors always charge so much?	2. Dodo
3. *Do v*entilate the new house better.	3. Dove
4. This pencil is a hal*f-inch* longer.	4. Finch
5. "Hit a *fly," catcher* Jones shouted from the dugout.	5. Flycatcher

6. Fred *started* up suddenly from his reading.   6. Redstart
7. You can't *kill deer* without a license.   7. Killdeer
8. Ralph patted *her on* the cheek jokingly.   8. Heron
9. I sent the past*or a V*enetian vase.   9. Raven
10. The boy left the porch with *awk*ward strides.   10. Hawk
11. He saw them b*oth rush* down the alley.   11. Thrush
12. The wind*ow l*ooks over the garden.   12. Owl
13. Her eye*s wand*ered over the curious crowd.   13. Swan
14. The *crow*n lay shattered on the granite floor.   14. Crow
15. Bungal*ow ren*ts are out of proportion to those of
    apartments.   15. Wren
16. The old horse seemed *to wheeze* worse than usual.   16. Towhee
17. The angry father threatened to *thrash* Erna.   17. Thrasher

Alphabetical Nature

Players sit at tables. Give each person a sheet of 8½ × 11-inch paper and a pencil. Ask everyone to write the letters of the alphabet in a column on the left side of the sheet.

On signal each player attempts to write the name of a tree, bird, animal, vegetable, fruit, wildflower, or garden flower to the right of each letter of the alphabet.

After a designated time call a halt to the game. Ask the person with a complete or the most complete list to read it. If it is correct, he wins the game.

A complete list may resemble the following:

A—Aster
B—Bear
C—Cauliflower
D—Dogwood
E—Endive
F—Fox
G—Grapefruit
H—Hepatica
I—Iris
J—Jack-in-the-Pulpit
K—Kohlrabi
L—Lily-of-the-Valley
M—Marten

N—Nectarine
O—Okra
P—Pumpkin
Q—Quince
R—Rose
S—Starling
T—Trillium
U—Umbrette
V—Vicuna
W—Watermelon
X—Xanthisma
Y—Yam
Z—Zebra

Nature Fill-Ins

Draw this diagram on a blackboard or large sheet of paper:

TREES						
BIRDS						
ANIMALS						
FLOWERS						

Select a five-letter word and enter the letters at the top of the columns in the diagram. For example, if the word chosen is "cards," place the letters C, A, R, D, S at the top of the columns. Have the players form groups of four and sit at tables. Give each group a sheet of 8½ × 11-inch paper and a pencil. Have each group appoint a member to copy the diagram and enter the letters of the word. Another member of the group records the group's answers in the spaces of the diagram.

On signal, each group attempts to fill in the spaces with words beginning with the letters at the top of the column and coming under the classification of trees, birds, animals, and flowers. At the end of a designated time call a halt to the activity. Ask the recorder for each group to read the answers. For each correct answer, the team scores one point. The team with the highest score wins.

Below is an example of a winning team's answers:

	C	A	R	D	S
TREES	cedar	apple	redwood	dogwood	sassafras
BIRDS	crow	avocet	robin	dove	sparrow
ANIMALS	cat	antelope	rabbit	dog	skunk
FLOWERS	cosmos	aster	rose	dahlia	salvia

Suggestion: A method of scoring which encourages the players to attempt to think of uncommon names is to award ten points for each correct name which no other group has used; seven for each name two groups have used; five for a name three groups have used; three for a name four groups have used; and one for a name used by more than four groups.

Instead of the four categories illustrated above try four of the following: fish, reptiles, insects, constellations, fruits, vegetables, grain, rivers, lakes, oceans.

Speedy Nature Replies

Select a category: bird, tree, flower, vegetable, animal, or fruit.

Players form two lines which sit facing one another. One line is Team 1; the other, Team 2. Ask each team to number off consecutively, beginning at the same end of the lines. Thus players with the same number will be opposite one another.

State the category and a letter of the alphabet. For example, "Vegetable. Name a vegetable starting with the letter C." The Number 1 player on either team who first states the name of a vegetable beginning with the letter *C*, for instance "Cauliflower," scores two points for his team; the other Number 1 scores one point for trying.

Continue by stating another category or the same and another letter. Ask Number 2's to respond. Play continues until each pair of opposing players has a chance to compete. The team with the highest score wins the game.

If the players on both teams fail to respond correctly, select the same or another category and a different letter and call on the next player of each team. For any of the categories players may use a name only once.

IDENTIFIERS

Plant Beginnings

Place a variety of seeds, bulbs, rhizomes, corms, tubers, and tuberous roots on individual plates on a table. Have a sheet of 8½ × 11-inch paper available for each group. Players are in groups of four.

Give each group a specified time in which to walk to the table, observe, and try to identify and remember the kinds of seeds, bulbs, rhizomes, corms, tubers, and tuberous roots. The players may not converse with one another at the table.

After each group views and tries to identify the displayed items, give one member of each group a sheet of paper and a pencil. Within a designated time the members of the group merge their ideas and one member records them.

Call a halt to the activity and request the recorder for the group with the longest list to read it. If the items on the list are correct, the group wins the game. In case of errors in identifying the items call on the recorder reporting the next longest list.

The following items may be included:

    bulbs—daffodil, tulip, onion
    corms—crocus, gladiolus
    tubers—potato, caladium
    tuberous roots—sweet potato, dahlia
    rhizomes—bearded irises, Rex begonia, calla lily, Solomon's seal
    seeds significantly different in appearance—corn, peanut, bean, watermelon,
        pea, apple, coconut, lettuce

Seeing and Hearing Nature

Players sit at tables. Give each player a sheet of 8½ × 11-inch paper and a pencil.

Within a specified time each person is to list the objects or creatures in nature he sees and hears on his way to work, school, or a particular place in the community.

Call time and request the person with the longest list to read it. If the objects or creatures are really found in nature, he wins the game.

CREATERS AND ACT-OUTERS

Flower Arranging

Have for each group a low bowl, flower holder, scissors or knife, garden flowers, and some twigs from a tree or a few cuttings from a shrub. Players form groups of four and sit at tables.

On signal, each group proceeds to originate an arrangement with the materials. After a designated time call the arranging to a halt. Have one member of each group return the remaining materials while the others place the arrangement on the table so that it is the center of interest.

Since everyone is on the committee of judges, allow the groups to view the arrangements and judge them on the sole basis of originality. Request each group to resume its place, and ask one member of each group to voice the members' selection.

Suggestion: If flowers are not available use fruits and vegetables.

Outdoor Scene

Cover the tops of the tables. Have for each group a pie tin, some moss, clay (for hills and mountains), artificial flowers (or garden flowers if available), a small mirror (for a lake), a few twigs from a tree or shrub, and a knife, pruning shears, or old scissors. Players form groups of four and sit at tables.

Within a specified time each group tries to create a miniature replica of an outdoor scene. At the end of the allotted time call a halt to the activity. Ask one person from each group to return the remaining materials while the others get their scene ready for exhibition.

Since everyone is a judge, ask the players to view each outdoor scene. Request one person from each group to voice the group's choice. The scene which most resembles nature wins the event.

Food's on the House!

Have for each group a piece of galvanized metal screening 12 inches square, four lengths of wire 24 inches long, and one length of wire 32 inches long. Players form groups of four and sit at tables whose tops are covered.

Within a designated time each group proceeds to create a bird feeder by folding up the four sides of the screening and making a square tray. A 24-inch length of wire is fastened at each corner to secure it, and the 32-inch length is wound around the tops of the four end wires to draw them together above the center of the feeder. The first group to add this finishing touch which makes the feeder ready to hang on a tree shouts, "Food's on the house!"

Check that the feeder is complete. If it is ready for the birds, announce the winner. Allow the other groups time to complete their feeders. The winners have the honor of helping anyone requesting it.

In hanging the feeder in a tree adjust the wire so the feeder is about 6 feet from the ground. This makes the tray safer for the birds and provides a reasonable reach for the individual filling the tray with food. If bread crumbs or wild bird seed is placed in the feeder, add a piece of fine screening to keep the food in the tray.

Birdhouse Building

Cover the tables and give to each group a ready-to-assemble birdhouse (available from hobby shops) and the equipment designated on the container to build the house. Players form groups of four and sit at the tables.

On signal, each group proceeds to read the directions for building the house and starts erecting the dwelling for a feathered friend.

The first group to complete a house shouts, "The house is ready!" Check, and if the house is complete, announce the winner.

A New Look!

Cover the tops of the tables with heavy paper or newspapers. Have for each group a lemon or an orange, four pipe cleaners, four round toothpicks, and some raisins or cloves. Players form groups of four and sit at the tables.

Within a specified time each group is to create an animal with the given supplies. The range of choice is limited only by the imagination of the group.

At the end of the designated time call a halt to the animal creating. Have one member return the remaining supplies while the others give the object of their imagination a prominent place on the table. Allow the members of all groups to view each creation. Ask one person in each group to announce the group's choice of the animal having "a new look!"

Flower Charades

On a 2 × 2-inch slip of paper for each group write the name of a flower which the members are to pantomime. Players form groups of four. Distribute to each group a slip bearing the name of a flower and assign an area where each group may plan and practice its pantomime without revealing the name of the flower to the others. Allow each group five minutes in which to prepare its presentation.

The performers pantomime the name of their flower by syllables. Request one of the groups to present its pantomime while the other groups try to guess the name of the flower that is being offered in pantomime. Any group that guesses the name wins the honor of presenting its pantomime.

If the groups fail to guess the name of a flower being pantomimed, the players announce it and select another group to offer its presentation.

The following list of flowers has pantomiming possibilities:

Carnation (Car/nation)
Sweet pea (Sweet/pea)
Dogwood (Dog/wood)
Marigold (Mary/gold, Marry/gold)
Lady-slipper (Lady/slip/her)
Lady finger (Lady/finger)
Foxglove (Fox/glove)
Touch-me-not (Touch/me/not)
Primrose (Prim/rose, Prim/rows)
Four-o'clock (Four/oh/clock)
Dutchman's Breeches (Dutch/man's/breeches)

Dutchman's Pipe (Dutch/man's/pipe)
Jack-in-the-Pulpit (Jack/in/the/pull/pit)
Catnip (Cat/nip)
Johnny-jump-up (Johnny/jump/up)
Forget-me-not (For/get/me/not)
Bittersweet (Bit/her/sweet)
Dandelion (Dandy/lie/on)
Goldenrod (Golden/rod, Goal/den/rod)
Skunk cabbage (Skunk/cab/age)
Honeysuckle (Honey/suckle)
Tulip (Two/lip)

Bird Charades. Use the name of birds and play the same as Flower Charades. The names of birds offering pantomiming possibilities include:

Sparrow (Spare/row)
Thrasher (Thrash/her)
Towhee (Tow/he)
Warbler (War/blur)
Woodpecker (Wood/peck/her)
Vireo (Very/oh)
Kingfisher (King/fish/her)
Killdeer (Kill/dear)
Catbird (Cat/bird)
Redstart (Red/start)
Ovenbird (Oven/bird)
Grosbeak (Gross/beak)

Bobolink (Bob/oh/link)
Flycatcher (Fly/catch/her)
Nighthawk (Night/hawk)
Whippoorwill (Whip/poor/will)
Waxwing (Wax/wing)
Cardinal (Card/in/all)
Junco (Junk/oh)
Blue Jay (Blue/jay)
Creeper (Creep/her)
Nuthatch (Nut/hatch)
Flicker (Flick/her)

Tree Charades. Use the names of trees and play the same as Flower Charades. The names of trees offering pantomiming possibilities include:

Basswood (Bass/wood)
Hornbeam (Horn/beam)
Box Elder (Box/elder)
Buckeye (Buck/eye)
Butternut (Butt/her/nut)
Buttonwood (Butt/on/wood)
Catalpa (Cat/tall/pa)
Chestnut (Chest/nut)
Dogwood (Dog/wood)
Hackberry (Hack/berry)
Hemlock (Hem/lock)

Hop Hornbeam (Hop/horn/beam)
Horse chestnut (Horse/chest/nut)
Redbud (Red/bud)
Sweet Gum (Sweet/gum)
Mulberry (Mull/berry)
Papaw (Pa/paw)
Sourwood (Sour/wood)
Sycamore (Sick/ah/more)
Tamarack (Tam/ah/rack)
Tuliptree (Two/lip/tree)
Walnut (Wall/nut)

Vegetable Charades. Use the names of vegetables and play the same as Flower Charades. The names of vegetables offering pantomiming possibilities include:

Cabbage (Cab/age)
Tomato (Tom/ate/oh, Tow/mate/tow)
Parsnip (Par/snip)
Pumpkin (Pump/kin)
Lentil (Lent/ill)

Radish (Red/dish)
Spinach (Spin/age)
Pepper (Pep/purr)
Lettuce (Let/us)
Turnip (Turn/up)

Outdoor Safety

On a 3 × 5-inch slip of paper for each group write an outdoor safety tip which is to be acted out. Players form groups of six members each. Give each group one of the slips and allow the players a designated time in which to prepare their pantomimes.

Call time and request one of the groups to present its pantomime. The other groups attempt to guess the action. If a group guesses correctly, it presents its pantomime. If the group has been on stage, it selects another group to perform.

If the players fail to guess the safety tip being pantomimed, the performers announce it and select another group to offer its presentation.

A few safety tips which have pantomiming possibilities:

Stay with a boat even if it fills with water or overturns.
Decide on a seat in the boat in advance and stay seated.
Avoid overloading a boat; a small outboard is not a luxury liner.
Build outdoor fires in prescribed areas.
Be sure that a fire is out before leaving it.

CHAPTER 5

BRAIN
TEASERS

CONTENTS

* See Chapter IV for description

100

CONTENTS (continued)

Adults as well as youth will enjoy brain teasers. Though no one will evolve as a genius as a result of participating in the teasers in this chapter, all players will discover that it is fun to think.

Association, guessing, and memory are the core around which the patterns for the brain teasers are fashioned. The games which require association appear under Associaters, Reassemblers, and Responders. For these activities, participants must write or state letters, words, or phrases which they relate to given ones (associators); use designated letters or rearrange given letters or items (reassemblers); or respond correctly before a player counts to a specified number or repeats a predetermined phrase (responders).

Those games which require a player to guess through questioning a word, activity, object, or character are grouped under Guessers. The memory games appear as Substituters, Repeaters, and Stretchers. For the substituters, a player must use a catch word for a regular word or number. The repeaters require alertness in remembering messages or lists as they grow in content and length. For the stretchers, participants are credited for the longest list of specified items prepared within a time limit.

The chapter concludes with race and relay teasers whose object is to have individuals or groups complete a designated action in competition with others. Races fall under the heading Race Eventers; relays under Relay Eventers. For ready reference, the games and activities are listed in alphabetical order at the beginning of the chapter.

Paper, pencils, a blackboard in some cases, chalk, and a few reference works are all that a leader must have to provide the pathway to playing these games and in setting the mental processes of the individuals in high gear.

ASSOCIATERS

Complete the Affinities

For each participant prepare a list of unfinished affinities on the left-hand side of a sheet of 8½ × 11-inch paper, for example:

Bread and _____
Salt and _____
Knife and _____

Players sit in a circle, preferably at a table. Distribute a list and a pencil to everyone.

On signal each person completes the affinities by adding the word he associates with it, for example:

Bread and *butter*
Salt and *pepper*
Knife and *fork*

After a designated time call a halt to the game. The player completing correctly the most affinities wins the game. See page 44 for affinities to use in playing the game.

Variation: Complete the Old Sayings. Give each player a list of incomplete old sayings. Play the same as Complete the Affinities.

See page 45 for a list of old sayings to use for the game.

Finish the Analogy

Compile a list of analogies (see suggestions below). For this game the players sit in a circle.

Read an analogy, omitting the last word; for example, "Father is to son as mother is to _____." The first person to complete the analogy by calling "daughter" scores one point.

Continue reading the analogies and allowing time for the players to respond. The person having the most points at the end of a designated time wins the game.

Some analogies to use in compiling a list include:

Father is to son as mother is to _____ (*daughter*).
Foot is to shoe as hand is to _____ (*glove*).
Dog is to pup as bear is to _____ (*cub*).
Cow is to calf as doe is to _____ (*fawn*).
Sheep is to lamb as frog is to _____ (*pollywog*).
Hen is to chick as goose is to _____ (*gosling*).
Hat is to head as coat is to _____ (*back*).
Coat is to vest as shoe is to _____ (*sock*).
Pencil is to paper as chalk is to _____ (*blackboard*).

Balloon is to gas as football is to _____ (*air*).
Scissors are to cloth as a razor is to _____ (*whiskers*).
Sailboat is to sail as canoe is to _____ (*paddle*).
Bow is to arrow as shotgun is to _____ (*shell*).
Baseball is to bat as tennis ball is to _____ (*racket*).
Pen is to ink as brush is to _____ (*paint*).

It Reminds Me

Players sit at tables. Give each player a sheet of 8½ × 11-inch paper and a pencil.

State a word, for example, "travel," and ask each person to list the words he associates with the word. After a designated time call the game to a halt and ask the person with the longest list to read it. If the associations are logical, the player wins the game.

Authors and Books

Prepare for each player, on a slip of 4 × 6-inch paper, the names of ten classics of literature. To the right of the titles but *not* in the correct order write the names of the ten authors, as illustrated:

Les Misérables	Robert Louis Stevenson
Oliver Twist	Nathaniel Hawthorne
Vanity Fair	Alexandre Dumas
Don Quixote	Sir Walter Scott
The House of the Seven Gables	Oliver Goldsmith
Wuthering Heights	Victor Hugo
The Count of Monte Cristo	Miguel de Cervantes
The Vicar of Wakefield	William Makepeace Thackeray
Ivanhoe	Emily Brontë
Treasure Island	Charles Dickens

Players sit in small groups. Give a slip bearing the mismatched titles and authors and a pencil to each player.

On signal, everyone tries to match the titles of the classics with the correct authors. After a designated time, call a halt to the game. Ask the person matching all or most of the titles and authors to read his list. If it is correct, he wins the game.

Keep a list of the titles and the correct names of the authors to use in checking the players' answers. The correct answers for the suggested classics and authors follow:

Les Misérables—Victor Hugo
Oliver Twist—Charles Dickens
Vanity Fair—William Makepeace Thackeray
Don Quixote—Miguel de Cervantes
The House of the Seven Gables—Nathaniel Hawthorne
Wuthering Heights—Emily Brontë
The Count of Monte Cristo—Alexandre Dumas

The Vicar of Wakefield—Oliver Goldsmith
Ivanhoe—Sir Walter Scott
Treasure Island—Robert Louis Stevenson

Composers and Compositions. Use titles of musical compositions and their composers. Play the same as Authors and Books. Remember to mix the names of the composers and compositions before giving the list to the players.

A list of compositions and composers to be used in playing the game might include the following. They are correctly combined:

The Barber of Seville—Rossini
The Pirates of Penzance—Gilbert and Sullivan
Robin Hood—De Koven
New World Symphony—Dvořák
Tannhäuser—Wagner
La Traviata—Verdi
Sonata No. 14 for Piano (Moonlight)—Beethoven
Scheherazade—Rimski-Korsakov
Scotch Symphony—Mendelssohn
Tales from the Vienna Woods—Johann Strauss

Advertising Phrases

Compile a list of well-advertised products and a descriptive phrase associated with each product. Players form two teams, face, and sit opposite one another about 10 feet apart. Appoint a scorekeeper for each team. Give each scorekeeper a 3 × 5 card and a pencil.

State the name of a well-advertised product. The first player to call out a descriptive phrase associated with the product scores a point for his team. Phrases need not be word for word. If the thought is correct, the player scores a point for his team. If there is a tie, each player scores a point.

Play continues for a designated time. The team with the highest score wins the game.

Significant Numbers

Write the following numbers on a blackboard or a large sheet of paper: 12; 7; 13; 100; 3; 60; 400; 14; 20,000; 40. Have the players sit in small groups. Give each player a sheet of paper and a pencil. Ask the players to copy the numbers on the left side of their paper.

Within a designated time everyone writes to the right of each number the expression or thought he associates with the number. Call a halt to the game and ask the player with the complete or most nearly complete list to read his associations with the numbers. If the associations are logical, he wins the game.

A list of associations with the above numbers might include:

> 12—Twelve men good and true.
> —A dozen.
> 7—Seven come eleven.
> —Seven ages of man.
> —*The House of the Seven Gables.*
> 13—Friday the thirteenth.
> —An unlucky number.
> 100—The first hundred years are the hardest.
> —I will not live to be one hundred.
> 3—*The Three Musketeers.*
> —Three's a crowd.
> 60—She ran like sixty.
> 400—He was one of society's four hundred.
> 14—"Fourteen men on a dead man's chest."
> 20,000—*Twenty Thousand Leagues Under the Sea.*
> 40—Forty fathoms deep.
> —Life begins after forty.

Symbolic Articles

Place a number of articles about the room (see the right-hand column of suggestions below). Assemble the players and give each one a copy of the phrases listed in the left-hand column of suggestions and a pencil.

On signal, the players scatter and seek the object that represents each listed phrase. Upon finding it, the player writes the name of the object opposite the correct phrase, as shown in the right-hand column of suggestions.

Reassemble the players and ask the person finding all or most of the objects to read his list. If the list is correct, the player wins the game.

A list of phrases to use in playing the game and the objects to represent them include:

A boy's ambition.	A wooden shaving made by a carpenter's tool. On the answer list this should be written as "shaving."
Commentators on *Ivanhoe*.	Two potatoes on a copy of *Ivanhoe*.
"Charge of the Light Brigade."	Electric light bill.
A hairless Irish terrier with his eyes not open.	An Irish potato.
A sower of tares.	Needle and thread.
For gentlemen only.	Suspenders.
Little bright eyes.	Small eyes used in sewing.
Collector of taxes.	Magnet.
What a boxer expects.	Sock on the nose (sock pinned on nose of a mask).

What young men often get.	The mitten.
What every girl strives for.	Beaus (a bunch of ribbon bows pinned to a card).
Famous Latin scholar.	Cicero (a row of girls pasted on a card).
A paradise on earth.	Two dice on a saucer of dirt.
A corncrib.	Old shoe.
A famous slipper.	Banana peel.
What a baseball team must have.	Pitcher.

Letters Equal to Words

Prepare a list of questions players can answer with a letter of the alphabet. Players form teams of four players each and sit in groups. Give each group a pencil, a sheet of paper, and a copy of the questions. Ask each team to select one person to act as recorder.

On signal, each team attempts to answer the questions by using letters of the alphabet. For example, to the question, What letter is a human organ? the player responds with the letter *I*. After a designated time call a halt to the activity. Ask the recorder for the team completing all or most of the questions to read the list. If the answers are correct, the team wins the questions and letters quiz.

The following are some questions which the players can answer with letters of the alphabet.

Questions	*Answers*
1. What letter is a beverage?	1. T
2. What letter is a bird?	2. J
3. What letter is a vegetable?	3. P
4. What letter is an insect?	4. B
5. What letter is part of a house?	5. L
6. What letter is a large body of water?	6. C
7. What letter is a cue?	7. Q
8. What letter is a sheep?	8. U
9. What letter is a command to oxen?	9. G
10. What letter is a verb of debt?	10. O
11. What two letters describe a possible condition of a road in winter?	11. I–C
12. What two letters name a county in England?	12. S–X
13. What two letters form a word meaning too much?	13. X–S
14. What two letters name a creeping vine?	14. I–V
15. What two letters name a verb meaning to deteriorate?	15. D–K
16. What two letters name a word meaning not difficult?	16. E–Z
17. What two letters form a girl's nickname?	17. K–T
18. What two letters name a written composition?	18. S–A
19. What two letters name a ribbed cotton fabric?	19. P–K
20. What two letters form a word meaning jealousy?	20. N–V

State in Question

Write a series of questions on a blackboard or large sheet of paper which the players can answer with the abbreviations of states (see below).

Players sit in a circle. Provide each player with a 4 × 6-inch card and a pencil.

On signal the players attempt within a designated time to answer each question by using the abbreviation of a state.

Call a halt to the game and ask the player who has all or most of the answers to read the questions and his abbreviations of the states. If his answers are correct, he earns the title of being the "best state abbreviator."

Following are some questions that can be answered by using the abbreviations of states.

Questions	States
1. Which state is the cleanest?	1. Wash.
2. Which state is the most religious?	2. Mass.
3. Which state never forgets itself?	3. Me.
4. Which state saved Noah and his family?	4. Ark.
5. Which state is a physician?	5. Md.
6. Which state is a grain?	6. R. I.
7. Which state seems to be in poor health?	7. Ill.
8. Which state is an exclamation?	8. O.
9. Which state is a parent?	9. Pa.
10. Which state is to cut long grass?	10. Mo.
11. Which state is to study carefully?	11. Conn.
12. Which state is a number?	12. Tenn.
13. Which state is metal in its natural formation?	13. Ore.
14. Which state is the happiest?	14. Ga.

A Motor Romance

Players form two teams and sit facing each other about 6 feet apart. Ask one of the players on each team to keep score. Give a 3 × 5-inch card to each scorekeeper.

Read the following poem but omit the italicized words. Any member of either team may call the missing word, which must rhyme with the last word of the preceding line. The first player to call the missing word scores one point for his team. The team with the highest score at the conclusion of the reading wins the poetic endeavor.

> Alice and her beau one day
> Went riding in his (*Chevrolet*);

Her beau was fat, his name was Frank,
And he was somewhat of a *(crank)*.
It was too bad he wasn't smarter,
He didn't know how to work the *(starter)*.
She showed him how, the little dear,
And also how to shift the *(gear)*.
Away they went, but something broke,
'Twas just the measly little *(choke)*.
He fixed it with a piece of wire,
Then something popped—it was a *(tire)*.
'Twas mended soon, but next—ker-plop
They struck a branch and smashed the *(top)*.
"Dear me," cried Alice, "that's too much!"
Then something happened to the *(clutch)*.
And next, poor Frank, unlucky dub,
Just grazed a rock and mashed a *(hub)*.
"Oh, Frank," cried Alice, with a squeal,
"I think we're going to lose a *(wheel)*."
They climbed a hill, and then 'twas seen
The tank contained no *(gasoline)*.
They coasted downward toward the lake
But Frankie couldn't work the *(brake)*.
They struck a post a moment later
That almost wrecked the *(radiator)*.
So both climbed out and poor old Frank
Bought gasoline and filled the *(tank)*
And gathered up from road and field
The fragments of the broken *(shield)*.
They fixed the engine tight and snug
And had to use a new *(spark plug)*.
Just then he slapped at a mosquito
And dropped a wrench on the *(magneto)*.
'Twas useless then to sweat and toil
Nothing would run except the *(oil)*.
They journeyed home with Frankie pushin'
While Alice sobbed upon the *(cushion)*.
So poor Frank's fate was really dreadful
And Alice married happy *(Edsel)*.

Riddles

Prepare a list of riddles to read to the players. Have the players form two teams and sit facing each other about 6 feet apart.

Read aloud the question part of a riddle, for example, "Why are weary people like automobile wheels?" The first team to respond correctly with "Because they are tired," scores five points; the other, one point for trying. In answering the riddle the player does not need to use the exact words of the suggestions which follow, but the thought must be similar and logically correct.

Play continues for a certain designated time. The team with the most points wins the game. A list of riddles of different kinds follows.

1. Why would Samson have made a good actor?
   Answer: He would have brought down the house.
2. Why is the nose in the middle of the face?
   Answer: Because it is the scenter.
3. What is full of holes and still holds water?
   Answer: A sponge.
4. Why is a caterpillar like a hot biscuit?
   Answer: Because it makes the butter fly.
5. What grows larger the more you take from it?
   Answer: A hole.
6. Why is the heart of a tree like a dog's tail?
   Answer: It is farthest from the bark.
7. How long did Cain hate his brother?
   Answer: As long as he was Abel.
8. What will go up a chimney down but won't go down a chimney up?
   Answer: An umbrella.
9. Which animal took most luggage into the ark and which took the least?
   Answer: The elephant, who took his trunk, and the fox and the cock, who had only a brush and a comb between them.
10. Why is an orange like a church belfry?
    Answer: Because you usually get a peel (peal) from it.
11. Why does a horse eat in an odd way?
    Answer: Because he eats best when he hasn't a bit in his mouth.
12. When is a doctor most annoyed?
    Answer: When he is out of patients.
13. When did George Washington first ride in a four-wheeled vehicle?
    Answer: When he took his first hack at the cherry tree.
14. At what time of the day was Adam created?
    Answer: A little before Eve.
15. What is the difference between a garden hose and a clothes hamper?
    Answer: One keeps the lawn wet and the other keeps the lawn dry (laundry).
16. What is the difference between an old penny and a new dime?
    Answer: Nine cents.
17. Why are fish considered well educated?
    Answer: Because they are generally found in schools.
18. Why is Ireland apt to become the wealthiest country in the world?
    Answer: Because of Dublin (doublin').
19. What table has no legs to stand on?
    Answer: The multiplication table.
20. What is the difference between one yard and two yards?
    Answer: Usually a fence.
21. What colors would you paint the sun and the wind?
    Answer: The sun rose and the wind blue (blew).
22. Why should you never tell secrets in a corn field?
    Answer: Because corn has ears and is bound to be shocked.

23. What is the difference between a cat and a comma?
     Answer: A cat has its claws at the end of its paws, and a comma its
     pause at the end of its clause.
24. When was money first mentioned in the Bible?
     Answer: When the dove brought the green back to Noah.
25. How are lollipops like race horses?
     Answer: Because the more you lick them the faster they go.
26. When a boy falls in water what is the first thing he does?
     Answer: Gets wet.
27. What would happen if a man should swallow his teaspoon?
     Answer: He wouldn't be able to stir.
28. Why is life the greatest of all conundrums?
     Answer: Because we all have to give it up.
29. What is it from which you may take away the whole and still have
     some left?
     Answer: The word "wholesome."
30. If a two-wheeled wagon is a bicycle, and a three-wheeled wagon a
     tricycle, what is a five-wheeled wagon?
     Answer: A V-hicle.
31. Why does a freight train need no locomotive?
     Answer: Because the freight will make a cargo (car go).
32. When is money damp?
     Answer: When it's due (dew) in the morning and it's missed (mist)
     at night.
33. When did Napoleon sleep five in a bed?
     Answer: When he slept with his forefathers.
34. Who are the two largest ladies in the United States?
     Answer: Miss Ouri (Missouri) and Mrs. Sippi (Mississippi).
35. What is the difference between a cloud and a whipped boy?
     Answer: One pours with rain and the other roars with pain.
36. What is the difference between a watchmaker and a jailer?
     Answer: One sells watches and the other watches cells.
37. What is the difference between a fisherman and a lazy schoolboy?
     Answer: One baits his hook and the other hates his book.
38. What is the difference between a man going upstairs and a man
     looking upstairs?
     Answer: One is stepping up the stairs and the other staring up the
     steps.
39. What is filled every morning and emptied every night except once a
     year, when it is filled at night and emptied in the morning?
     Answer: A stocking.
40. What is the keynote of good manners?
     Answer: B natural (be natural).
41. What kind of a noise annoys an oyster?
     Answer: A noisy noise annoys an oyster.
42. What is it that goes from New York to Albany without moving?
     Answer: The road.
43. Why is a dog biting his tail a good manager?
     Answer: Because he makes both ends meet.
44. Why wasn't the Statue of Liberty placed on Brooklyn Bridge?
     Answer: Because she liked her bed low (Bedloe's Island).

45. Who is the first man mentioned in the Bible?
    Answer: Chap one (Chap. I).
46. Which is the longest word in the English language?
    Answer: Smiles. It has a mile between the first and last letters.
47. Why is *U* the jolliest letter?
    Answer: Because it is always in the midst of *fun*.
48. What sea might be used for a bedroom if the house were crowded?
    Answer: Adriatic (a dry attic).
49. There was a girl in our town,
    Silk *an'* satin was her gown,
    Silk *an'* satin, gold *an'* velvet
    Guess her name, three times I've tell'd it.
    Answer: Anne.
50. Sometimes I am very sly;
    Other times a trade I ply;
    Over the billows swift I fly;
    Now, pray tell me, what am I?
    Answer: Craft.

Trade Riddles. Use trade riddles and play the same as Riddles.
A list to use might include the following.

1. What trade is it whose best works are trampled upon?
   Answer: Shoemaker.
2. What trade does the sun follow?
   Answer: Tanner.
3. What trade does the president follow?
   Answer: Cabinetmaker.
4. Of what trade can it be said that all its members are men of letters?
   Answer: Printer.
5. Of what trade is a little tin dog?
   Answer: Tinker (tin-cur).
6. Of what trade is the preacher at a wedding?
   Answer: Joiner.
7. Of what trade is the sun in May?
   Answer: Mason (May-sun).
8. What trade is best qualified to cook a hare?
   Answer: Hairdresser.
9. What trade is the name of an author of English literature?
   Answer: Goldsmith.

Nut Riddles. Use nut riddles and play the same as Riddles. A
list might include the following.

1. What nut is spread on biscuits and griddle cakes?
   Answer: Butternut.
2. What nut is a picture hung on?
   Answer: Walnut.
3. What nut is painful?
   Answer: Acorn.
4. What nut is used for a trunk?
   Answer: Chestnut.

5. What nut borders the sea?
    Answer: Beechnut.
6. What nut do people drink?
    Answer: Coconut.
7. What nut makes a noise like a sneeze?
    Answer: Cashew nut.

Tree Riddles. Use tree riddles and play the same as Riddles. See list on page 87.

Flower Riddles. Use flower riddles and play the same as Riddles. See list on page 88.

REASSEMBLERS

Aunt Nellie's Cat

Players form two teams and sit opposite each other about 10 feet apart. For groups over twenty players have additional teams.

Call on the first player of Team 1. He must say, "Aunt Nellie's cat is _____," and add an adjective describing the cat which begins with the letter *a,* for instance, "arrogant." If the adjective is correct, the player scores three points for his team. Next call on the first player of Team 2. He must repeat the statement and first adjective, as well as add an adjective beginning with the next letter of the alphabet.

Continue by calling alternately on the members of the two teams, who repeat the statement, the preceding adjective, and add an adjective beginning with the next letter of the alphabet.

When a player's answer is incorrect, he scores one point for trying and the next player on the opposing team has a chance to state an adjective with the letter. If a player omits an adjective, fails to answer, or as the list grows repeats the adjectives in the incorrect order, he scores a point for trying and the opposing team has a turn. The team with the most points at the end of a designated time wins the game.

Word Lightning

Secure a blackboard and chalk or a large sheet of paper and a black crayon for keeping score. Have a watch. Players form two teams, face, and sit opposite each other about 10 feet apart. Ask each team to number off consecutively.

Call on one of the teams, follow it with a player's number, for example, "Team 1, Number 4," and add a letter of the alphabet, for instance, *b.* The player immediately states as many words beginning with the letter *b,* as he can within a half minute. Count the words and record the number on a blackboard or large sheet of paper. Players may use a word only once.

Alternate teams called on and letters given. Omit the letters *u, x, y,* and *z.* The team with the highest score at the end of a designated time wins the game.

I Love My Love

On a 3 × 5-inch card for each team write the following lines with the exception of the letter and words in parentheses:

I love my love with an (*A*) because he is (*amusing*).
I will send him [or her] to (*Aurora*).
And feed him on (*applesauce*).
I will give him an (*autograph*).
And a bunch of (*asters*) for a nosegay.

Give an index card to the first player of each group.

Ask the first player of each group to recite the lines and fill in the blanks with words beginning with the letter *a* as shown in the example. The second player recites the lines as soon as he receives the index card from the starter. He fills in the blanks with words beginning with the letter *b*. In turn each person passes the card to the next person, who repeats the lines and fills in the blanks with words starting with the next letter of the alphabet.

If a player fails to think of a correct word, he scores a point against himself. After each player on the team has a turn, ask the members to state their points. The team with no or the fewest points wins the title of the "best blank-filling lovers."

Words and Things

Players sit in a circle. Give each a 4 × 6-inch card and a pencil.

Select a word containing six letters, for example, "salted." Ask each player to make a chart by writing the letters of the word in a column down the left side of his index card and then on the right side reverse the order of the letters, for example:

```
s_____d
a_____e
l_____t
t_____l
e_____a
d_____s
```

Within a designated time the players attempt to fill in the blanks with words starting and ending with the given letters. The first line requires a word which starts with *s* and ends with *d*, such as "simplified" or "syncopated." The players should use the longest words they recall, because the object is to fill in the blanks with words having the greatest number of letters as well as starting and ending with the given letters.

Call a halt after a designated time, and ask the players to count the letters in each of the words they have used. Request the player having the most letters in his words to read his fill-ins. Check the number of letters, and be sure that the words begin and end with the given letters. If the list is correct, the player wins the title of being the "best stretcher of words."

Pro and Con

Players form two teams which face and sit opposite each other about 6 feet apart. Call one team the Pros and the other the Cons.

On signal, the first member of the Pros must state a word beginning with "pro," for example, "program." As soon as he names a word, the first player on Team 2 gives a word beginning with "con," for instance, "concert."

Play continues in this manner with the teams alternating in responding. If a player fails to respond or gives an incorrect answer, he scores a point against his team. The team with no or the fewest points at the end of a designated time wins the game. When the game does not move rapidly enough, place a ten-count limit on the time allotted to each player to give his word.

Some of the words beginning with "pro" and "con" which the players might list include:

proceed	concave
probe	conceit
procedure	conceal
proceeder	concentrate
procession	concept
procrastinate	concern
procure	concerto
procedural	concession
producer	conclave
productive	conduct
profess	concoct
profession	concord
professor	concordance
profile	concourse
profound	concrete
problem	concurrent
progression	concussion
progressive	condense
projector	condemn
proportion	condition

Roll the Words

Secure six half-inch cubes of wood for each group of four players. Print a letter of the alphabet on the sides of each of the six cubes. Use each of the vowels three times. Players sit at tables in groups of four. Give each player a pencil and a 3 × 5-inch card for keeping his score.

For a designated time the players take turns in rolling the cubes and trying to form words from the letters which are on the upturned faces. When a player forms a word, he writes it on his scorecard. The next player immediately starts rolling the cubes.

At the end of the allotted time call a halt to the cube rolling and ask each player to count the number of words and the number of letters in the words. The player who forms the greatest number of words using the greatest number of letters wins the word-rolling activity.

Unscrambling Words

Write the following list of scrambled words on the blackboard or on a large sheet of paper.

Players sit within reading distance of the blackboard or sheet of paper on which the scrambled words are written. Give each player a 4 × 6-inch index card and a pencil.

1. btamleiuoo
2. elintovsei
3. etrhate
4. tablel
5. dgenrgina
6. ehengorues
7. cnpeli
8. vscnoinretao
9. wlrsofe
10. kosbo
11. portss
12. rmcefroenap
13. scnortce
14. smicu
15. sagem

On signal, each player tries within a specified time to unscramble the jumbled letters and to form words.

After the allotted time call a halt to the game and ask the player who unscrambles all or most of the words to read his list. If his list is correct, he wins the game.

The unscrambled words noted above are the following:

1. automobile
2. television
3. theater
4. ballet
5. gardening
6. greenhouse
7. pencil
8. conservation
9. flowers
10. books
11. sports
12. performance
13. concerts
14. music
15. games

Jumbled Sentences

Ask the players to sit in a circle. Give everyone a pencil and a 4 × 6-inch card.

Request each player to think of a sentence containing a specified number of words; jumble the words (not the letters); and write them on the card. Punctuation marks and capitals must be indicated in the correct place. For example, a player decides on the following sentence: *Unscrambling sentences is fun, although the hashing of words is sometimes too complicated.* In its scrambled form it appears: *too complicated. Unscrambling is sentences although fun, sometimes of hashing the is words*

After each player writes a jumbled sentence, he passes the card to the player on his right. On signal, each player tries to reassemble the words to form the original sentence. The first player to correctly reassemble the sentence wins the contest.

Advertisement Cut-Ups

From some magazines cut out advertisements of well-known products. Cut each advertisement into several pieces, and place the pieces in an envelope. Have one envelope for each group. Players form teams of four, and each group sits at a table. Give one envelope to each group.

On signal, each group removes the cut-up advertisement from the envelope and proceeds to reassemble it. The first group to succeed in correctly completing the advertisement wins the activity.

Suggestion: To carry out themes for parties, use illustrations that are appropriate for particular holidays or special occasions.

Mixed Sentences

In advance, on a slip of paper for each team, write a sentence which has a word for each member of a team. If each team has six members, the sentence will contain six words. Cut up each sentence, shuffle the pieces, and give one word to the members of every team. Be careful not to mix the words from one sentence with the words from the other sentences. Players stand in single files behind the starting line, which is 15 feet from a blackboard or large sheet of paper. Give the first player of each team a piece of chalk, or a black crayon if the paper is substituted for the blackboard.

On signal, the first player of each team hustles to the blackboard, writes his word, hurries back to his team, gives the chalk to the second player in line, and goes to the end of his team.

Play continues with each player hastening to write his word and return to his team. The first team to have its members place all words on the board wins five points; all others, one point for trying.

Allow the remaining teams time to write all their words on the board. Now, announce that members of each team should get together and unscramble the sentence. On signal the first player on each team, who has the chalk, rushes to the board and writes the complete sentence. The first team to write its sentence correctly wins five points; all others, one point for trying.

Building Words

Write a word containing a generous number of vowels, for example, "commensurate," on the blackboard or on a large sheet of paper. Players form groups of eight and sit in circles. Give a 4 × 6-inch card and a pencil to one player of each group, who acts as the recorder.

On signal, each group tries to form as many words from the given word as it can within the designated time. Players may use only the letters appearing in the word and only as often as they appear in the given word.

After the allotted time call a halt to the game and ask the recorder of the group which has the longest list to read it. If the list is correct, the team wins the word-stretching game.

Special Occasion Words. Write the name of a holiday, special occasion, or a word associated with either of them on the blackboard or large sheet of paper. Play the same as Building Words.

Alphabet-Macaroni Words

Secure a box of alphabet macaroni and some paper cups. Players form groups of four and sit at tables. Give each group a cup of the macaroni.

Within a designated time each group tries to form as many words as possible containing four or more letters. At the end of the allotted time call a halt to the game and ask the groups to count the number of words and letters in each word. Request one person from the group which has assembled the most words and letters to read the list. If they are bona fide words, the group wins the honor of being the "best alphabet macaroni word-makers."

Doublets

Write on a blackboard or large sheet of paper two words having the same number of letters, for example, "pig," and "sty." Players sit facing the blackboard or sheet of paper. Give each a 3 × 5-inch card and a pencil.

On signal, the players try within a designated time to change one word to the other by changing one letter at a time. By changing one letter he makes a new word. He continues changing one letter at a time and forming new words until the other half of the doublet is achieved. For example, in changing "pig" to "sty," the following words are achieved: "pig—pit—pat—pay—say—sty."

After the allotted time call a halt to the activity, and ask the player making the change-over in the least number of words to read the links or intervening words that he used. If the words are correct, he scores five points. All others score one point for trying.

Announce another doublet and give the signal; the players proceed to change one word to the other. The person having the highest score at the end of a specified time wins the game.

Additional doublets to use in playing the game include:

sad to fun	poor to rich
wet to dry	rest to sofa
pen to ink	black to white
elm to oak	flour to bread
blue to pink	tears to smile
hold to have	fat to pig

RESPONDERS

Letter Response

On a slip of 2 × 2-inch paper write one letter of the alphabet. Have one slip and a pin for each player. Letters may be duplicated if necessary. Do not use the letters *u, v, x, y,* and *z.* Players form a circle. One player, "it," stands in the center. Give each player a letter and pin, and ask him to pin the slip on the front of his clothing.

"It" approaches one of the players in the group and asks him a question. The first word of the player's answer to the question must start with the letter he wears. "It" immediately starts counting to ten. Before he reaches ten the person must respond correctly.

If he succeeds, "it" moves on to someone else. If the player fails to respond correctly, he and "it" exchange places. If after three tries, "it" fails to catch a player, he selects someone else to take his place.

Bird, Beast, or Fish

Players sit or stand in a circle. One player, "it," stands in the center.

"It" approaches one of the players and says, "Bird, beast, or fish." Immediately "it" repeats one of the categories, for example, "bird."

The player must respond with the name of a bird before "it" counts to ten. If the player succeeds in responding correctly, "it" approaches another player and tries to catch him. If the player gives an incorrect answer or no reply, he and "it" exchange places.

When "it" follows the three categories with "Beast," the player must state the name of an animal. If "it" says, "Fish," the player gives the name of a fish. If after three attempts to catch a player, "it" fails, he selects someone to take his place.

Earth, Air, Fire, or Water. Call "Earth, air, fire, or water." If "it" says, "Earth," the player must name an animal. For "air," the player gives the name of a bird; for "water," the name of a fish; for "fire," the player remains silent. Play the same as Bird, Beast, or Fish.

Animal, Vegetable, or Mineral. Call "Animal, Vegetable, or Mineral." Play the same as Bird, Beast, or Fish.

Opposites

Players sit in a circle. One player, "it," stands in the center.

"It" approaches anyone in the circle and points to some part of his body and says, "This is my _____," but he names some part of the body other than that to which he points. For example, "it" points to his eye and says, "This is my nose."

The person whom he approaches responds, "This is my eye," while he points to his nose. When the player correctly points to the part of the body which "it" has named and states the "opposite" before "it" counts to ten, "it" moves on to someone else. If the player does not respond correctly, he exchanges places with "it." If "it" fails to catch someone after three attempts, he selects another person to take his place.

Prince of Paris

Players sit in a circle. Select an "it," who remains in place. Ask all of the players except "it" to number off consecutively.

"It" says, "The Prince of Paris lost his hat. Have you found it, Number 4, sir?"

Number four jumps to his feet and replies, "Who, sir, I, sir?"

"It" remarks, "Yes, sir, you, sir!"

Number 4 says, "No, sir, not I, sir!"

"It" asks, "Well, sir, who then, sir?"

Number 4 says, "Number 7, sir," or any other number within the group. Number 7 must respond in the same manner as 4. If a player fails to answer correctly, he exchanges places with "it," who takes the number of this individual. The game proceeds as it did previously.

Shout the Number

Everyone sits on chairs in circle formation. Ask the players to number off consecutively.

Ask player Number 1 to start the activity by stating his number and calling another number, for example, "Number 1 calling 6." Immediately Number 6 replies by stating his number and calling another number, for example, "Number 6 calling 9."

If, however, Number 6 hesitates, calls a number which is not represented, or calls his own number, he must leave his chair and go to the last chair, in which case the others move up one place. If the wrong person responds, that person takes the last seat.

When the players move they change numbers, each assuming the number of the seat to which he moves. Since the enviable position is the first seat, everyone aspires to reach it and retain the place of honor.

Shout the Name and Number. Assign names to the first four players, for example, John, first player; Jack, second; Jim, third; and Joe, fourth. Starting with the fifth player, everyone numbers off consecutively, beginning with number one. The game might start: "John calling Number 5." Number 5 responds, "Number 5 calling Jim." Jim responds, "Jim calling Number 1." Play the same as Shout the Number.

Rock, Scissors, Paper

Explain to the group that rock (designated by closed fist) is superior to scissors (two fingers crossed) because the rock will break the scissors; scissors are superior to paper (all fingers extended) because the scissors will cut paper; paper is superior to rock, because paper will wrap and conceal rock. Players sit in a circle facing center. One player, "it," stands in the center.

"It" approaches one of the players in the group, extends his right arm, and gives the sign for either rock, scissors, or paper. "It" immediately starts counting to five. The player must retaliate with the sign which is superior to the one "it" gives before "it" reaches the count of five. If the player succeeds, "it" tries another player. When the player fails, he exchanges places with "it." If after three attempts, "it" fails to catch someone, he selects another person to take his place.

Example:
"It" displays a closed fist (rock);
    Reply: all fingers extended (paper).

"It" displays all fingers extended (paper);
   Reply: two fingers crossed (scissors).
"It" displays two fingers crossed (scissors);
   Reply: closed fist (rock).

Under the Count

Players form two teams, face, and sit opposite each other about 10 feet apart. Each team numbers off consecutively.

The first player of Team 1 states the name of a city, for example, Chicago, and immediately starts counting to ten. Before he reaches ten the first player on Team 2 must respond by giving the name of a city whose first letter is the same as the last letter in the given city, in this case, for example, Omaha. If the player succeeds, he scores five points for his team. When he fails to respond correctly, he scores one point for trying.

Play continues with the first player of Team 2 naming a city and trying to count to ten before the first player of Team 1 responds correctly by naming a city whose first letter is the same as the last letter of the given city. In turn each member of the teams attempts to state the name of city before the member of the opposing team counts to ten. The team with the highest score after everyone has a chance to participate wins the activity.

Know Your Geog?

Secure an atlas to use for reference. Players form a circle. One player, "it," stands in the center.

"It" approaches someone and names a city, river, or mountain and immediately starts counting to twenty. The person must reply with the state in which the city, river, or mountain is located before "it" reaches the count of twenty. If he fails, he exchanges places with "it." If he succeeds, "it" approaches another player. If after three trials "it" fails to catch anyone, he selects someone to take his place.

Around the World. "It" names a city, river, or mountain located anywhere in the world. The player responds with the name of the country where the city, river, or mountain is located. Play the same as Know Your Geog?

States and Capitals. "It" names a state. The player responds by stating the capital of the state. Play the same as Know Your Geog?

Capitals of the World. "It" names the capital of a country anywhere in the world. The player responds by giving the country whose capital was cited. Play the same as Know Your Geog?

The King's Dinner

On sheets of paper print a series of *t*'s. Make each letter 6 inches and cut them out. Provide one *t* for each player who is to participate. Players sit in a circle. Announce that the players are to suggest a menu for a king. He is a peculiar individual and dislikes all food or drink containing the letter *t*.

In turn each player suggests a beverage or food he thinks the king will enjoy. Any person suggesting a food or beverage containing the letter *t* or failing to name one receives a letter *t* to remind him of the king's peculiar dislike for anything that contains the letter. The player with no letter at the conclusion of the game earns the title of being a member of "His Majesty's Chief Corps of Chefs."

Suggestions: A menu which the king enjoys because it contains no items having the letter *t* in them includes:

Pea soup	Gravy
Olives	Cabbage salad
Pickles	Beans
Fried chicken	Cauliflower
Macaroni	Rolls
Shrimp	Bread and jam
Veal	Milk
Pork	Coffee
Beef	Cherry pie

If the game is repeated, use another letter which is tabooed from being included in the menu suggested for the king. Be sure to prepare the letters in advance.

GUESSERS

Coffeepot

Players sit in a circle. Select an "it" and ask him to leave the room.

Have the other players select some activity, for example, swimming, which "it" is to attempt to guess when he returns. Recall "it." He starts questioning the players in the group, who must answer his questions truthfully. In asking the questions, "it" must use the word "coffeepot" to represent the activity, and the players he queries also must substitute "coffeepot" for the activity. The questioning and answering might resemble the following:

> *"It":* How often do you *coffeepot?*
> *Player:* I *coffeepot* frequently during some parts of the year.

"It":   Do you *coffeepot* in the house?

Player: I don't, but some individuals *coffeepot* indoors.

"It":   Do you *coffeepot* for fun?

Player: Yes, but *coffeepotting* can be done professionally.

"It":   What time of the year do you *coffeepot*?

Player: Depending upon where a person lives he might be able to *coffeepot* all year. I *coffeepot* outdoors during only a small portion of the year.

"It":   Is it swimming?

Player: Yes.

Questioning and answering continues until "it" names the activity. The person making the remark that enables "it" to guess the activity is "it" for the next round of the game.

If after a reasonable length of time "it" fails to guess the activity, reveal what it is. Allow "it" to select someone with whom to exchange places.

Teakettle

Players sit in a circle. Select an "it" and ask him to leave the room.

Have the players select some homonyms (words pronounced alike but different in meaning and spelling), for example, "so, sew, sow."

Ask two individuals to plan a short bit of conversation in which they use the words "so, sew, sow." However, instead of stating the words they substitute for them the word "teakettle."

Recall "it," who listens to the following type of conversation and attempts to guess the homonyms:

"Teakettle? I can't *teakettle* well."
"I thought you could *teakettle*."
"I can *teakettle* if I must, but Betty *teakettle* beautifully."
"I will *teakettle*, if you agree to *teakettle* the grass."
"All right, while we will *teakettle* differently, both of us will *teakettle*."
"I should say *teakettle*."

The conversation continues until "it" discovers that "teakettle" is being substituted for the homonyms "sew, so, sow." "It" selects someone to take his place, and he joins the group. Select two other conversationalists and repeat the activity.

If after a reasonable time "it" cannot guess the homonyms, ask the two individuals who "out-teakettled" "it" to announce them. "It" and the two conversationalists join the group. Select another person to be "it" and two conversationalists. While "it" is out of the room, select another set of homonyms which the twosome incorporates in the conversation.

Homonyms which might be used include:

in—inn	cellar—seller
by—buy—bye	cereal—serial
to—too—two	dew—due
dear—deer	flea—flee
vain—vane—vein	kernel—colonel
rain—rein—reign	sent—scent—cent
shoe—shoo	some—sum
plain—plane	sun—son
principal—principle	stake—steak
ant—aunt	tail—tale
ate—eight	way—weigh
base—bass	week—weak

Six Guesses

Provide a blackboard and chalk, or mount a large sheet of paper and use a crayon. Players sit facing the blackboard. Select one individual to be "it," and ask him to leave the room. Appoint one other player to act as recorder at the blackboard.

While "it" is out of the room, have the group decide on a word which "it" is to guess when he returns, for example, the name of a fruit—"raisin."

Recall "it." State the category (fruit) from which the word has been selected. Have the recorder draw a series of lines to represent the number of letters in the word. Since there are six letters in the group's selection (raisin), the recorder draws the following arrangement of blank lines: _ _ _ _ _ _ .

"It" starts questioning the group; for example, "Does the word have an e in it?" Since it does not, the recorder draws a hatch mark (/) on his scorecard to indicate one chance is gone. Then "it" might ask, "Does it have an i in it?" The recorder writes i in its proper place: _ _ i _ i _ . "It" then may ask, "Does it have a u in it?" Since it does not, the recorder adds another mark (/) to his scorecard, making //, which indicates that two turns have been used. Guessing continues until "it" fills in all the letters (r a i s i n) or he uses up his six opportunities.

If "it" fills in all the letters, he has another turn. He leaves the room while the group selects another word. If he completes the second word, he selects someone to take his place and chooses a new recorder. If "it" fails to guess correctly within his six chances, he joins the group. Select a new "it" and recorder.

Suggestions: Words may be selected from the following types of subjects:

Nature

Birds
Trees
Animals
Flowers
Fish
Fruits
Vegetables

Geography

Countries
Rivers
Mountains
States
Capitals
Cities
Lakes
Oceans

History

Presidents
Kings
Famous men
Famous women
Famous statesmen
Famous events

Music

Musical instruments
Famous composers
Musical terms
Well-known songs
Famous operas
Instrumental selections

Physiology

Organs of the body
Bones of the body

Art

Famous artists
Famous paintings
Famous sculptors
Famous statues
Famous architectural structures
Style of architecture

English

Famous authors
Famous poets
Famous playwrights
Poems
Famous characters of fiction
Famous orators
Famous works of fiction

Indian Lore

Tribes of Indians
Famous Indians
Articles of Indian clothing

Twenty Questions

Everyone sits in a circle. Select an "it."

"It" decides on some object he wants the others to attempt to guess using twenty questions or less. For example, "it" chooses "sailboat." In turn, each player asks "it" a question in an attempt to guess the name of the object "it" has chosen. "It" must answer the questions with "Yes," "No," or "I do not know." The questions and answers may run as follows:

"Is it in the animal kingdom?" "No."
"Is it found on the American Continent?" "Yes."
"Is it confined to one particular section of the United States?" "No."
"Is its use usually confined to any particular season of the year?" "Yes."
"Is it characteristic of city life?" "No."
"Is it characteristic of rural life?" "No."
"Is it related to woods activity?" "No."

"Is it connected with a sport?" "Yes."
"Is it related to the wind?" "Yes."
"Is it related to the water?" "Yes."
"Is it propelled by hand?" "No."
"Is it a sailboat?" "Yes."

The player asking the last question which helps the group to guess the object exchanges places with "it." He selects another object for the players to guess.

When the players fail to guess the object within the twenty questions, "it" announces the object and selects another person to take his place while he joins the group.

On the Spot. Have "it" leave the room while the group decides on some object "it" is to try to guess when he returns. Recall "it." Have him question the players in an attempt to discover the name of the object. If he guesses the object within the twenty questions, the individual answering the last question which helps "it" to guess the object exchanges places with "it."

If "it" fails to guess the object, announce the group's choice, and allow "it" to select someone to take his place.

Third Degree

Have the players form groups of six. Ask each group to sit in a different section of the room. Each team selects a representative. The representatives meet and select some object from any place in the universe which the other players will attempt to guess. Each representative goes to a group other than his own.

The members of the group immediately query the representative in an effort to discover the name of the object. In responding, the representative may use only "Yes," "No," or "I don't know." The players may ask any number of questions. However, the object is to guess the name of the item before the other teams succeed. The first team to guess it scores five points; all others score one point for trying.

Play continues with each group selecting another representative, who helps choose another object for the groups to guess. When groups are unable to guess an object, ask one of the representatives to announce the item. Every team scores one point for trying, and the game proceeds in the previous manner. The team with the highest score at the end of a designated time wins the game.

What's My Job?

Everyone sits in a circle. Select an "it."

"It" leaves the room while the group decides on some occupation he is to guess. Recall "it." He may use ten questions in his attempt to discover his supposed occupation. The players may answer the questions with "Yes," "No," or "I don't know."

If "it" succeeds in guessing the occupation, the player answering the last question exchanges places with "it." If "it" fails to guess the occupation with ten questions or less, announce his position, and allow "it" to select someone to take his place.

Am I? Have "it" leave the room while the group selects a character from fiction or real life whom "it" supposedly represents.

Recall "it." Within ten questions he is to guess for whom he is doubling. The players must answer his questions with a truthful statement. The person giving the answer immediately preceding the naming of the character by "it" exchanges places with "it." If "it" fails to guess the character, announce the name. Allow "it" to select a person to take his place.

Murder

Have a playing card for everyone. Be sure there is an ace of spades and a joker among the cards. Scatter the cards face down on a table. Explain to the group that the person drawing the ace of spades is the Prosecuting Attorney and the one drawing the joker, the Murderer.

Ask everyone to come up to the table and to draw a card without revealing its face to anyone. After everyone has a card, turn off the lights. The person who drew the joker, the Murderer, moves about the room and taps a player on the back. The victim screams. To give the Murderer a chance to escape from the scene and to give the others an opportunity to move about the room, count to ten before turning on the lights.

The person who drew the ace of spades now functions as the Prosecuting Attorney. He calls anyone he wishes to the witness stand and questions him. Everyone except the Murderer must truthfully answer all the questions. The Murderer may lie to any or all of the questions except the one: "Are you the Murderer?" The Prosecutor may ask this question only three times in the course of the entire game. When he obtains a "Yes" to this question, he has won his case.

If the Prosecutor does not discover the Murderer within the time he has asked three individuals, "Are you the murderer?" or if the questioning tends to lag, the Prosecutor places the case in the hands of the group. The elusive Murderer identifies himself.

Collect the cards and repeat the action if the group seems receptive to another case.

Found: One Body! Ask one individual in advance to be the Murderer and another to be the Informant. The Informant announces to the group that he has found a body outdoors. Everyone in the room is subject to questioning. Appoint a Prosecuting Attorney, who attempts to solve the crime in the same manner as in Murder.

Ghost

Players sit in a circle.

Ask one individual to start the game by calling the first letter of a word of more than two letters without revealing the word. The player next to the starter thinks of a word beginning with the letter and adds the second letter. The third player adds a third letter, and in turn the other players continue to make additions. Each player must take care that the letter he adds does not complete a word. For example, the first player calls "t," the second "r," the third "o." The fourth player unable to think of any word but "Troy" is forced to add the "y," completing the word. He becomes a half-ghost.

A player must always have in mind a word of more than two letters when he gives a letter. Frequently, a player unable to think of a word using the letters passed on to him calls a letter regardless in an attempt to bluff. Any player suspecting a bluff can challenge the player to state the word he has in mind, and if that player is unable to, he becomes a half-ghost. If he can name an actual word, however, the challenger becomes a half-ghost. For example, if the letters which have been named are t–r–i–n–i–t and the next player states the letter *a*, a player who cannot think of a word with those letters might suspect the previous player of bluffing and therefore challenge him. If the challenged player can give a word in which the *a* fits—for example, "trinitarian"—the challenger becomes a half-ghost. When anyone is already a half-ghost, he becomes a full ghost, and a point is scored against him. If anyone speaks to a half-ghost, he becomes a half-ghost; if he speaks to a ghost, he becomes a ghost, and one point is scored against him. Ghosts remain in the game and continue to participate. No player scores until he is a ghost.

With the completion of each word the game continues with the next player thinking of a word of more than two letters and calling the first letter. At the end of a designated time, the player with no points or the least number of them wins the game.

Suggestion: Cut holes in the centers of old clean sheets so that players can slip them over their heads. When a player becomes a ghost, he dons the ghostly garb, which he wears throughout the game.

SUBSTITUTERS

Fizz

The players sit in a circle.

On signal, the players start the game by counting off in a counter-clockwise direction, beginning with the number one. When the players come to the number five or any number which is a multiple of five, the word "fizz" is said instead of the number. The count would therefore be as follows: "1–2–3–4–fizz–6–7–8–9–fizz–11, etc."

When the fifties are reached, the count becomes more amusing: "fizz-0" (for fifty)—"fizz-one—fizz-two, etc." Fifty-five is "fizz fizz."

Buzz. Use the word "buzz" in place of numbers containing seven and numbers which are multiples of seven. Play the same as Fizz.

Fizz Buzz. Combine the rules for Fizz and Buzz and proceed as in both. When a number is both a "fizz" and a "buzz," say "fizz buzz."

Buzz Bang. Substitute "bang" for numbers containing six and numbers which are multiples of six. Use the word "buzz" as in Fizz Buzz and proceed as in that game.

Succotash. Substitute "beans" for any number containing seven and any number which is a multiple of seven. Seventy is "beans-0"; seventy-one, "beans-one"; seventy-seven is "beans beans."

In place of numbers containing nine and numbers which are multiples of nine, use the word "corn."

For any numbers that contain either seven or nine or multiples of them substitute the word "succotash." For example, twenty-seven is "succotash" because it contains seven and is a multiple of nine.

For numbers which are both "beans" and "corn," use the word "succotash."

REPEATERS

Gossip

Prepare a brief news item. Have the players sit in a circle.

Whisper the brief news item to the player on the right. He whispers it to the next player. In turn each individual relays the bit of news to the neighbor on his right. Players may not whisper the message more than once. When the last player hears the news, he states aloud what he has heard. The difference between the original news item and the item as reported by the last player is usually greatly amusing.

Gossip Relay. Write a sentence on a 3×5-inch card for each team. Provide one blank card and a pencil for each group. Have the players form teams and stand in single files.

Give the card with the gossip item to the first player of each team. After each head player reads the sentence, collect the cards. Distribute a blank card and pencil to the last player on each team.

On signal the starter of each team whispers the sentence to the player behind him. Whispering continues until the last player hears the message and writes it on his card. He rushes to the leader and presents the sentence as he heard it. The team that is first to have all of its members participate and whose statement is nearest the original sentence wins the whispering competition.

Shopping

Players sit in a circle.

The game is started by one player's saying, "I went to the store and bought _____," and adding an item beginning with the letter *a*, for example, "apples." The player on the starter's right repeats the statement and adds an item beginning with the letter *b*, for instance, "I went to the store and bought apples and beets." Each player buys an article in the store beginning with the next letter of the alphabet and repeats all the articles purchased by those preceding him.

If a player omits an article, misnames one, mixes the alphabet, or is unable to think of an article beginning with the letter he is required to use, he scores one point against himself. When a person makes an error, the next person must correct it before continuing the grocery list. The player with no points or the fewest points at the end of a designated time wins the game.

When I Inherit That Million. Start the game by saying, "When I inherit that million, I will buy _____," and add a word beginning with the letter *a*, for example, "airplane." Play the game the same as Shopping.

Pack My Trunk for Klondike

Players sit in a circle.

One of them starts the game by saying, "I packed my trunk for Klondike, and I put in it _____," and inserting the name of an appropriate item, for example, "a pair of boots." The second player repeats the statement and adds another item: "I packed my trunk for Klondike and I put in it a pair of boots and a jacket." Any item appropriate for the trip to the Klondike is acceptable. Play continues by repeating items and adding a new item. If a player omits an article in his recitation, he scores one point against himself. The person who can recall the most items in the proper order wins the game. Second place goes to the player who has the fewest points.

Visiting Aunt Marie. Start the game by saying, "I am going to visit Aunt Marie; I'm taking her a _____." Each player adds the name of a gift for her and repeats the foregoing presents. Gifts must be appropriate. Play the same as Pack My Trunk for Klondike.

Rigmarole

Prepare a list of phrases or sentences of the tongue-twister type. Players sit in a circle.

Start the game by stating a twister. Have each player repeat it in turn. Then add to the first saying another twister. Have everyone repeat both of the twisters in turn. Each round add a new twister phrase. The players must repeat all twisters in the correct order.

For tongues that twist or memories that become confused the player scores one point against himself, but he remains a participating member of the group. As his turn comes up after a miss, the player may try again. If he foregoes the opportunity, he scores another point. The player with no points or the fewest points at the end of a designated time wins the tongue exercise.

Some phrases of the tongue-twisting type to use in playing the game include:

1. One old ostrich
2. Two tree toads twisting tendrils
3. Three tiny titmice tapping trees
4. Four fat fellows fanning flames
5. Five fluffy finches flying fast
6. Six of Susie's sisters sewing shirts
7. Seven sea shells in Sarah's shawl
8. Eight elves eating Easter eggs
9. Nine nimble noblemen nibbling nuts
10. Ten throbbing thrush thriving thither
11. Albert Applebeck's awful apples
12. Big black bugs biting bears

STRETCHERS

Sights to See!

Players form groups of four and sit at tables. Ask each group to appoint a Tourists' Guide. Give each Guide a sheet of 8½ × 11-inch paper and a pencil.

Within a designated time the players in each group name the places they wish to visit in the United States. The Guide lists the places on the sheet of paper. In stating the names of cities and states the group must specify a point of interest found in each of them, for example, New York—Madison Square Garden; Chicago—Hull House; and Florida—Marineland. Merely listing a city or state does not count.

After an allotted time, call a halt to the game and ask the Tourists' Guide having the longest list to read it. If the list is correct, the group wins the game.

World Travel. Have players name any interesting places in the world which they want to visit. Play the same as Sights to See!

Know Your Slang?

Players form groups of four and sit at tables. Ask each group to appoint a recorder. Give each recorder a sheet of 8½ × 11-inch paper and a pencil.

Within a designated time, the recorders for each group list as many slang expressions and words as the members of the groups can recall. At the end of time have the recorder with the most expressions read his group's list. If all the expressions are recognized slang words or phrases, this group wins.

Name the Trees. Have the recorder list as many names of trees as the members can recall. Play the same as Know Your Slang?

House Plants That Count. Have the recorder list as many names of house plants as the members can recall. Play the same as Know Your Slang?

Superstitious? Have each recorder list as many superstitions as the members of the group can recall. Play the same as Know Your Slang?

How Many Flowers? Have each recorder list as many names of flowers as the members can recall. Play the same as Know Your Slang?

List the Birds. Have each recorder list as many names of birds as the members of the group can recall. Play the same as Know Your Slang?

RACE EVENTERS

Words on Foot

Prepare two sets of alphabet cards on sheets of 8½ × 11-inch cardboard. Use a brown crayon for making one set of cards and a green one for the other set. Have as many letters as there are players in each group (see suggestions below). Divide the players into two teams. Have each team sit facing opposite each other, about 10 feet apart.

To the left and a few feet outside, the players on Team 1 mark a line perpendicular to the team; Team 2 does the same. These lines are the spelling lines (see Figure 5–1). Distribute the brown letters to Team 1, the green to Team 2—one letter to each player. Have available a large sheet of paper and a black crayon for recording the score.

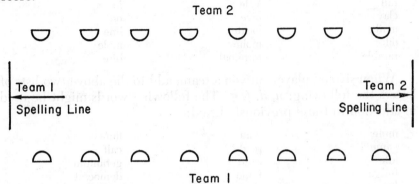

FIGURE 5–1. Formation of players and location of spelling lines for Words on Foot

Call out a word. The players from each team holding the letters in that word rush to their spelling line, quickly arrange themselves in the order in which the letters appear in the word, and hold up their letters in front of them. The team which is first to spell the word correctly and hold the letters in plain view scores three points. The other scores one point for trying. Record the score. The team first to score fifteen points wins the speedy spelling race.

Suggestions: Select the letters to be used beforehand, and retain a list of the words that the players can spell with their letters of the alphabet. Take letters which appear most frequently in the English language, and use words in which the same letter appears only once. Announce the words very distinctly.

When there are eight players on a team, use the following letters: *a, e, t, r, m, b, o, c.* The words to use might include:

care	more	era
tore	bear	rate
mob	mace	boat
race	team	amber
Rome	beam	trace
mate	brat	cream
come	tear	moat
tame	comb	brace

When there are twelve players on a side, add the following letters to the above list: *i, l, y, n.* Words to use in addition to those listed above might include:

bait	lace	moaner
omit	only	rain
mice	lame	bale
neat	malt	meal
boil	boy	lice
rice	main	real
rail	Yale	in
clay	nice	on
mail	locate	line
oil	money	mole
ramble	terminal	bite

When sixteen players are on a team, add to the above two lists of letters the following: *u, d, f, g.* The following words might be used in addition to those previously listed:

mule	done	flute
game	ready	calf
idle	cage	geranium
fudge	fame	democrat
fig	made	urbanity
route	lunatic	fraction
date	fortune	country
long	draft	comedy
young	yearling	ramble
faint	left	dance

Letter Scramble

Prepare a list of words of from four to ten letters long, and make up two sets of alphabet cards containing all the letters used in the list of words. Have the players form two teams of at least ten members each and sit facing each other about 12 feet apart. Place a table in the center between the two teams, with the letters essential to spelling all the words face down on each team's side of the table. Mark a spelling line for each team.

Announce the number of letters in the word to be spelled by the two teams so that the players can prepare for action; for example, if there are five letters, the first five players on each team will be involved. Now call out the word. Each fivesome hustles to its alphabet cards and locates the five letters needed to spell the word. Finding them, the players rush to their spelling line, and holding up the letters, they quickly arrange themselves in the correct order to spell the word. The first team to complete the word correctly scores a point. The five players then go to the end of their respective teams, and the other players move ahead so the next set

of players is ready to respond. The team with the most points at
the end of a designated time wins the game.

Word Spelling Race

Prepare four sets of alphabet cards. Players form four teams
and sit in a hollow square (see page 9).

Have the players on all teams number off in consecutive order.
Place each set of alphabet cards face down on a table. Make certain
that each team member knows which pile of cards belongs to his
team.

Announce a word which the teams are to spell. Immediately,
Number 1 on each team rushes to his team's alphabet cards, finds
the first letter of the word, places the other letters face down, hurries
back to his place, and holds the card up in front of him. Number 2
on each team then rushes for the second letter of the word, comes
back to his place, and holds up his letter.

All the players needed to complete the spelling of the word
hurry in turn to secure the necessary letters. The number of players
going into action to spell a word is dependent upon the number of
letters in the word; for example, in a five-letter word only Numbers
1 to 5 of each team participate. The first team to spell the designated word scores three points; the other team, one for trying. The
first team to score fifteen points wins the spelling competition.

After each word is spelled and scores are tallied, ask a player of
each team to return the letters to the proper pile on the table,
shuffle the letters, and place them face down on the table. As soon
as one word has been spelled, the players who participated go to
the end of their team while the others move into readiness for the
next word to be called and spelled.

In the following list of words containing eight letters or less,
each letter appears only once:

judge	worship	geranium
claim	caution	feudal
shingle	shield	discount
author	captive	hexagon
country	senator	urbanity
dynamo	hoist	travels
conquer	fraction	jaundice
dynastic	teapot	unsavory
journey	impulse	jeopardy
virulent	scarlet	laughter
spoilage	homage	javelin
republic	aversion	sluice
scenario	harmonic	jocular
poetry	frowzy	terminal
sidewalk	mucilage	group

Suggestion: To increase the variety of words use some in which the letters appear more than once. To compensate for the extra letters, the players use additional leg work. For example, in the word, "contest," the person having the letter *t* gets himself in position between the *n* and *e* and then hustles to the end of the word to add the final *t*. If a letter is repeated, as in "affect," the person having the letter *f* gets in position and moves the letter in pendulum fashion to indicate the letter is repeated.

RELAY EVENTERS

Add a City

Have an atlas available for checking the names of cities. Players form teams and sit in single files. Give the first player of each team a pencil and a 4 × 6-inch card.

On signal, the first player of each team writes on the top of his team's paper the name of any city in the United States (example, Los Angeles). He quickly passes the card and pencil to the second player, who must write beneath it the name of a city whose name begins with the last letter of the preceding name. As soon as he writes the name (for example, Sarasota), he passes the paper and pencil to the third player, who writes the name of a city beginning with the last letter of the second player's city (for example, Atlanta).

Play continues until the last player adds a city. He takes the list and pencil to the head player, who stands and waves the card to indicate his team has finished. The first team to complete a correct list wins the game. Check to see that each city except the first one begins with the last letter of the preceding one. If the team makes an error, the group having the longest correct list wins the relay. All names may be used only once.

Famous Writers. Have each player write the name of a well-known writer. In this version the name of the writer may begin with any letter of the alphabet. Play the same as Add a City.

Long- and Short-Haired Composers. Have each player write the name of either a classical or nonclassical composer. In this version the name of the composer may begin with any letter of the alphabet. Play the same as Add a City.

Painters to the Fore. Have each player write the name of a famous painter either of the past or contemporary. In this version the name of the painter may begin with any letter of the alphabet. Play the same as Add a City.

Automobiles on Display. Have each player write the name of an automobile. In this version the name of the automobile may begin with any letter of the alphabet. Play the same as Add a City.

Vegetarian Menu. Have each player write the name of a vegetable. In this version the name of the vegetable may begin with any letter of the alphabet. Play the same as Add a City.

Gardens. Have each player write the name of a flower. In this version the name of the flower may begin with any letter of the alphabet. Play the same as Add a City.

Wings. Have each player write the name of a bird. In this version the name of the bird may begin with any letter of the alphabet. Play the same as Add a City.

Trip to the Zoo. Have each player write the name of an animal found in the zoo. In this version the name of the animal may begin with any letter of the alphabet. Play the same as Add a City.

Potted Beauty. Have each player write the name of a house plant. In this version the name of the house plant may begin with any letter of the alphabet. Play the same as Add a City.

Forests. Have each player write the name of a tree. In this version the name of the tree may begin with any letter of the alphabet. Play the same as Add a City.

Celebrities. Have each player write the name of a famous person of the past or present. In this version the name of the person may begin with any letter of the alphabet. Play the same as Add a City.

Favorite TV Programs. Have each player write the name of a television program. In this version the name of the program may begin with any letter of the alphabet. Play the same as Add a City.

Favorite Radio Programs. Have each player write the name of a radio program. In this version the name of the program may begin with any letter of the alphabet. Play the same as Add a City.

Building Sentences

Use a blackboard and chalk, or substitute a large sheet of paper mounted on a wall and a black crayon. Indicate a starting line 12 feet from the blackboard. Players form groups of eight or less, and each team stands or sits in a single file behind the starting line. Give the first player of each team a piece of chalk.

On signal, the first player of each team moves forward and writes on the blackboard the first word of a sentence, then immediately hurries back to his line, hands the chalk to the second player in line, and goes to the end of his team. The second player rushes forward to the blackboard and adds the second word to the sentence.

Play continues as each player adds a word. The last player on the team concludes the sentence. The first team to have its members participate and build a real sentence (containing a subject and predicate and expressing a complete thought) wins the game.

SENSE ALERTERS

CONTENTS

Sense alerters give the players an opportunity to check on the efficiency of their basic senses of sight, hearing, smell, taste, and touch. These senses take the leading roles in the games, and mental processes are in the supporting cast. For ready reference the list preceding this chapter groups the games into categories according to the sense used.

Sensibility to outward impressions can be rewarding. The players may gain real appreciation for their perception while participating in the sense alerters.

In addition to paper and pencils most of the supplies needed to put the senses on the alert come from the kitchen cupboards, the refrigerator, or the food store.

OBSERVERS

Do You Observe?

Select ten articles which offer possibilities for testing powers of observation, such as a pencil, a spool of thread, a page from a newspaper, a printed wrapper from a loaf of bread, a wrist watch that has stopped, an illustrated advertisement of an automobile, the illustrated cover of a magazine, a postmarked envelope, an electric light bulb, and a book jacket. Players sit in a circle. Give each player a 3 × 5-inch card and a pencil.

Pass the items, one by one, around the circle and request the players to examine each article carefully. When everyone has had a chance to examine the items, collect the articles. Ask the players a series of questions or request information about the items which test their powers of observation. The first player to respond with a correct answer scores three points. Each player keeps his own score on the card. The person having the highest score at the conclusion of the questioning wins the game.

Some questions and statements to check on the players' observations might include:

1. Pencil
   What was the name of the pencil?
   What was the name of the pencil's manufacturer?

What was the color of the pencil?
Did the pencil have a sharp point?
Was the eraser new or used?

2. Spool of thread
   What was the name of the thread's manufacturer?
   What was the number on the spool?
   What was the color of the thread?
   What kind of thread was on the spool?

3. Page from a newspaper
   What was the date of the page?
   From what section was the page?
   What was the number of the page?
   How many columns made up the page?
   Was any bold-face type used on the page?
   Did any of the stories carry a by-line?

4. Wrapper from a loaf of bread
   What kind of bread had been in the package?
   What was the weight of the loaf?
   What was the baker's name?
   What was the name of the bread?

5. Wrist watch that has stopped
   What was the make of the watch?
   Did it have a second hand?
   At what time did the watch stop?
   Of what material was the band or bracelet made?
   Of what material was the watch made?

6. Illustrated advertisement of an automobile
   What was the make of the car?
   Who manufactured it?
   What was the color of the vehicle?
   What was its body style?

7. Illustrated cover of a magazine
   What was the subject of the illustration?
   Give the date of the magazine.
   State the name of the magazine.
   Name the title of an article or story featured on the cover.

8. Postmarked envelope
   Name the place where it was postmarked.
   What date was it postmarked?
   What was the color of the stamp on the envelope?
   Was it a commemorative stamp? Name the occasion.
   What was the denomination of the stamp?

9. Electric light bulb
   What was its wattage?
   What was its voltage?
   What was the trade name appearing on the bulb?

10. Book jacket
    What was the title of the publication?
    Who was the author?
    Give the name of the publisher.
    What was the basic color used in the jacket?

Reproducing the Picture

Secure two duplicates of a picture having many details. Have a watch for timing and a blackboard and chalk or a large sheet of paper and a black crayon for recording scores. Have a 3×5-inch card and a pencil for each group. Players form two lines and sit facing one another about 10 feet apart. Designate one line as Team 1; the other is Team 2. Give a picture to the head player on each team.

On signal, the first player observes the details in the picture: subject, color, technique. Allow each player one minute to study the picture; then call time and ask the first player of each team to pass the picture to the second player. When everyone has had a turn, gather the pictures. Distribute a card and a pencil to each team.

Have each team list its observations. After an allotted time call a halt to the listing and ask one member of each team to read its combined observations. Give each team one point for each correct observation. The team with the highest score wins the picture observation game.

Four Wheels in Detail. Arrange in advance to have an automobile available for observation. Send each team outside for three minutes to look at the automobile and observe and remember as many details about it as they can. They may not raise the hood or enter the automobile. Play the same as Reproducing the Picture.

Note the Change

Place twelve items on a table. Make a diagram of the placement of the articles. Then change the arrangement and make a diagram of this second arrangement. Cover the items. Have two $8\frac{1}{2} \times 11$-inch sheets of paper and a pencil for each group. Have a watch for timing.

Players form groups of six. Seat players in such a position that they cannot see the items from their places at any time.

Uncover the items. Each group in turn comes to the table and observes the items on the table for one minute.

After every group has had a turn, arrange the items according to the first diagram made prior to playing the game. Allow each group another turn of one minute to observe the changes in placement. Then distribute a pencil and the two sheets of paper to each group. Within a designated time each group makes a diagram of the original and the reorganized placement of the objects.

Call time and ask one member of each group to present the diagrams. The group presenting the two diagrams most similar to the actual arrangements as shown on the leader's diagrams wins the game.

Items which might be used in playing the game include:

book	pencil
deck of playing cards	clock
three pieces of silverware	shoe with laces
scissors	newspaper turned to editorial page
aspirin	toy automobile
six paper clips	folded handkerchief

Different Bouquets. Have the players view an arrangement of flowers. Play the same as Note the Change. Instead of rearranging the bouquet while the game is in progress have two arrangements, so the second bouquet can be used as soon as everyone views the first display. Make two diagrams to use in checking the players' powers of observation.

Rearranged Fruit. Arrange fruit in a basket. Play the same as Different Bouquets.

Rearranged Vegetables. Arrange vegetables in a basket or on a table. Play the same as Different Bouquets.

Describe the Stranger

Arrange in advance to have an individual unknown to the group arrive at a designated time. Arrange players so that they will face the visitor, but do not call their attention to the fact that they are to observe him and write a description of him. Have a 4 × 6-inch card and a pencil for each player.

When the visitor arrives, talk with him for a few minutes. Shortly after his departure give each player a card and a pencil. Ask everyone to write a description of the person: approximate age, height, weight, color of eyes, color of hair, type of face, color of clothes, kind of shoes, and any other noticeable features.

After a designated time ask each person to read his description. The player having the most accurate description asks the individual to re-enter the room to verify his accuracy in observation.

Eye Them

Place twenty or thirty assorted objects on a table. Cover the objects with a cloth or large sheet of paper. Have a 4 × 6-inch card and a pencil for each player. Seat players in such a position that they cannot see the items at any time from their places.

Uncover the items. Ask small groups of players to come to the table to view the objects for one minute. The players may not discuss the items with anyone.

After everyone has had a turn distribute a card and a pencil
to each player. Within a designated time everyone lists as many
items as he can recall seeing during his minute of observation. After
the allotted time call a halt to the game and ask the player with the
longest list to read it. If the items he included are actually on the
table, he wins the observing game.

Checker Placing

Provide for each group a checkerboard or a cardboard copy of
one, four red checkers, and four black checkers. Have another
checkerboard on a table placed so the players cannot see it from
their tables. Place four red and four black checkers at random on
the board and cover it with a newspaper or cloth.

Players form groups of four and sit at tables. Uncover
the checkerboard and ask each group to come to the table and
view the placement of the checkers on the board. The players
may not converse with one another about the placement of the
checkers.

After everyone views the checkers distribute a checkerboard
and four red and four black checkers to each group. Within a
designated time the members of each group attempt to place the
checkers in the same positions as the ones set up on the display
board.

At the end of the allotted time check each group's placement.
The one which placed the most checkers correctly wins.

Quick Sight

Have ready for each player six ¾-inch black disks and an
8½ × 11-inch piece of cardboard marked off into squares. Mark off
an additional cardboard piece for display and pin six black disks of
¾-inch diameter in various places on the display cardboard.

Players form groups of four and sit at tables. Hold up the display
card with the attached disks and ask the players to view it. Count
slowly and quietly to thirty. Conceal the card. Distribute a cardboard and six disks to each player. Request the players to place
their disks on the cardboard in the same relative position as those
they observed on the display card. The player wins who has the
most disks accurately placed.

Window Shopping

Select five shop windows displaying different kinds of merchandise and make a list of the items in the windows. (Make sure that
the window displays will not be changed before the group is to

play the game.) Provide a sheet of 8½ × 11-inch paper and a pencil for each group. Have a watch for timing.

Players form groups of four. Take the groups to the designated shops and allow every group to view each window display for two minutes. When everyone has had a chance to observe the displays, return to your meeting place. Give each group a sheet of paper and a pencil. Request each group to select one person as a recorder.

On signal each group is to list within a designated time the items which the members saw displayed in the five windows. The merchandise from each window must be listed separately.

At the end of the allotted time call a halt to the listing and ask the recorder of the group having the longest list to read it. If the group's observation is correct, the members earn the title of "Best Window Shoppers."

SNIFFERS

Sniff Sniff

Secure eighteen half-ounce bottles and eighteen liquids with a characteristic odor (see list below). In each bottle place a few drops of one of the liquids. Wrap each bottle with enough tissue paper so that contents are not visible, but allow an opening so the cork can be removed. Number the bottles and make a list of the contents each bottle contains. Have a 4 × 6-inch card and a pencil for each player.

Players sit in a circle. Give each player a card and a pencil. Uncork the bottles and pass them around the circle, one at a time. Ask each player to sniff each one. As soon as he thinks he recognizes the liquid, he writes the number appearing on the bottle and the name next to it on his card.

After everyone has a chance to sniff each bottle, ask the player with the longest list to read the number of each bottle and the liquid he thinks it contains. If his list is correct, he wins the title of the "Best Sniffer."

Some liquids with characteristic odors that might be used are:

Vanilla extract	Coffee
Wintergreen oil	Milk
Lemon extract	Chocolate milk
Orange extract	Olive oil
Almond extract	Vinegar
Peppermint extract	Camphor
Strawberry extract	Castor oil
Pineapple extract	Witchhazel
Tea	Cologne

Spicy Sniff. Place a sample of different spices in individual paper nut cups. Play the same as Sniff Sniff. The eyes cooperate with the nose in helping the players to identify the spices.

Some spices with characteristic odors are:

Cloves (ground)	Allspice
Cinnamon (ground)	Bay leaves
Pepper (ground)	Caraway seed
Ginger (ground)	Celery salt
Nutmeg (ground)	Chili powder
Mustard (dry)	Mint leaves (dried)
Celery seed	Poppy seed
Anise seed	Pumpkin pie spice blend
Thyme	Sage

Nosegay

Secure a variety of flowers which have significant aromas, for example: marigold, nasturtium, rose, phlox, sweet alyssum, and chrysanthemum. Secure a roll of paper towels for blindfolds. Obtain a 3 × 5-inch card, a pencil, and two paper clips for fastening blindfolds for each player.

Players sit in a circle. Have two players assist in blindfolding each person. Blindfold the assistants.

Pass the flowers, one at a time, around the circle. Ask the players to smell each one, try to identify the flowers, and remember the names of them.

After everyone has a chance to smell the flowers, ask the players to remove the blindfolds. Distribute a 3 × 5-inch card and a pencil to everyone and ask the players to write the names of the flowers he thinks he identified. Ask the player with the longest list to read it. If his "smeller" has served him correctly, he wins the game.

The sense of touch also may assist in this game, for individuals who know flowers are able to identify some of them by touch.

Identifying Vegetables. Have the players pass vegetables which have been cut in half around the circle, one at a time. Play the same as Nosegay. Vegetables which may be used include the following: carrot, kohlrabi, radish, potato, onion, pepper, celery, cabbage, parsley, and peas in a pod.

HEARERS

Who Is Speaking?

Have two paper clips and a roll of paper towels for blindfolds.

Players sit in a circle. Designate an "it" who stands in the center. Blindfold "it" using a piece of paper toweling fastened with two paper clips. Then ask the players to change seats to increase the difficulty "it" will have in identifying them.

Point to one of the players in the group and say, "Speak to it, please." The person must respond with a remark or two, and "it" tries to identify the player's voice and give his name.

If the identification is correct, "it" exchanges places with the player. Place a fresh blindfold on the player and continue the game in the same manner.

When "it" fails to identify a player, select another person whom "it" must try to name. If "it" fails to identify two players consecutively, he removes the blindfold and selects a member of the group to take his place while he joins the circle.

Suggestion: Use this game if players know one another well enough that they are able to identify one another's voices.

Find the Watch

Have a stop watch and a blindfold.

Players sit in a circle. Blindfold one player, "it," who stands in the center. Hold the watch at face level and stand within "its" hearing range.

Start the stop watch. "It" attempts to locate the watch by listening to its ticking. When he discovers it he places his hands on it. Keep a record of the time it takes him to find the watch. Announce the time to him. He selects someone to take his place and joins the group.

After everyone has a turn, the player finding the watch in the shortest time wins the title of "Keenest Ears."

Sound Effects

Secure a number of items which will make a characteristic sound when dropped on the floor, for example: a pie plate, a shoe, six pieces of silverware, a woman's handbag loaded with the usual, five pennies, a magazine, a handful of paper clips, a deck of cards, and a basketball. Also have a watch. Obtain a screen or an old sheet (but not so old that the players can peer through it). Suspend the sheet, making sure that it goes down to the floor. Place the items on a table behind the screen or sheet. Have a 3 × 5-inch card and a pencil for each player. Appoint an assistant in advance to perform as Chief Dropper behind the screen and drop the items, one at a time, at half-minute intervals.

Players sit and face the screen or sheet. Pass out the cards and pencils and ask each player to write the numbers one through ten on the left side of his card. On signal, the Chief Dropper starts the activity. As he drops each item, the players try to identify the object dropped. They write the name of each object they identify to the right of the corresponding number.

After the tenth item is dropped, ask the player with the most complete list to read the objects he identified. As he reads each item, the Chief Dropper steps from behind the screen or sheet and presents the item. The player with the most correct identifications wins the game and is complimented for possessing the "best pair of listeners." If the players are unable to identify some of the items, ask the assistant to present them after a winner is declared.

Recorded Sounds

Secure a record player and a sound effects record. Have a 3 × 5-inch card and a pencil for each player. Players sit in a circle.

Ask the players to listen to the record and try to identify the various sounds which they hear. After playing the record, distribute a card and a pencil to each player. Within a designated time the players list on the cards the sounds which they recognized.

After an allotted time call a halt and ask the player with the longest list to read it. If he heard correctly, he wins the listening activity.

Recognizing Bird Songs. Have the players listen to a recording of the songs of various birds and try to identify them. Play the same as Recorded Sounds.

Music Box. Have the players listen to a pianist play a medley of well-known selections and try to identify them. Play the same as Recorded Sounds. In lieu of a pianist use a record player and play short portions from a varied group of well-known records.

Listen for the Whistle

Secure a record player, a recording of a march, and a whistle.

Players form teams of ten. Members of each team stand in a single circle, facing in a clockwise direction. Appoint an assistant to watch each circle and to keep score.

To the rhythm of the march and on one blast of the whistle the players proceed around the circle in a clockwise direction. When the whistle is blown twice, the players must reverse and march in a counterclockwise direction. On the sound of three blasts the players face the center, halt, and mark time. With four blasts of the whistle everyone turns his back to the center and faces out, marking time.

After the first blast of the whistle which initiates the marching action, a score of five points is awarded for each change of direction which an entire team performs correctly. All others score one point for trying. The team with the most points at the end of a designated time wins the game.

Blow the whistle frequently so that the groups must continue to change from one direction to another.

TASTERS

Team Tasters

Make a list of half as many items with characteristic tastes as there are players. Obtain two of each item. Wrap each article in waxed paper. Secure a roll of paper toweling for making blindfolds and two paper clips for fastening each blindfold. Have two 3×5-inch cards and two pencils.

Divide the players into two teams. Appoint an assistant from each team to help blindfold the players. Then blindfold the assistants. Distribute an item to be tasted by each player, making sure that both teams receive identical items.

On signal, each player unwraps the item he is to taste and identify. As soon as each player tastes and eats his sample, call the activity to a halt. Ask the players to remove the blindfolds. Give one player on each team a card and a pencil. Allow each group a few minutes to list the items everyone thinks he tasted.

At the end of the allotted time call a halt, and ask the team having the longest list to have one member read it. If the list is correct, the group earns the title of "Best Tasters."

Items to identify in the tasting contest might include:

Piece of peppermint-flavored candy
Piece of wintergreen-flavored candy
Piece of licorice
Slice of banana
Slice of orange
Slice of lemon
Small piece of bitter chocolate

Do You Know Your Nuts? Distribute a wrapped shelled nut to members of the teams. Play the same as Team Tasters. While some of the nuts suggested in the game are actually fruits, to many individuals they are known as nuts, so it should not alter the tasting contest. Some nuts to use include:

peanut	hickory
walnut	almond
pistachio	piece of coconut
cashew	pecan
brazil	filbert

Edible Plants. Distribute a small sample of a vegetable wrapped in waxed paper. Play the same as Do You Know Your Nuts? Vegetables to include in the game:

carrot	green pepper
kohlrabi	celery
radish	parsley
potato	peas
onion	bean
cauliflower	

FEELERS

The Rural Touch

Secure a roll of paper toweling to use for blindfolds. Have a 3 × 5-inch card, a pencil, and two paper clips for fastening the blindfold for each player. Place a variety of vegetables in a basket or carton and cover the vegetables with a paper.

Players sit in a circle. Ask two players to assist in blindfolding the others; then blindfold the two assistants.

Pass the vegetables, one at a time, around the circle. The players try to identify and remember the names of the vegetables. When all have had a chance to touch the vegetables, put the vegetables back in the basket or carton and cover them with the paper. Have the players remove their blindfolds. Distribute a card and a pencil to each player, and ask everyone to list the vegetables he thinks he identified. After a designated time call a halt, and ask the player with the longest list to read it. If it is correct, he wins the title "Best Truck Farmer."

Some vegetables to use in playing the game include:

carrot	onion
beet	green pepper
radish	bunch of celery
Swiss chard	cauliflower
parsley	stalk of asparagus
cabbage	pod of peas
potato	eggplant

Finesse in Identifying Fruits. Use fruits instead of vegetables. Play the same as The Rural Touch.

Fruits to use in playing the game might include:

peach	cantaloupe
pear	apricot
banana	nectarine
avocado (alligator	cherry
pear)	lemon
unripe plum	orange
apple	lime

MYSTIFIERS

CONTENTS

In the first section of the mystery games, the Intriguers, conspiracy is necessary between the performer of the mystifying feat and an accomplice. The success in playing the mystifiers depends upon how well the performer and his accomplice play their mysterious roles. To keep the observers in suspense, the duo must work as a unit and know exactly what each is to do. A trick should be practiced several times before the twosome presents it to a group so that there will be no mistakes.

While the observer may assume that the performer is psychic or possesses supernatural insight, the pattern for playing mystery games is very much down to earth: the performer and his accomplice have a predetermined signal which enables the performer to respond correctly.

In the second part of the chapter, Number Tricksters, the players perform a series of calculations, which the leader initiates, and find the numbers playing tricks on them. To their amazement the numbers in some of the games reveal the cold facts, such as the player's age, month of birth, or even the amount of change he is carrying.

For all of the games the players sit in a small group except in the activities which specify a circle formation or those in which the players sit at tables.

An alphabetized list of the games precedes the chapter.

INTRIGUERS

What Time Is It?

The performer leaves the room while the group decides upon an hour which he is to try to guess when he returns.

Recall the performer. As he enters, he asks, "What time is it?" The accomplice answers, "Well, I forgot to bring my watch; I can't say exactly." The performer then replies, "A watch isn't needed. It is six o'clock."

CLUE: The key for telling the time is the following:

The first letter in the *third word* of the accomplice's answer tells the secret. The third word in the above example is "forgot." *F* is the sixth letter of the alphabet, hence the hour is six o'clock.

Hour	Key Letter	Hour	Key Letter
1	A	7	G
2	B	8	H
3	C	9	I
4	D	10	J
5	E	11	K
6	F	12	L

After the stunt has been performed a few times the key may be changed by a prearranged signal between the two principals. For example, one o'clock could be represented by the letter M:

Hour	Key Letter	Hour	Key Letter
1	M	7	S
2	N	8	T
3	O	9	U
4	P	10	V
5	Q	11	W
6	R	12	X

Black Magic

The performer leaves the room while the group selects some object which it wishes the performer to guess. When the performer returns, the accomplice asks him a series of questions. For example, if the object chosen was table, the accomplice may ask: "Is it a chair?" "Is it a book?" "Is it _____'s shoe [the shoe referred to is black]?" The performer replies "No" to all of these questions. Then the accomplice asks, "Is it a table?" and the performer says, "Yes, that is it."

CLUE: The performer answers correctly because the accomplice names the correct object immediately after he names a black object.

Red, White, and Blue. Play the same as Black Magic except for the clue.

CLUE: The first time the performer returns to the group name the selected object immediately after an item which is red; the second time, after something white; and the third time, after something blue.

Suggestion: In place of colors, use a creature or object which flies or a four-legged creature or object as the clue name.

Mystery City

The performer leaves the room. One member of the group names the city where he was born. Recall the performer and inform him he is to discover the name of a town or city. Through a series of questions about cities, the accomplice secretly informs the performer of the correct one. If the city is Syracuse, for example, the questioning may go this way:

Accomplice: Is it Miami?
Performer: No.
Accomplice: Is it Los Angeles?
Performer: No.
Accomplice: Is it Detroit?
Performer: No.
Accomplice: Is it Syracuse?
Performer: Yes.

CLUE: The correct city is the second one named after a two-word city. In this example, Los Angeles is the key name.

Revealing the Number

The performer leaves the room and the group selects a number from one to one hundred. This number the psychic performer will reveal to them upon his return. When the performer returns, the accomplice calls out a series of numbers. The performer knows which is the right one through the clue.

CLUE: Suppose the group selects the number 36. The accomplice gives the clue by the first number he calls out. If the first number is 59, for example, the first digit, 5, means that the fifth number in the next group of numbers the accomplice calls out must be multiplied by the second digit, 9, to determine the selected number. The accomplice calls four numbers at random, say 84, 68, 8, 91; then says 4 for the fifth number; then another random number or two before he says 36. The performer has mentally multiplied the fifth number, 4, by 9; the result, 36. Therefore when the accomplice calls out 36, the performer stops him by saying "Thirty-six is the number."

Mysterious Cup

The performer places a penny on a table and places a cup upside down over it. He then says that he will leave the room. He tells the group that while he is gone one of the players is to remove the penny, and when he returns the cup will tell him who has taken it. After the performer leaves, some player takes the penny and keeps it out of sight. The group recalls the performer, who asks that the players touch the cup one at a time. When all have touched it, the performer, who has the clue, picks up the cup, places it to his ear, listens, and then names the player who holds the penny.

CLUE: The accomplice gives the clue by touching the cup immediately after the person who holds the penny.

Magic Cane

The accomplice secures a cane, stick, or umbrella ahead of time.

The performer leaves the room while the group selects a short verb which he can act out easily, for example: walk, run, sing, dance, or hop.

Recall the performer. The accomplice must employ showmanship to confuse the observers while secretly relaying the word to the performer through a series of comments and taps on the floor with the cane. When the performer has discovered the verb, he acts it out.

CLUE: The first letter of each of the accomplice's remarks represents a consonant in the word, while the vowels are represented by taps on the floor: A, E, I, O, and U are symbolized by one, two, three, four, and five taps, respectively.

If, for example, the word which the group selects is "dance," the word might be revealed to the performer in the following way:

The accomplice says, "Do not stand too far away, Mr.
_____."   (D)
Then he taps on the floor once.   (A)
He says, "Now, we must all be very quiet. Concentrate, my
    friend."   (N, C)
He taps the floor twice with the cane.   (E)

Spirit Photography

The performer asks all the players to sit in a circle. Holding up a spoon, he informs the group that the spoon is magic and will take photographs. He says that he will leave the room while a picture is taken and then return and name the photographed player by looking at the spoon. He asks for a player to be "photographer," gives him the spoon, and tells him how to take the picture.

After the performer leaves the room, the "photographer" holds the spoon in front of any player, then places the spoon on the floor in the center of the circle and returns to his place. When the performer is recalled to the room, he picks up the spoon, studies it carefully while looking around the circle (and secretly watching the accomplice for clues), and finally points out the photographed player.

CLUE: When the performer returns, the accomplice indicates to him by a slight movement of a hand or finger on which side of the circle the photographed player sits. This eliminates half of the group. Then the accomplice assumes the exact pose of the photographed player, changing his position whenever the player does.

If the accomplice was the player photographed, he indicates this fact to the performer by sitting with his feet or legs crossed, a sign which has been determined in advance.

Reading Temples

The performer says he will leave the room while the group selects a number between one and ten. He announces that when he returns he will determine the number the group selected by merely placing his hands on a player's temples.

The performer leaves, the group selects a number, and the performer returns. Naturally, he places his hands on the accomplice's temples. After considerable "stage business" to deceive the group while he gets the clue, the performer states the number.

CLUE: The accomplice secretly reveals the number by tensing and relaxing his jaws the required number of times. The performer, with his hands on the accomplice's temples, feels the movement and determines the number.

This One, That One

The accomplice places four books on the floor in the position illustrated below (Figure 7–1). He does *not* label them.

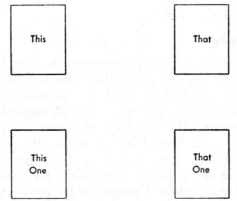

FIGURE 7–1. Book arrangement for This One, That One

The performer is asked to leave the room while the group selects one of the four books. On his return he is to point out the selected book. When the performer is called back, the accomplice points to any of the books except the chosen one and says "Is it this one?" or "Is it that one?" The accomplice replies, "No." Then the accomplice points to the correct book and says, "This?" The accomplice replies, "Yes."

CLUE: The chosen book is indicated by *This* (or, in another instance, it may be *That, This One, That One*). The clue word is decided on beforehand. The introduction of additional words in some cases, such as "is it," is to confuse the group.

Which Book?

Place six books on the floor in a row. While the performer is out of the room, the group is to select one of the books. When the performer returns he will be expected to name the right book. After the performer has been recalled, the accomplice makes no remarks, but points to one book after another. The performer surprisingly says, "No," until the selected book is pointed out.

CLUE: The performer picks the correct book because he knows that his accomplice will point to it immediately after he points to one of the books which is next to either end.

Which Match?

Scatter a half-dozen safety matches on the floor in the center of the group. The performer leaves the room. The players decide upon one match. The accomplice recalls the performer and tells him he must discover their selection. Pointing to one match after another the accomplice says, "Is it this match?" The performer says "No" until the accomplice secretly gives the clue that the match is the one selected.

CLUE: The accomplice stands still when he points to the wrong matches. When he singles out the selected match, he makes a very slight movement with his right foot. The performer detects this movement and can name the correct match.

Three in a Row

The performer places three matches in a row on the floor. He tells the group that after he leaves the room they are to select one match, which he will discover as their choice when he returns. After the performer has been recalled, he ponders for a while, looking about the room and secretly noting his accomplice's clue. Then he chooses the correct match.

CLUE: If the left match in the row has been chosen, the accomplice places his left hand over his right on his lap. If it is the right match, he places his right hand over his left. When it is the center match he does not place either hand on the other.

Suggestion: Instead of giving hand clues, the accomplice may give the clue when recalling the performer. He calls out "All right" for the match to the right, "Ready" for the middle one, and "Come in" for the left match.

Who Has the Match?

Players sit in a semicircle. The performer leaves the room. After he leaves, one of the players takes a match. Then all players fold their hands in the same way in their laps.

After the performer has been recalled, he walks slowly in front of the players, intently gazing at their folded hands. Occasionally he looks forward and backward along the semicircle as though to check the other players but actually watching for the accomplice's signal. When he gets the clue, he points out the person who holds the match.

CLUE: When the performer stands in front of the person holding the match, the accomplice makes a slight movement with his foot. Detecting this movement, the performer knows who has the match.

Mystifying Reader

Obtain two small boxes. Label one *"Mystic Messages."* The performer, known as the Mystifying Reader, sits at a table. Each player is given a piece of 3 × 5-inch paper and a pencil.

Everyone writes on his paper a short sentence of four or five words and folds the paper twice, showing the sentence to no one. The Mystifying Reader gathers the slips in the box labeled *"Mystic Messages"* and gives it to one of the players, who is to be the Guardian of the messages. Then the Reader asks the Guardian to hand him one of the messages.

Closing his eyes, the Mystifying Reader places the *folded* paper against his forehead and remains in supposed deep thought momentarily. Then he states a sentence of four or five words, which he has just made up, and asks who wrote it. His accomplice admits authorship.

The Mystifying Reader then unfolds the paper, apparently to verify that the message is the one he "read," but his real motive is to read the sentence which is really on the paper. Placing the slip in the empty box with his left hand he extends his right hand to the Guardian of messages and says, "Give me the next message that I may ponder on the unseen words and give them expression."

Closing his eyes he places the second folded slip against his forehead and supposedly goes into a deep thought. He reveals the message written on the *previous* paper which he read when he pretended to verify the message of his unknown accomplice. Since this sentence was actually on the first slip, one of the guests will have to admit writing it. This helps enhance the mysterious atmosphere. The Reader continues his mystifying performance, revealing more of the supposedly unseen messages.

CLUE: The accomplice does not give his sentence to the Reader at the time he collects the slips. However, he admits having written the sentence the Reader invents. Part of the success in doing the trick depends upon the accomplice's carefulness in concealing from the group the fact that he has not given the Mystifying Reader a message for the container.

NUMBER TRICKSTERS

Revealing Ages

Secure a blackboard and chalk, or a large sheet of paper and a black crayon. Players sit at tables. Distribute a sheet of 8½ × 11-inch paper and a pencil to each player.

Request each player to write on his sheet of paper his age or any other number he wishes. Ask him to double it, add one, multiply by five, add five, and multiply by ten. For example:

Age or number selected	32
Double	64
Add one	65
Multiply by 5	325
Add 5	330
Multiply by 10	3300

Call on someone to announce the total he has achieved in his mathematical gymnastics. Write the number on the blackboard or large sheet of paper. Subtract one hundred, strike off the last two digits and the result is the individual's original number or age. For example:

Subtract 100	3200
Strike off the last two digits	32

Announce the surprising result and ask the person to verify the answer.

Magical Threes. Play the same as Revealing Ages except have the players use the following calculations: multiply the age or selected number by three, add one, multiply by three, and add the original number. Call on someone to reveal the total. Cross off the last digit, and the result is the player's original number or age. For example:

Number or age	27
Multiply by 3	81
Add 1	82
Multiply by 3	246
Add the original number	273
Strike off the last digit	27

Month and Age. Play the same as Revealing Ages except with different calculations. Ask each person to write down the number of the month in which he was born (2 for February, for instance), multiply it by two, add five, multiply by fifty, add his age, subtract 365, and add 115. In the resulting number, the first digit or two tells the month in which he was born and last two digits reveal his age. For example:

Month (February)	2
Multiply by 2	4
Add 5	9
Multiply by 50	450
Add age (32)	482
Subtract 365	117
Add 115	232

The first digit, 2, indicates he was born in February, and the last digits reveal his age, 32.

Age and Money. Play the same as Revealing Ages except with different calculations. Ask each person to write his age, multiply it by two, add five, multiply by fifty, and then subtract 365. Each player then adds to the result the amount of change he has with him, and then adds 115. In the resulting number the first two digits tell his age and the last two the amount of change that he possesses. For example:

Age	16
Multiply by 2	32
Add 5	37
Multiply by 50	1850
Subtract 365	1485
Add change (12¢)	1497
Add 115	1612

The first two digits indicate he is sixteen years old, and the last two digits show that he has twelve cents in coins.

Number Magic

Players sit in a circle. Give each player a sheet of 8½ × 11-inch paper and a pencil. Without revealing the figure to the group, write the number 1,089 on a 3 × 5-inch slip of paper. Fold the slip, give it to one of the members of the group, and ask him to put it in his pocket without looking at it.

Have each player write on his paper any number of three digits that he chooses. Then have the players reverse their numbers and subtract the smaller from the larger to find the difference. Then reverse the difference and add the difference and its reverse together. For example:

Number chosen	842
Reversed	248
Difference	594
Reversed	495
Added	1,089

Call on the person who put the slip in his pocket. Ask him to read the number on the paper. To his and the group's amazement the number is the same as the total each player achieved through his mathematical maneuvering.

Naming the Figure

Players sit at tables. Give each player a sheet of 8½ × 11-inch paper and a pencil.

Ask each player to write a number on his paper, double it, and record that figure. State any even number and ask everyone to add it to the doubled number. Then request the players to divide the result by two, and subtract the original number. Select any individual and to his and the group's surprise tell him the exact remainder that is on his paper. It will be half of the even number which he was requested to add. For example:

Number selected	20
Doubled	40
Even number added	12
Total	52
Divide by 2	26
Original number subtracted	6

Ever Nine

Players sit at tables. Give each player a sheet of 8½ × 11-inch paper and a pencil.

Ask everyone to write a number containing three different digits, reverse the number, and then subtract the smaller number from the larger to find the difference. For example:

Number	843
Reversed	348
Difference	495

The middle digit in the difference between a number and its reverse is always 9, and the sum of the first and last digits is always 9.

Call on a player and ask him to state the last digit of his resulting number (difference). Then mentally subtract that digit from 9 to find the first digit. In the example above, 5 from 9 yields 4. Since the middle digit is always 9, the player's result is revealed as 495.

Triple Digits. Request each player to write on his paper any number with three different digits, reverse that number, and subtract the smaller number from the larger to find the difference. Then tell any player the middle digit in his answer. This is possible because the middle digit will always be 9. For example:

Number selected 123
Reversed 321
Difference (smaller number subtracted from larger number) 198

One of Nine

Memorize the following number combinations or write them on a small card which can be held in the palm of the hand: 99, 198, 297, 396, 495, 594, 693, 792, 891.

Players sit at tables. Give a sheet of paper and the pencil to one of the players. Ask him to write any number containing three different digits on his paper, then to reverse the number and subtract the smaller from the larger figure. Without looking at his paper state the answer. This supposedly amazing feat is possible, because there are only nine possible answers, which are listed above. As he subtracts be in a position to watch his pencil carefully. By detecting the first figure which he writes it is possible to know that it is one of the above answers, for the first digit is not repeated in any of the nine possible answers.

Trick Adding

Ask the group to add four 2's together so that the result will be 5.

If no one finds the way to achieve this after a brief period of frustration, write the solution for them:

$$2 + 2 + \frac{2}{2} = 5$$

CREATIVE
FUN MAKERS

CONTENTS

Creative games provide some of the most spontaneous fun, because they motivate the players in a group to express themselves, and everyone possesses a desire for self-expression. Expressing oneself is fun; it permits an individual to put his imagination into action. Even those who feel that they possess little or no imagination find creative activities enjoyable, if the atmosphere for fun prevails.

The games in this chapter do not stress artistic perfection or a need for unique talent; they are the fun-way approach to creative activities.

It is this approach which the leader of social recreation employs in teaching and conducting the creative games. If the leader places the emphasis on artistic perfection, a creative game that is intended solely for fun becomes a competitive chore for the individuals who lack experience in self-expression. The leader is not concerned with how well a group pantomimes or dramatizes, tells or writes a story to which everyone contributes a portion, or creates some picture or object. His objective is to help the individuals to participate and enjoy creative expression in a group atmosphere.

Perhaps the most familiar games are those activities which are based on pantomime and dramatization. The flare for "let's pretend" starts when the young begin to mimic the oldsters and continues until the oldsters mimic the young.

To assist the leader in choosing and varying his program, the activities are grouped as follows: pantomiming or dramatizing an action (Skit Stimulaters); creating a story or poem or expressing an idea in a specified manner (Imagination Inducers); and illustrating or creating an object (Arty Awakeners). The list preceding this chapter groups the activities alphabetically within the main categories.

Surprisingly few materials are necessary to conduct these activities. Most important are pencils, paper, and crayons. The leader will discover that adults as well as children will respond to these games and activities which call upon their "undeveloped" creative talents.

SKIT STIMULATERS

Charades ✓

Divide the players into groups of five. To each group assign a word which its members will pantomime (see list of suggestions below). Do not let the other groups hear the word. Allow each group a few minutes in which to prepare its pantomime.

Ask one of the groups to pantomime its assigned word by syllables and then act out the entire word. The other groups attempt to guess the word, and the first group to guess it has the honor of pantomiming next.

If the others cannot guess the word which the acting group presents, they may request the group to re-enact some of the syllables or all of them. If after three performances the audience cannot guess the word being pantomimed, the acting group announces the word. Select another group to perform.

The following words offer possibilities for pantomiming:

Automobile (Ought/oh/mob/eel)
Airplane (Air/plane)
Stationary (Station/airy)
Handkerchief (Hand/cur/chief)
Infancy (In/fan/sea)
Forswear (Four/swear)
Antidote (Aunt/I/dote)
Penitent (Pen/eye/tent)
Cribbage (Crib/age)
Masquerade (Mass/cur/aid)
Bookworm (Book/worm)
Knapsack (Nap/sack)
Handicap (Hand/eye/cap)
Pilgrimage (Pill/grim/age)
Sausage (Saw/sage)
Melancholy (Melon/collie)
Definite (Deaf/in/ate)
Caravan (Car/ah/van)
Bandage (Band/age)
Tennessee (Ten/I/see)
Catering (Kate/her/ring)
Microscope (My/crow/scope)
Innuendo (In/you/end/oh)
Caricature (Carry/cat/your)
Decorate (Deck/oar/ate)
Eyelash (I/lash)
Cannibal (Can/eye/ball)

Ingratiate (In/gray/she/ate)
Shylock (Shy/lock)
Mayflower (May/flower)
Pupil (Pew/pill)
Penmanship (Pen/man/ship)
Princeton (Prince/ton)
Attenuate (At/ten/you/ate)
Heroes (He/rows)
Necklace (Neck/lace)
Pantry (Pan/tree)
Horsemanship (Horse/man/ship)
Welcome (Well/come)
Antarctic (Aunt/ark/tick)
Buccaneer (Buck/can/ear)
Charlatan (Char/lay/tan)
Hornpipe (Horn/pipe)
Independence (Inn/deep/end/dense)
Kingdom (King/dumb)
Phantom (Fan/Tom)
Feline (Fee/line)
Alternate (All/turn/eight)
Metaphysician (Met/a/physician)
Paradox (Pair/o'/docks)
Milwaukee (Mill/walk/key)
Shakespeare (Shake/spear)
Cicero (Sissy/row)
Benjamin (Ben/jam/in)

Animated Proverbs

Give each group a slip of paper on which a proverb has been written (see list of proverbs on pages 42–44). Allow each group time to prepare its presentation of the proverb either in pantomime or with spoken lines. In preparing their presentations the groups should not divulge their proverbs to the other groups.

Call on one of the groups to portray its proverb. The first of the nonperforming groups to guess the proverb is next to go on stage. If the same group guesses the proverb twice, the members select a group which has not had an opportunity to perform. When no one guesses the words of wisdom, allow the group to announce the proverb and select another group to perform.

Titles! On Stage!

Assign to each group of five players the title of a moving picture, play, book, musical selection, radio program, or television program. Explain to the groups that each word in the title must be pantomimed separately. The entire title is pantomimed in the final presentation. Allow each group a short time to decide upon the action.

Call on one of the groups to portray its title. Of the remaining groups, the audience, the first group to identify the title takes the center of the stage to pantomime its title. Continue until all have performed. If one group guesses first twice, the members of this group select a group which has not had an opportunity to perform.

Animated Nursery Rhymes

Assign to each group of five a nursery rhyme which it is to pantomime, for example: Little Miss Muffet, Little Jack Horner, Mary Had a Little Lamb, Jack and Jill, Old King Cole, Humpty-Dumpty, Hickory Dickery Dock, Little Bo Peep, or Polly Put the Kettle On. Allow the groups time to plan the action.

While one group is acting, the others attempt to guess the nursery rhyme they are portraying. Give each group a chance to perform.

Animated Musical Terms. Proceed as for Animated Nursery Rhymes, except assign to each group one of the following musical terms:

sharp	rests	time
flat	quarter	notes
scale	half	chord
staff	natural	key

bars	slur	measure
major	beat	accent
minor	air	whole

Props—Not the Play

Have the players form groups of eight or less. Give each team a bag containing several items such as a screw driver, pencil, paperweight, dog's collar, book, paper clip, coin purse, flowerpot, pruning shears, or other available miscellaneous items.

Allow each group about ten minutes to prepare a creative play in which everyone participates. The properties for the drama are in the bag, and each item must come into use, not merely be displayed, during the production. Whether properties for the groups are the same or different frequently depends upon the availability of the items. Even if the properties are the same for all groups in these creative productions, the results will be widely different.

In turn each group presents its original play. After the final production have the players decide which group was most imaginative in its use of the props.

On-the-Spot Drama

Ask one member of each group of five to collect an item from each member of his group. The items which he obtains become the props for the creative play which the members of the group must originate. Allow about ten minutes' preparation time.

Have each fivesome in turn present its creative play. After the final production have all players decide which group was most original in the use of its properties.

Search for Properties

Divide the participants into groups of five. Give each group a list of ten properties which the members must secure within a designated time. The lists may be the same or different for every group, but the items must be readily available to the players. For example, a list might include: can of soup, old chair, bandage, miniature automobile, picture of a bird, tire tool, broom, old lamp shade, magazine, and a spoon.

When the groups have gathered their ten items, allow the participants about ten minutes in which to prepare an original dramatization in which they will use all the collected properties. Then have each group present its play. Upon the completion of the creative dramatics, let the players decide which group should be voted the cleverest in its use of properties.

Be sure that one member from each group accepts responsibility for returning the props after the activity.

America's Greatest Event

Divide the players into groups of eight or less. Without divulging their choice to the other groups, the members of each unit select within a designated time the occasion in American history that they consider of most significance and decide how they wish to present it. All members must participate.

Ask one of the groups to present its dramatization. The first group to guess the momentous event takes the center of the stage and presents its drama.

If everyone fails to guess the event, the historical revivers announce the occasion, and they select another group to stage its production. When any group succeeds in guessing the greatest event twice, it selects any unit which has not had an opportunity to perform.

An Embarrassing Moment

Players form groups of four. For each group write an embarrassing situation on a slip of paper. Fold the slips and place them in a container. Ask one member of each foursome to take a slip for his group. Allow the players about five minutes to prepare their presentations of embarrassing situations.

Have each group in turn present its embarrassing situation. The other groups try to identify the situation being enacted. If a group guesses correctly, it scores five points. When the audience is unable to discern the situation, the actors announce the embarrassing moment. Each group scores one point for trying. The group with the most points at the conclusion of the acting wins the game.

Some embarrassing situations that anyone might encounter are:

Coming into a dark theater and mistaking a seat in which someone is sitting for an empty place.

Trying to impress someone and then ungracefully stumbling over an object.

Sitting on a gentleman's hat, crushing it, and then trying to get the hat back into what one hopes was its original shape.

Stepping on someone's clean white shoes and trying to remedy the situation.

Spilling soup on one's necktie and observing that the spot remains quite obvious in spite of a rubbing or two.

Spilling a glass of water at the dinner table and being faced with a dual tragedy: a broken glass and a miniature river winding its way down the table.

Passing an unmanageable gravy bowl which slides and sends the gravy on your lap.

Driving a car in heavy traffic and having the engine stall. Trying to get it to start to the tune of the honking horns of impatient drivers who shout and glare as they zoom around the stalled car.

Treating someone to luncheon and discovering when taking the check that it's the day handbags were changed (or for boys and men—suits) and your wallet was left at the home post.

Passing someone on the sidewalk and then thinking it's someone you should know. While looking back to try to establish his identity, charging full speed into a person carrying a load of parcels which fall and scatter here and there.

Spur of the Moment

Players form groups of four. Give each group a slip of paper on which is written an incident which will lend itself to dramatization. Allow about five minutes for the groups to create the dramas.

In turn, ask each group to present its incident. Following the production, one member of the foursome should read the incident so the others who have witnessed the action can evaluate the drama just presented. After each group has produced its drama take a vote to determine which group receives the most acclaim.

A few incidents which might be used follow:

Two customers in a supermarket race their carts to the checker who seems least busy. The disgruntled loser keeps riding the wheels of her cart on the heels of the winner, who greatly resents the action.

It's bargain day in the basement of a large department store. Women's dresses hold the greatest interest. Unfortunately there are only a few of the popular sizes, for most of the dresses are for the "beanpole" or the newest member of a reducing club.

While out for a walk, a dog and his master meet a cat, which becomes frightened and climbs a tree. The dog's master tries to persuade Pussy to come down, but the dog barks in an effort to keep him aloft. Pussy's owner comes out with a ladder and is very angry. The neighbors coach him about placing the ladder and approaching Pussy. As the dog and his owner leave, Pussy comes down on his own four feet.

A group bound for work awaits the bus on a rainy day. As they step from the curb, a honking motorist sends them back to the sidewalk and splashes them with messy rain water. Anger mounts as the bus, which is filled with passengers, does not stop for them.

A home run at a baseball game creates an outburst of excitement. The fans who are enjoying "between hit snacks" are so enthusiastic about the play that they spill their liquid refreshments on the fans below, whose enthusiasm is dampened but whose ire is kindled.

In a millinery shop at Easter time the clerk is trying desperately to sell one of the dozens of hats that she has shown to her hard-to-please customer. While she turns on her salesmanship, the husband of the customer amuses the children by wearing some of the women's hats and letting the children try those which daddy doesn't find suitable.

Crambo

Divide the players into groups of five. Each group takes a turn at being the actors while the others are the audience. Ask one five-some, who are to be actors first, to leave the room while the audience selects a verb or a noun. Recall the actors and let them know that the word is a verb or a noun and give them a word it rhymes with. For example, if the word is the verb "sell," inform the actors that the word is a verb which rhymes with bell.

Allow the actors a few minutes to consult one another in their attempt to guess the word and decide on the action for dramatizing it. They might assume the word is "tell," and each member pretends to be a gossip on the telephone. Each person in the troupe repeats, "I tell you that's what I heard."

Since it is the wrong word, the audience expresses its disapproval. The actors form a huddle and decide on another word and the action for expressing it. When the actors succeed in guessing and acting out the word "sell," they exchange places with another of the groups.

If after three attempts the actors cannot guess the word, the audience announces the word. The acting group selects any fivesome to take its place while it joins the audience.

Active Adverbs

Have the players form two teams of ten. Call one team the Actors, and the other, the Askers. Teams sit facing one another about 12 feet apart. If there are more than twenty players, have the extra players form additional teams of Actors and Askers which sit in the same formation in another section of the area. Have each team number off consecutively from one to ten. Team members participate in pairs; so one and two, three and four, five and six, seven and eight, nine and ten on each team are partners. Give each couple on the Actors and Askers teams a slip of paper on which an adverb has been written.

Call on the first two players of the Actors to perform in the manner of the adverb on their slip any task the Askers will request. The Askers try to discover the adverb by requesting the couple to demonstrate the adverb through their actions. For example, the first couple of the Actors may have the adverb "furiously." When the first twosome of Askers requests them to walk around the room in the manner of the adverb, they proceed to walk furiously. The second couple of Askers tells them to shake hands with two of the players on their own team. They shake hands furiously.

Each couple on the Askers team continues to make a request until one of them discovers the adverb assigned to the players. The Askers score two points; the Actors, one for trying. If after five attempts to guess the adverb the Askers fail, the Actors announce the adverb and each team scores one point for trying. Roles are then reversed. Play continues with teams alternating roles of Actors and Askers until every twosome has a chance to present an adverb. The team with the highest score wins.

Drama for the Occasion

Have the players form groups of ten or less. Give each group a different list of words that are associated with a holiday or some particular occasion. Provide each player with a sheet of 8½ × 11-inch paper and a pencil.

Allow the dramatists about ten minutes to prepare a play in which they will use every word that appears on the list at least once or more. Using the technique of voice over action the group may decide to have one person narrate the story while the other troupers act out their parts.

Each group in turn presents its dramatization while the members of the other troupes record the words that they think they identify. After each presentation allow time for the groups to read the words that they recorded. For each word the viewing teams identify they score two points. The team with the most points at the end of the dramatizations wins.

Name the Occupation

Ask the players to form teams of ten or less. Allow each group time to select a trade or profession and to plan how to present it in pantomime.

At the end of a designated time the first group gives its presentation. The others attempt to guess the trade or profession being enacted. The first team to guess correctly scores three points; the performing group, two points for its presentation; all others, one for trying. If after three attempts no one guesses correctly, the performers announce the occupation. Their team scores three points; every other group, one point for trying.

Continue to call on the groups until each troupe has presented its occupation in pantomime.

IMAGINATION INDUCERS

Continue, Please!

Players sit in a circle. Distribute to everyone a sheet of 8½ × 11-inch paper and a pencil or, preferably, a black crayon. Ask each person to print his name on the paper in large bold letters, so the persons in the circle can read it. If the group is large, have several circles. Request the players to hold up their papers so that everyone can read them.

Begin telling a story. At any interesting place in the imaginative tale call on one of the players thus: "Florence Heimick, continue, please!" Florence Heimick continues to weave the yarn until she reaches a stopping point and calls on someone else to embark on the sea of imagination. As she does this, she places her paper face down, which means she has had a turn. Each person follows this procedure; as he finishes his episode he asks someone else to continue. The story proceeds until the person who holds the final name card is called on to "Conclude, please!" He takes hold of the tale and brings it to its end.

Stories may be fanciful or ordinary everyday happenings, as this opening portion of a tale indicates:

> The Brown family planned on having a very relaxing and enjoyable vacation. Pop was chief packer of the family's car, and Mom was special dispatcher of which items should come and which should remain at home; but even then . . . Florence Heimick, continue, please!
>
> Sue and Tom hated to leave anything at home, for they were certain that the item they did not take would be just the thing they would want to use while they were on vacation. Bill Thompson, continue, please!
>
> Pop was packing the bags when he heard a "Meow, Meow, Meow." After listening carefully he said to Sue and Tom, "Did you hear a cat's meowing?" They both responded negatively. Muriel McLuen, continue, please!
>
> Dad persisted, "Where is Fluff?" Tom remarked, "Our cat is over at the neighbors'." "Yes," said Sue, "that's what you told us to do." "I know; but I wonder . . ." Mary Brown, continue, please!

With each person's imagination keeping the creative flame aglow the story goes on until the last person brings it to a conclusion. The kind of vacation the Browns have depends entirely upon the creative storytellers.

Initialed Tales

Select two initials, for example, *L* and *M*. Begin telling a story, using these letters in each sentence. For example, the first person to start the story may say, "*L*ouis *M*artinez, the *l*ocal *m*iser, lived in a *l*onely *m*ansion overlooking *L*ake *M*iserable."

In turn each player on the right adds a sentence giving one incident in the life of Louis Martinez, but he must use the initials *L* and *M* at least once in the sentence. Play continues until the last player adds his contribution to the tale.

This is the pattern that one *L* and *M* tale followed:

> Louis Martinez the *l*ocal *m*iser, lived in a *l*onely *m*ansion overlooking *L*ake Miserable. He *l*oved *m*oney so well that he *l*ost *m*any hours of sleep counting

the large mounds of the lovely musty "green stuff." When at last morning came, he looked mighty peaked.

After treating himself to a breakfast of a little mush, he was off to the lone mission of large muscle activity which consisted of piling, re-piling, and loading money.

This was the daily existence of Louis Martinez until one day a labeled man from a large mint came calling. He said, "Louis Martinez, I have longed mightily to help you count your large mounds of limitless money."

After he did Louis Martinez was a long-faced man gazing at the little mounds of limited money he now possessed; for the labeled man from the large mint now was counting the large mounds of long-due money.

Then the little mush that Louis Martinez ate became less mush, for he no longer needed energy for his large muscle activity of piling, re-piling, and loading money.

Substitute Adjectives

Select a well-known children's story or a short story. Make a copy of it, but omit all adjectives in the story, leaving a space for them on the paper.

Begin to read the story, stopping at each blank space. Each player in turn names an adjective which is written into the blank in the story. After all of the blanks are filled read to the group the strange tale that evolves through substituting adjectives.

New Nouns. Eliminate the nouns from the story. Fill in the spaces with the nouns which each member suggests. Read the new version of the tale.

Describing the Party

If the players are well acquainted, write an original story about them and the party. Make a copy of it, but in the copy omit all adjectives, leaving blank spaces for them.

Read the story, stopping at each blank space. Request that each member of the group, in turn, name an adjective which is to be entered in the blank space. When all the blanks are filled the story is complete. Read the entire tale over again with the substituted adjectives.

An original tale with the substitution of a group's adjectives might begin like this:

An (insipid) crowd of (sour) guests gathered at the (outlandish) home of the (boring) Mrs. Phillips and the (snoring) Mr. Phillips. A more (catty) group could not be imagined. The (snippy) Mrs. Phillips and the (dopey) Mr. Phillips received the (repellent) guests in their (messy) attire. The (outrageous) dinner included: (weather-beaten) soup, a (frolicsome) salad · with (lifeless) lettuce, (indecisive) potatoes, (skimpy) roast, (bouncing) beets, (rubbery) rolls, (anemic) butter, (cold) coffee, and (devastating) dessert.

A tale of this kind can terminate or continue, depending upon the number of persons in the group.

Consequences

Have the players form groups of eleven. Give everyone a pencil and a sheet of 8½ × 11-inch paper.

Each player writes an adjective describing a woman, folds the top of the paper down so that the writing is covered, and passes the paper to the person on his right. Each person also receives a paper from the player on his left. Then the following are written, one at a time, and after each word, phrase, or sentence is written, the player folds the paper and sends it on to the next person.

1. An adjective describing a woman
2. A woman's name
3. An adjective describing a man
4. A man's name
5. Where they met
6. What she did
7. What he did
8. What she said
9. What he said
10. The consequences
11. What the world said

After each person writes the eleventh item on his slip, "What the world said," call a halt. Ask each person to unfold the paper he holds. In turn, everyone reads the contents from his slip.

The following tale is an example of what might result from the group's contributions:

Timid Kitty Huffy and dashing Mr. Slither met in the Museum of Antiques. She wiped a speck out of her eye. He fell to the floor. She said, "Oh, it wasn't a rock."

He said, "It must be Leap Year."

They decided to return the antique pearl necklace to its case. The world said, "There is a place for everything."

√ Last Will and Testament

Players sit in a circle. Each player has a sheet of 8½ × 11-inch paper and a pencil. Inform each participant that he is about to prepare his last will and testament.

Have each person write on the top of his sheet of paper "The Last Will and Testament of _____." He folds the sheet over the first statement and passes the paper to the person to his right. This person adds a name to the blank space; for example, he might add

"Willie Watkins." He then folds the slip so that it hides the name and passes it to the player on his right. This third player writes: "I bequeath to ———— the following items:" and enters a name in the space, for example, "Slim Slugger." Then he folds the slip and passes it on to the next person on the right. This fourth person adds an item to the document. Play continues with each player adding an item. After all participants have made an addition to the documents, each will should be back in the hands of the person who started making it out. Ask each person to read the will he holds.

The will started above and "reproduced" here is a boon to Slim Slugger:

> The Last Will and Testament of Willie Watkins. I bequeath to Slim Slugger the following items: 1930 Ford, bottle of hair oil, half a tube of tooth paste, six shares of Phony and Phony stock, next appointment with the dentist, box of paper clips, a large box of dog biscuits.

Critics, Beware!

Players form groups of six or more, and each group sits in a circle. Give each player a pencil and a piece of 8½ × 11-inch paper.

Ask everyone to make up a title for a book. After writing it, each player passes his unfolded slip to the person to his left and receives one from the player to his right. This time everyone adds a subtitle under the name of the book. On the third passing each player writes the name of the author or authors; fourth, a passage from the book; fifth, another passage from the book; sixth, a statement from a critic.

Call a halt and ask each person in turn to present his book.

A group might evolve the following description:

1. Title of a book:	The Way to the Poorhouse
2. Subtitle:	How to Arrive Quickly
3. Authors:	N. O. Silver
	N. O. Greenbacks
4. Passage from the book:	With installments due only on Monday, Tuesday, Wednesday, Thursday, Friday, and Saturday, believe me it's a short way to the poorhouse.
5. Another passage from the book:	To facilitate the speed of entrance by all means watch the enticing advertisements. Get those little feet running to the bargains, especially when sales resistance is low, and you are bound to get to the poorhouse quickly.
6. Critic's statement:	At last a book that is practical. It gives one the ways to enter the poorhouse quickly and positively. Until the publication of this book everyone has been postponing going. Now, with its arrival—why wait?

If there are more than six players in a group, have the players write additional imaginative passages from the book and reviews from various critics instead of one.

Turnback's Improvements

Each group of eight players sits in a circle. Give one member of the group a pencil and a sheet of 8½ × 11-inch paper.

On signal, the first player in each group writes one sentence stating the improvements he feels the town of Turnback needs in order to put it on the map. As soon as he completes the sentence he folds the paper to cover the writing and passes it to the player on his right who makes his contribution to improving Turnback.

When the last player writes his suggestion, he passes the list to the person who started Turnback's project. He reads the recommendations for improving the town.

Progressive Poems

Each group of six players sits in a circle. Each player has a sheet of 8½ × 11-inch paper and a pencil.

Have each player write the number 1 on the left side of his paper and next to the number attempt to write a line of poetry. He folds the paper over the line, writes the number 2 on the left side of the sheet, and passes it to the person on his right. As he gives the player the paper, he tells him the last word in his line of poetry.

The "poetic bug" continues until the sixth or concluding line has been written for each creative endeavor. In turn, each person reads the "very free verse" to which he has put the finishing touch.

Suggestions: If the group needs more than the last word of the preceding line to inspire it to write poetry, have the first person pass the sheet unfolded to the second person, who writes his line and then folds the paper over the first line. In this way the individual who receives the paper knows the entire preceding line instead of merely the last word.

In some instances it is fun to keep the paper unfolded completely. This gives each player an opportunity to read all of the preceding lines before he adds his line. Usually in this version sense takes precedence over nonsense.

Changing Proverbs

For everyone who is to participate write a proverb on a 3 × 5-inch slip of paper (see list of proverbs on pages 42–44). To each player give a proverb, another 3 × 5-inch slip of paper, and a pencil.

Within a designated time ask each person to rewrite the proverb in the style in which it is written and expressing the same idea. Call time and ask each person to read his innovation.

The proverb, "You can't eat your cake and have it," in the rewritten form may become, "You can't waste natural resources and have them."

High-Brow Proverbs. Within a specified time have everyone rewrite a proverb in an elegant manner of expression.

The simple proverb, "Haste makes waste," in its dignified form might read, "An unwise accentuation of speed in performing a given task frequently results in an undesirable retardation in the rapidity with which the completion of a task is achieved, and a reduced output in the resultant commodities for which the task is performed."

Slang Tabooed

Have a slang expression on a 3 × 5-inch card or slip of paper for every member of the group. Distribute an expression, an additional blank card, and a pencil to each participant.

Within a designated time ask each person to express the thought in the slang expression in a more "cultured" manner. Have each person read the original expression and his reworded contribution to the group.

The humble expression "That's for the birds" might evolve as "Your exalted opinion is destined for the residents of the aviary."

Editing "The Corny Currier"

Players sit in groups of four at separate tables. Give each group four pencils and a dozen sheets of 8½ × 11-inch paper. Select an editor for each group and assign each of the other members a section of the newspaper which he must write in a humorous style. The editor must add the finishing touch to the material to make it readable. Sections to assign include:

Local News	Book Reviews and Chats about Authors
National News	Fashions, Beauty, Household Items
Society Section	Gardening Advice
Personal News	Theatrical Section (Drama, Dance, Music)
Sports	Television, Radio, Movies
Advice to the Lovelorn	Editorials

Allow twenty minutes for each group to prepare its section of *The Corny Currier*. If the members of the group know one another well, suggest that the reporters and editor inject a personal element into the stories. Fun is accentuated if the copy is a burlesque of the average material appearing in the newspapers.

Suggestion: Provide each group with a sample section or column from which the members are to write their humorous version of the copy.

Clipped Letters

Players are in groups of four, with each group at a separate table. Provide each group with some old magazines, sheets of 8½ × 11-inch paper, scissors, and paste.

Within twenty minutes have each unit compose a letter to the other members of the groups. The letters should be a composite of words, phrases, and sentences clipped from the magazines and pasted on the sheet or sheets of paper.

When the time is up, ask one person from each group to read the letter that the members composed. Allow the groups to decide on the cleverest letter.

Mixed Advertisements

Arrange the players in groups of four, each group at a separate table. Give each foursome a classified advertisement section from a newspaper, scissors, paste, and some sheets of 8½ × 11-inch paper.

Have each group decide on a subject for its proposed advertisement. The members of each group find words, phrases, or sentences that they need to create their new advertisement and paste them on the sheets of paper.

Within a designated time call the advertisement assembling to a halt. Ask one member of each group to read the newly created advertisement.

The following mix-up is the result of combining words, phrases, clauses, and sentences from advertisements for the sale of a home, a farm, and an automobile:

Stone House For Sale

Ideal for large family. Huge barn: dining area, wall to wall carpeting, walnut paneling, drapes, crystal and brass lighting fixtures.

Enclosed yard for the little pigs. Wonderful place for the youngsters to play.

Recreation room for the children and chickens.

Beautiful acreage—entirely air conditioned.

Many additional features: ducks with automatic transmission; turkeys with tubeless tires; cows good for many trouble-free miles.

The tractor which goes with the property has airfoam de-luxe upholstered seats; built-in barbecue; electric ovens; also disposal and dishwasher.

Make an appointment to see this very unusual property!

Story of Songs

Have the players form groups of four, each group in a different section of the room. Give each group a pencil, several sheets of 8½ × 11-inch paper, and at least one copy of a book of songs that have maintained their appeal through the years. Appoint one individual in every group for the recorder.

Within ten minutes each group is to write a story by using the titles of songs. Players may use the titles they find in the song book or names of top hits of the day. Not more than two words may be used to connect the titles. As the members weave their story the recorder writes it on a sheet of paper.

Call time, assemble the groups, and ask the recorder for each group to read the story evolving from connecting the titles of songs.

The cooperative efforts of a group may produce something like the following story:

> In the Gloaming Long Long Ago When You and I Were Young, Maggie, after meeting Annie Laurie, Little Annie Rooney, and Sweet Genevieve Comin' Through the Rye, we sat Down by the Old Mill Stream where Old MacDonald Had a Farm to admire The Last Rose of Summer.
>
> We heard Three Blind Mice say, "Good Night, Ladies," had a Lovely Evening in your Home on the Range. After Seeing Nellie Home it is Home, Sweet Home.

Telegrams

Give each player a pencil and a sheet of 8½ × 11-inch paper. Dictate ten letters of the alphabet, for example, O, P, A, T, W, M, Y, E, H, B. The players write a telegram using the letters in the given order as the first letter of the words in the message.

In using the above letters, here are some messages that might evolve:

> OUR PEANUTS AWFUL TASTY. WILL MATCH YOU EATING HALF BUSHEL.
>
> OUR POCKETS ARE THREAD WORN. MAIL YOURS. EDDIE'S HAVE BLOWN.
>
> OLD PIPES ARE TREASURES. WORTH MANY YEARS' ENJOYMENT. HAPPY BIRTHDAY.
>
> OLD PANTS AT TAILOR. WILL MAIL YOUR EVERY-DAY HAT BACK.
>
> OLD PIES ARE TERRIBLE. WHY MUST YOU EAT HEARTY BRUNCH?

Meet the Poets

Paper and pencil for everyone. Assign a number to each player. Ask each player to compose a four-line rhyme containing his name and the assigned number.

At the end of five minutes ask everyone who has completed his rhyme to read it in turn to the group. Some of the creations might include:

> My number is four
> And my name is Stone
> I've been here before
> And I'd rather stay home.

> My name is Bill Stokes
> And my number is one
> I do not mind jokes
> If they lead to fun.

> I never was a lucky soul
> Good fortune ne'er was mine
> For what will rhyme with Davidson
> Or even with number nine?

Custom Rhymes

For each person write a question on a 3 × 5-inch slip of colored paper and a noun on a 3 × 5-inch slip of white paper. Give everyone a colored slip with a question, a white slip with a noun, an 8½ × 11-inch sheet of paper, and a pencil.

Within a designated time have each person write a four-line rhyme which answers the question on the one slip and includes the noun appearing on the other.

With the question "When were you born?" and the noun "bulldog," a player might create the following rhyme:

> In the month of May
> When the days were bright,
> My bulldog and I
> First saw the light.

ARTY AWAKENERS

Art Consequences

Eight players sit in each circle. Give one person in each group a sheet of 8½ × 11-inch paper and a pencil.

Ask the first person in each group to draw the head of a man, woman, or child on his paper. He folds the paper over his drawing, being careful that the bottom of the head extends below the fold so the next person can continue the drawing. He passes the paper and pencil to the player on his right who draws the neck, folds the paper, and passes it and the pencil to the third player who draws the shoulders. Four draws the body; five, an arm and hand; six, an arm and hand; seven, a leg and foot; and eight, a leg and foot.

Place the drawing from each group on exhibition and allow the players to choose the funniest drawing. The group whose combined artistic attempts produce the greatest laughter wins the title "Ye Artists of Great Mirth."

Strange Animals

Provide each person with a sheet of paper and a pencil.

Ask everyone to write his name on the top of the sheet, draw the head of an animal, fold the paper over the drawing, and pass it to the person on his right. The second person draws the neck, folds the paper, and passes it to the third person, who draws the body and tail. Four draws a leg; five, a leg; six, a leg; seven, a leg; and eight, without unfolding the drawing, puts a title on the bottom of the sheet.

On signal the players unfold the drawings and return them to their original owners. Each person holds his strange animal so that everyone can see it. Allow the group to decide which composite has a title which seems most appropriate for it.

Growing Masterpiece

Give each player crayons and a large sheet of drawing paper. Determine the subject for a drawing, for example, an outdoor scene. With the subject decided upon, have everyone start his masterpiece by drawing something that is appropriate for the setting.

On completing the initial bit of art, the player passes the drawing to the person on his right, who makes some addition to the "masterpiece-in-the-making" and sends it on to the next person. Each player continues to add something to the scene: tree, flowers, grass, lake, river, sky, sun, bird, animal, person, campfire, or other appropriate contributions. Players proceed to add to the drawings and pass them until everyone has his original sheet.

Ask each individual to hold his drawing so that everyone can see it. Allow the members of the group to decide which drawing really resembles the outdoors.

Add a Line

Give everyone a pencil and a sheet of 8½ × 11-inch paper. Ask the players to write their names on the sheets.

On signal, each person draws a line on his paper—curved, horizontal, vertical, or diagonal. Everyone passes his paper to the person on his right. Players continue adding a line to the drawings and passing them until the unusual creations are back with their originators. The object in this "free-for-all art" is to try to create some recognizable subject with the miscellaneous lines.

Ask each person in turn to hold up his drawing while the members of the group tell what they find in the creation.

Hobby Artistry

Give everyone a pencil and an 8½ × 11-inch sheet of paper. Ask each person to write his name on his sheet.

Request each person to exert his creative imagination in portraying one of his hobbies on the reverse side of the paper.

At the end of the designated time collect the drawings and distribute them so that no one has his own creation. Each person analyzes the drawing that he holds. In turn, everyone tells what hobby he thinks the artist has portrayed. After each announcement the person reads the artist's name on the back of the sheet and asks him if he guessed the hobby correctly. Each individual who names the subject correctly is acclaimed "A Connoisseur of the Arts."

Speedy Illustrators

Players form groups of eight. Give each group eight sheets of 8½ × 11-inch paper and a box of crayons.

On signal, one member from each group, the Chief Illustrator, comes to the leader, who whispers to him the name of a well-known musical selection. The Chief Illustrator hurries back to his group and attempts to draw a picture which will help the other members of his group to guess the title of the musical selection. His only medium for expressing the idea is his drawing; he may neither speak nor write any words which disclose the title.

Any member of the group who thinks he knows the title hurries to the leader and states the name of the selection. The first group to identify the title from the Chief Illustrator's drawing scores three points. Each of the others scores one point for trying. Another player from each group becomes Chief Illustrator and goes to the leader for another title to illustrate.

When a player reports to the leader a title which is incorrect, he must return to his group and ask the illustrator to do additional drawing until someone thinks he knows the title. If, after a reasonable time, no one guesses the title, the leader announces it, and each group scores one point for trying. The group with the most points at the end of a designated time earns the title "Top Musical Illustrators."

Suggestion: Instead of the titles of musical selections use the titles of books, poems, plays, movies, radio or television programs, or a current event.

Illustrated Songs

Players are in couples. Give each twosome a sheet of 8½ × 11-inch paper, a 3 × 5-inch card, and a pencil.

Each couple selects a well-known song and proceeds to draw a simple illustration which depicts the title of the selection. Couples should be careful not to disclose the title to the others. After a prearranged number of minutes, call time. Assign a number to each couple, which they write on the upper right-hand corner of the drawing. Ask the couples to place their drawings on display.

Each couple views the drawings and attempts to guess the titles of the songs from the illustrations. One of each twosome records on the card the number of the drawing and writes the supposed title to the right of it.

At the end of a specified time call the guessing to a halt and ask every couple to get its drawing. Assemble the players. In turn, one member of each couple holds up their illustrated song, gives the number appearing on the right-hand corner, and states its title. Any couple which guessed the title correctly scores five points; everyone else, one point for trying. The couple with the highest score wins the game.

A few of the time-tested songs which lend themselves to illustration are:

Song	Illustration
Home, Sweet Home	A house, a bag with sugar printed on it, and another house
The Lost Chord	A shade covering a window and having no cord
Three Blind Mice	Three mice wearing dark glasses
Row, Row, Row Your Boat	A person rowing a boat
The Long Long Trail	A winding trail through some woods
The Old Spinning Wheel	Father Time, a top with lines indicating that it is spinning, and a wheel

Unseen Wildlife

Players sit at tables. Give everyone a pencil and an 8½ × 11-inch sheet of paper.

Allow a few minutes for each player to decide on a bird or animal which he will attempt to draw with his eyes closed. The players do not reveal their choices to anyone.

On signal, each player begins drawing the bird or animal of his choice. After a designated time call a halt. Ask each person in turn to hold up his drawing and allow the others to guess the subject of the "closed-eye" masterpiece. For every correct guess the guesser scores five points. The person with the highest score wins the game.

Guess: What?

Players sit at tables which are covered with heavy paper. Give each person a portion of modeling clay. Allow everyone a few minutes to decide on the subject for his creation.

On signal, each person begins modeling some object of his choice. After everyone completes his clay model, each modeler in turn makes three statements about his handiwork without revealing the name of his creation. After each remark he gives the others a chance to identify the model.

Anyone who identifies the creation after the first clue scores five points; after the second statement, four points; after the third, three. If no one guesses the identity of the model after the third statement, the modeler reveals the name of his work, and everyone scores one point for trying. Play continues until everyone has presented his creative attempt.

Find Yourself! ✓

Give everyone a sheet of drawing paper and crayons. In addition distribute to each player a 2 × 2-inch slip of paper on which he writes his name. Have the players fold the papers and deposit them in a container which is passed among the players. After everyone deposits his name, pass the container again and ask each person to take one slip. If anyone selects his own name, he folds the slip, puts it back in the container, and draws another slip.

Each would-be artist is to attempt to draw a portrait of the person whose name he drew. If he does not know the individual, he must find him, make a quick observation of his features, and then employ his imagination in attempting to draw the portrait.

After a designated time ask the artists to put their portraits on display. Everyone tries to find himself, which may be quite a task, for the resemblances may be remote. When everyone has discovered his portrait, have everyone in turn hold up his likeness and allow the group to decide on the three portraits which most resemble the individuals. Ask the recognizable trio to present the three responsible artists.

High Adventures

Players are in groups of fifteen, each group in a circle. Give each player a sheet of 8½ × 11-inch paper and a crayon.

Assign to each player the name of something that he can illustrate for a melodramatic tale about the thrilling days of the Old West. Allow the players about five minutes to complete their illustrations.

At the end of the allotted time call the illustrating to a halt. Ask one member to start telling a hair-raising tale about the Old West. Upon reaching a point in the story that he can illustrate with his drawing he holds it up in view of the group and concludes his portion of the exciting tale. The player on his right continues the story. He adds to the tale until he reaches a place where he can use his illustration. Storytelling proceeds until everyone participates. The last person brings the narrative to a conclusion.

In the thrilling tale of a journey in a stagecoach the following offer possibilities for illustrations: stagecoach, wheel, door, horse, whip, driver, gun, road, ruts, cowboy, girl, old lady, old man, young man, desperado, pay-roll bag, suitcase, lariat.

Creative Costuming

Have the players work in groups of four. Each group selects one member for its model. The other three create a costume for the model. Give each group crepe paper, artificial flowers, ribbons, pins, scissors, paste, and an old clean sheet which may be cut if necessary.

On signal, each trio uses its ingenuity in costuming its model. After a designated time call a halt to the activity. Ask the model from each group to promenade around the room. Allow the costumers to decide which group exerted the most originality in costuming its model.

Chapeau for Monsieur

Two boys and two girls form each group. Since the girls in each group are to create hats for the boys, give them pins, paste, scissors, artificial fruits and vegetables, feathers, ribbon, crepe paper, small ornaments, inexpensive unwanted jewelry, and a clean cloth, head size, to form the basis for the hat. Each boy in the group is to make up the other fellow's face to harmonize with his feminine chapeau, so give each pair face powder, rouge, lipstick, and eyebrow pencil. Also provide cleansing cream and tissues for removing the makeup.

Each foursome goes into action to create hats and apply makeup within a designated time. The boys vie with one another in the art of makeup, while each girl creates a hat that she feels is most becoming to one of the gentlemen.

After the creations are complete ask the models to promenade around the room and allow the girls to select the individual whose makeup and chapeau seem to epitomize the latest Paris creations.

PART II

PARTIES

THEME PARTY

FUN MAKERS

CONTENTS

CONTENTS (continued)

Special Occasions Calendar

Building a party around a theme provides an opportunity for creativity by the leader of social recreation and the groups which assist him in planning the special occasion. A theme can take the party-planners to the Arctic, as illustrated by Exploring the Arctic, and zoom down to the other end of the globe, as the party-goers do in South of the Equator.

To give the leader and his assisting party-planners a start to the scores of possibilities that may be the bases for building theme parties, the Special Occasions Calendar was formulated and is included in this chapter. Many of the occasions in this calendar may generate precisely the idea needed to create a variety of original party games, whether or not the games are played on the date given in the calendar. For example, Gregory XIII's work on the calendar inspired the Time's A-Fleeting Party. Benjamin Franklin's philosophy of thrift not only was the springboard for the Thrifty Tips party but also contributed the basis for the Franklin Quips game. Alexander Graham Bell's invention of the telephone sparked the Tell-Tale party.

Many of the novelists, poets, painters, and composers whose birthdays are included in the Special Occasions Calendar are present in spirit at the Creative Corral party.

Fulton's steamboat gave the first puff to the On the Go party. Starting with something ordinary produced the Buttons Aglitter, and a trend, the Do-It-Together party. Since somebody has a birthday during one of the months of the calendar each year, thus, Everybody's Birthday evolved.

The explorers in the calendar, as well as Skimo, a pet Siberian Husky, inspired Exploring the Arctic. Another clever pet, Skipper, a budgereegah, displaying his colorful tropical plumage, suggested the idea for South of the Equator.

Exploring the Arctic

Amazing happenings take place while the players explore the Arctic. In the opening defroster, Interage Expedition, the first miracle occurs, permitting the players—explorers for the occasion— to meet other courageous individuals who lived in different periods.

In the creative game, Flight Preparation, the players have a chance to become acquainted as they cooperate in making the team's map to use in the socializer, Flight to the Arctic. A second socializer, Pack Dog Relay, precedes the next creative game, Eskimos' Sun Spectacles. If the players' enthusiasm seems geared for more activity, use either or both of the socializers, Snowshoe Relay and Snowshoeing in the Sun.

Depending upon the group, play either the brain teaser Ursa Minor, in which Greek letters are used with astronomical precision, or the simplified version, Little Dipper Relay. Both these games give the players a chance to catch their breaths.

Another miracle transpires as the individuals play the role of intelligent Siberian Huskies in the next two socializers. Depending upon the available space, choose either Mush the Dogs' Relay, requiring 20 feet between the goal and starting lines, or the Siberian Husky Dog Race, necessitating 40 feet between the two lines.

Sight-Seeing in the Arctic and Leaping Crevasses are two socializers which precede the creative game Expressive Exploring, the final game in the Exploring the Arctic party.

For this expansive trip to the Arctic the supplies include in general: paper, cardboard, pencils, crayons, an air-route map for the Arctic, a map of the Arctic region, gunny sacks or holeless pillow cases filled with clean rags, several lengths of rope, some strips of old cloth, string, scissors, single-edge razor blades, darning needles, and shoe boxes. For specific details about the supplies refer to the preparation and formation preceding each activity.

Interage Expedition

For each player print the name of an Arctic expedition at the bottom of a 4 × 6-inch piece of paper, for example, "Richard E. Byrd Expedition." Give each player a sheet of 8½ × 11-inch paper, a pencil, a pin, and the name of an Arctic expedition. Have each player write his name on the top of both slips of paper. He pins the smaller paper on his clothing.

On signal, the players take the larger sheets of paper and the pencils and try to acquire the signatures of the members of the interage Arctic expeditions. They secure the players' own signatures and the names of the expedition of which they are a party.

At the end of a designated time, call a halt to the game. Each person counts the signatures on his list. Invite the person having the longest list to the front of the room to read the names he acquired, for example, "Roy Ludwick of the Lincoln Ellsworth Expedition." As he reads each name, the person arises. The person having the longest correct list wins the game and becomes the Interage Expedition Specialist. Any person whose name is not read stands and introduces himself.

Suggestion: A list of leaders of Arctic expeditions to use might include the following:

Roald Amundsen	Henry Hudson
William Baffin	D. B. Macmillan
Vitus Bering	N. A. E. Nordenskjold
Richard E. Byrd	Robert E. Peary
John Davis	Eric the Red
Lincoln Ellsworth	Vilhjalmur Stefansson
Adolphus Greely	

Flight Preparation

From an airline company or the library obtain for each team an air-route map showing the nearest airport and an air route to the Arctic region. For each team mount a piece of 17 × 22-inch paper on cardboard. Against the wall place tables on which to stand the maps completed in the Flight Preparation game. Divide the group into teams of six, and have the teams sit at the tables. Give each player a piece of paper $1 \times \frac{1}{2}$ inch. Place the large mounted paper, a pencil, a box of crayons, and the air-route map on the table for each team.

On signal, each team makes a map of the country over which the members will fly to the Arctic region. Ask each team to locate national and state boundaries, large lakes, rivers, and six cities on the map. Each player selects one of the six cities and prints the name of his city on his piece of paper.

One player of each team takes the completed air-route map, the reference map, and the six city slips to the leader for inspection for relative accuracy. The team representative returns the city slips to the players for use in the Flight to the Arctic game. Delay announcing the winner until all the maps and city slips are complete. The first team showing a correct air-route map and six city slips to the leader wins the game. While the other teams complete their maps, the winners have the honor of arranging the completed air-route maps on the tables against a wall for use in the game Flight to the Arctic.

Flight to the Arctic

See that a map for each team from the Flight Preparation game is on a table at the goal line. Fifteen feet from the goal line establish the starting line. Keep the players on the same teams as in the Flight Preparation game. Have the teams in single files behind the starting line opposite the maps they made in the Flight Preparation game. Each player holds the name of the city on the slip he made in the Flight Preparation game. Give a pin to each player.

On signal, the first member of each team walks quickly to the map and pins his city in the correct location. Arriving at the starting line, he shakes the hand of the next passenger on the flight before going to the end of the team. The flight continues until one team is first to have all its players pin the six cities in the correct locations on the map and win the Flight to the Arctic.

Pack Dog Relay

For explorations on mountains and glaciers where teams of dogs cannot travel, pack dogs carry the supplies not borne by the explorers. Pack dogs can carry forty pounds of supplies all day. In this game each couple becomes acquainted with both the explorer and his pack dog, for each plays one of the roles.

Fill gunny sacks or holeless old pillow cases with rags. Have two sacks for each team. Tie the top of the sacks so that the rags will not fall out. Secure a piece of sturdy old material 4 feet long and 4 inches wide to tie around the Pack Dog's waist. Provide two pieces of rope, each 2-feet long, for tying the packs on the cloth at the waist of the player representing the pack dog. Place a chair at the goal line opposite each team. Ten feet from the goal line indicate the starting line. Give the two pieces of rope, the 4-inch material, and the two packs to the first couple on each team. Ask each couple to decide who will play each of the roles—Explorer or Pack Dog. The couples stand in relay formation behind the starting line.

On signal, the Explorer of the first couple ties the material around the waist of the Pack Dog. He uses the ropes to tie one pack on each side of the material around the waist of the Pack Dog. As soon as the Pack Dog is ready for the trip, he bends at the waist and walks with hands hanging down. The pair then heads for the goal line in character: the Explorer encouraging his burden-bearing companion and the dog dramatizing his role. Reaching the chair, the goal, the Pack Dog puts a front paw (hand) on the chair and returns with the Explorer to the starting line in pack dog posture. The Explorer unties the packs, passes all the supplies to the next couple, and he and his Pack Dog go to the end of the line.

The relay continues until each couple has enacted the Pack Dog and Explorer pantomime. The first team to have its members complete the trip wins the Pack Dog and Explorer scurry.

Eskimos' Sun Spectacles

Besides being skilled artisans in bone, ivory, and stone, the Eskimos show ingenuity in making articles contributing to their survival in their severe climate. Some explorers have found the thin wooden spectacles of the Eskimos superior to the more modern eye protectors. Without sun spectacles the explorer may suffer from snow blindness, a temporary condition caused by the reflection of sunlight on the snow. Profiting by the experiences of the Eskimos and explorers, each player follows the example of the resourceful Eskimos as he makes the sun spectacles shown in Figure 9–1.

Supply pieces of 2 × 6-inch cardboard for each player. At each table have a ball of string, scissors, a single-edge razor blade, and a darning needle with an eye large enough to pass the string through. Have teams of six sit at each table.

Each player uses the razor blade to make two slits in his cardboard in such a position that he can see but will still be protected from the glare of the sun on the snow. When he fits the cardboard sun spectacles to his eyes, he securely fastens double string to each end, allowing enough string to tie behind his head. The members of the team may help each other, since the first team with each

FIGURE 9-1. Eskimo with sun spectacles

member wearing his sun spectacles wins the game. Do not announce the winners until all the players are wearing the Eskimos' Sun Spectacles.

Snowshoe Relay

While explorers use snowshoes purely as a means of transportation over soft snow, snowshoe races have become so popular in winter carnivals that the International Snowshoe Congress governs the sport in the United States and Canada.

Mark a starting line, and 20 feet from it indicate a goal line. Place a chair at the goal line opposite each team. Players stand in teams of six in single file formation behind the starting line. Give two large shoe boxes to the first player on each team. Have several extra shoe boxes on hand to replace those damaged in the snowshoe relay. Suggest that each person pretend he is wearing snowshoes as he walks with each foot in a shoe box.

On signal, the first player walks in his imaginary snowshoes to the goal, circles the chair, and returns to the starting line. He gives the second player the boxes and goes to the end of the team. Continue until all members of the snowshoe team participate. The team first to have all its members complete the Snowshoe Relay earns the title "Snowshoe Champions of the Arctic" for the duration of the party. The game offers the best fun when played on a floor that does not have carpeting or a rug.

Snowshoeing in the Sun. Have the players wear the sun spectacles they made in the Eskimos' Sun Spectacle activity as they proceed on the snowshoes. Play the balance of the game in the same way as Snowshoe Relay.

Ursa Minor

Constellations have helped guide explorers for many years. Locating Ursa Minor, also known as the Little Dipper and the Little Bear constellation, is particularly helpful and easy, because the North Star, a common guide, constitutes the tip of the Little Dipper handle and the end of the tail of the Little Bear.

For each relay team provide a sheet of 17×22-inch paper mounted on cardboard and place it on a table. Give a crayon to each team—any color which will show on the paper. Permit the players time to study a drawing of the constellation (see Figure 9–2). A Greek letter is assigned to each star in the constellation, beginning with the brightest star. Polaris, therefore, is alpha in the Ursa Minor constellation. Tell the players to note the Greek letter used to label each star as well as the position of the Greek letter in the diagram of the Ursa Minor constellation. Then indicate a starting line 10 feet from the table. Have the players form teams of seven and line up in single-file formation behind the starting line. Give the crayon to the first player on each team.

On signal, the first player proceeds to the paper on the table at the goal line, draws the Greek letter alpha (α) in the position of the North Star, Polaris, in the Ursa Minor constellation. He brings the crayon to the next player on his team before going to the end of the line. Constellation building continues with each player mark-

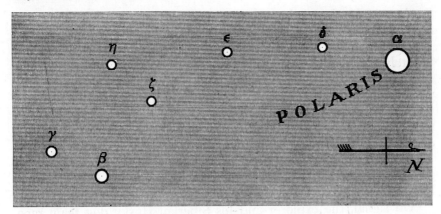

FIGURE 9–2. The Ursa Minor constellation

ing the Greek letter for the next star in the constellation in the correct relationship to the North Star, Polaris. The team which is first to complete placing the Greek letters in the correct positions for the Ursa Minor constellation wins the relay.

Little Dipper Relay. Have players use an asterisk (*) instead of the Greek letters to mark each star in the Little Dipper constellation. Proceed as in Ursa Minor.

Mush the Dogs' Relay

Establish a goal line 10 feet from the wall so that the dog team can swing around the goal. Indicate a starting line 20 feet from the goal line. Divide the group into teams of six players. Have each team stand behind the starting line in a modified dog team position: the first player, the Lead Dog, standing at the front of the team; the next four players, as couples, joining hands and standing directly behind the Lead Dog. The sixth player, the Explorer, stands on the back runner of the imaginary sled in line with the Lead Dog. Give a 12-foot rope to the Explorer on each team.

On signal, all five dogs bend forward from the waist in order to slightly resemble a dog stance. The Explorer remains in a standing position. The Explorer gives one end of the rope to the Lead Dog, who holds the rope with both hands behind his back. Next the Explorer passes the rope between the two pairs of "dogs," who hold the rope with their inside hands. Pretending to stand on his shortened 12-foot sled, the Explorer holds the rope, as he prepares to guide his team of Huskies.

Since dogs become very restless once they are in harness, as soon as the Explorer is in his position he gives the signal and starts mushing, encouraging his team. The Lead Dog must take the team around the goal and back to the starting line.

As soon as the dog team returns to the starting line, the Explorer unhitches his team and gives the rope to the player on his team who is to be the next Explorer. They exchange roles. The relay continues with hitching, racing, and unhitching until all six members of one team have taken the part of Explorer. The first team to have the six players successfully complete the dog team relay wins the title of the "Champions."

Siberian Husky Dog Race. Have each dog team and its explorer stand ready behind the starting line, which is 40 feet from the goal line.

On signal, the explorer and his Siberian Husky dog team race to the goal line and return to the starting line. The explorer and team finishing first win the title of the "Champion Siberian Husky Dog Team."

Sight-Seeing in the Arctic

Prepare a set of ten slips of paper for each team. Write the names of the same ten islands, oceans, or cities in the Arctic region on each set of slips. Provide a map of the Arctic region for each team so that the members can locate the ten places listed on the hidden slips. Be sure the ten places are shown on the maps available to each team. Distribute the slips around the room so that they are partially visible and the players will not have to open drawers or move items to locate them. Have the players form teams of ten. Ask each team to select a sight-seeing Guide.

On signal, everyone except the sight-seeing Guide starts sight-seeing, looking for the hidden slips. When a player finds a slip, he brings it to the sight-seeing Guide, who checks to see that it is not a duplicate of any slip already found by a member of the team. If the sight-seeing Guide already has the Arctic sight slip, the latest finder replaces the slip and looks for another Arctic sight slip.

As soon as the team members have located ten different Arctic sight slips, the Guide calls his team members together, and they find the location of each place on the map. The first team to correctly locate on the map the ten different sights wins the game.

Suggestions: The leader might write any of the following on slips after checking that they can be found on the maps available to the teams: Arctic Ocean, Baffin Island, Barrow, Beaufort Sea, Ellesmere Island, Etah, Godhaun, Mackenzie River, Peary Land, Prince of Wales Island, Upernivik, Victoria Island.

Leaping Crevasses

A necessary part of exploration in the Arctic is finding a route suitable for travel. Crevasses, or large cracks in the upper surface of a glacier, often must be crossed. The adventure of Leaping Crevasses will increase if the player imagines there is a 300-foot drop beneath him as he leaps across the crevasse. To make the leap successfully, however, he must not look down as he jumps.

Place a tape on the goal line, which must be at least 8 feet from a wall. Establish a starting line 3 feet from the goal line. Provide a sturdy rope 30 feet long for each team. Have players form teams of four and stand in file formation behind the starting line. Give the rope to the first player on each team. Each player ties the rope around his waist, allowing 4 feet of rope between himself and the next player.

On signal, the first player leaps across the 3-foot crevasse without glancing down at the 300-foot drop below him. As soon as the first player arrives safely, the second player makes the dangerous leap. After reaching the other side, each player moves back far enough to allow the next leaper to land over the tape line at the goal, but not so far as to reduce the amount of rope between the members of the team. Crevasse-leaping continues until all four members of the team safely make the jump. Players untie themselves, helping each other if necessary. The winning team is the first team with all its members safely over the crevasse and its rope neatly arranged for carrying until needed for the next leap.

Expressive Exploring

For each group write on a slip of 3 × 5-inch paper a brief description of a pantomime possibility associated with exploring the Arctic, for example: "Walk along a 10-inch ledge in a glacier ridge with a 300-foot drop on one side and a tough scrub balsam growth on the inside of the ledge." Have players form teams of six. Give each team one of the pantomime possibility slips. Allow time so that each team can decide which actions will best dramatize the Arctic exploration activity on its slip. Actions may be simultaneous, with each player showing the same activity; or individuals may give different interpretations of the Expressive Exploring. All members must take part in the team presentation and use actions, gestures, and facial expressions to convey the point of the dramatization.

At the end of a designated time, each team takes a turn presenting its version of the Arctic exploration activity on its slip. The other teams try to guess which exploring activity is being pantomimed. When the members of a team correctly guess the activity, they score five points and are the next actors unless they have had a turn—in which case they may choose the next dramatists. If no one guesses the title of the pantomime, the actors announce the title and have the honor of asking the next group to express the exploring activity assigned to its group. The team having the highest score after all the groups have performed wins the activity.

Suggestions: Other activities associated with the Arctic which offer pantomiming possibility include:

Crawling into a sleeping bag for the night while a blizzard rages.

Constructing a summer tent of imaginary caribou or sealskins.

Catching fish after chopping through 5 feet of ice after other sources of food are exhausted.

Carrying on the back 120 pounds of photographic equipment, food, and other necessities at the beginning of a mountain expedition.

Gathering specimens of Arctic plants and minerals near a recently active volcano.

Packing a komatik—an Eskimo sledge—to be pulled by a dog team, and arranging all the expedition supplies on the sledge. (A komatik is 10 to 12 feet long and 30 inches wide. It has wooden sides and crossbars lashed with rawhide.)

Paddling a kayak—an Eskimo canoe—by sitting in an opening, amidship, with the covering of sealskin laced about the paddler.

On the Go

In the party On the Go, the players find that the desire to be on the move is not a recent development, but that it has been the basis for urging individuals to develop various forms of transportation throughout the ages. By engaging in the activities, which range from a Chariot Relay to Flight Talk, the players learn that the on-the-go spirit is ageless.

To start the On the Go party, use the defroster Cities Meet, in which each player finds a partner by locating a person having a city beginning with the same letter as the city on his slip.

Continue with the socializer New Territory, and then allow the players to test their Air Age keenness in the sense alerter Aircraft Show before reversing the times for the socializer Chariot Relay. Return the players to the modern On the Go jargon by playing Flight Talk, a brain teaser.

By again flipping the clock—this time to the 1836-1896 era, in the socializer the Red Flag Relay—the players share the feelings of both the English drivers of mechanical vehicles and the red-flag bearers who preceded them at four miles an hour. Representative means of road transportation through the ages meet in the socializer Road Open, while the players relive one phase of early American freighting in the socializer Captains of the Road or, if appropriate for the group, Pioneer Loads.

In the sense alerter Signs of the Road, the players test their memories and powers of observation, while in the brain teaser Advantages, the players attempt to think of the benefits of each means of transportation they list. Conclude with the final creative fun maker, Troupe on Tour.

The supplies needed for the On the Go party include: paper, cardboard, pencils, crayons, small boxes, glasses without lenses, road maps, pictures of various types of aircraft, cloth reins, a record player, records, green crepe paper crowns, a yardstick, and thumb tacks.

Cities Meet

Provide a slip of paper for each player. On each pair of slips write the names of two cities beginning with the same letter, for example, Winnipeg on one slip and Washington, D.C., on the other one of the pair. Put the first slip of each pair in one box, the second in another box. Give one slip to each player. Be sure to distribute both slips of each pair but not consecutively.

On signal each player seeks the person having a city beginning with the same letter as the city on his slip. When the players with the names of the two cities beginning with the same letter meet, they are partners.

Some pairs of cities beginning with the same letter include:

Boston	Brownsville
Chicago	Cleveland
Cincinnati	Calgary
Denver	Dallas
Minneapolis	Moose Jaw
Montgomery	Montreal
Memphis	Mexico City
New York	New Orleans
Oklahoma City	Ottawa
Portland	Port Arthur
Phoenix	Pittsburgh
Salt Lake City	St. Louis
Seattle	Saskatoon
Tulsa	Toronto
Tallahassee	Tampico
Washington	Winnipeg

New Territory

On a dark night a person arrives at a strange airport 50 miles from his destination. There is no bus or taxi service between the airport and his destination, so renting a car is the only course even though the person is unfamiliar with driving the make of car that is available for rental. In the following game the players share this individual's experience.

Have available an old pair of glasses without the lenses and a road map for each team. Place a chair on the goal line, and 20 feet from it establish a starting line. Have the players stand in teams of six in single files behind the starting line. Designate the first player of each team as Starter. Give a road map and glasses to each Starter.

On signal, the Starter of each team pantomimes driving a car: leaving the airport's Rent-a-Car office (starting line), proceeding to his destination, and then returning to the airport. He holds the road map and glasses in his hand; he cannot wear the glasses for driving—they are useful only for reading the road map.

While proceeding to the goal line and back to the starting line, the player must stop three times, put on the glasses, refer to the road map, take off the glasses, and continue. Stopping and referring to the map occurs once en route to the goal, once at the goal, and once before reaching the starting line. Before going to the end of his team, the player gives the glasses and the road map to the next player in the file. Pantomiming driving, making the three road map reference stops, using the reading glasses, continue until the six drivers on one team are first to complete the trip to and from the goal. This team wins the game, and the members are acclaimed the "Best Horsepower Explorers."

Aircraft Show

Procure pictures of aircraft from an airline company. Place the pictures on a table and cover them until it is time to play the game. Have the players sit so that they cannot see the table from their places. Obtain a 4 × 6-inch card and a pencil for everyone.

Uncover the display of the pictures of the aircraft. Have small groups of players come to the table and view the pictures of the aircraft without discussing the models with one another. After everyone views the pictures and is back in place, distribute a card and a pencil to each player. Have everyone write the names of as many types of aircraft as he can recall seeing. After an allotted time, have the player with the longest list of aircraft read it. If the list is correct, he wins the aircraft recognition game.

Some of the models for which pictures might be shown include:

gliding machine	hydroplane
steam flying machine	airship
monoplane	gyroplane
biplane	helicopter
triplane	amphibian

Chariot Relay

As background information, and to augment the interest of the players in this game, recall for them the tenseness, excitement, and color of the chariot races of ancient times. Many will have seen these races enacted in motion pictures or illustrated in history or other books.

Place a chair opposite each relay team at the goal line, and 20 feet from the goal establish a starting line. Provide 3 yards of sturdy 4-inch cloth for each horse on each team. Make a green crepe paper crown for each driver to wear—a representation of the laurel wreath with which the victor and other distinguished persons in ancient times were crowned. Have a record-player and some music with a galloping rhythm. Instruct the teams, of twelve players each, to stand in groups of three behind the starting line. Two players are the horses; the third is the driver for each trio. Give two cloth reins to the first threesome of each team. Give each driver a green crepe paper crown. Use the galloping rhythm for background music.

On signal, the first three on each team tie the cloth reins around the waist of each horse and give the end to the chariot driver, who stands in his imaginary chariot. The driver places the substitute laurel crown on his head to show he is a Grecian of distinction. As soon as the two horses and the driver are in position, they start racing to the goal. Circling the goal, they hurry back to the starting line, remove the reins, give them to the next threesome, and go to the end of the team. Each driver wears his own crown.

Continue with each threesome hitching, crowning, racing to and from the goal, unhitching, giving the reins to the next trio, and going to the end of the team. The first team to have its horses and drivers complete the action wins the relay.

Flight Talk

Make two sets of alphabet cards, printing one letter on each sheet of 8½ × 11-inch cardboard. Use a blue crayon for making one set and an orange one for the other set. Omit *J, Q,* and *X.* Have the players form two lines of fourteen and sit facing one another about 10 feet apart. Designate one line as Team 1, the other, Team 2. Give the orange letters to the first player on Team 1 and the blue ones to the head player on Team 2. Have the first player on each team distribute the vowels to the last five players on his team and two consonants to the others.

Explain to the players that when two consonants held by any one player are needed to spell a word, he gives one to a player whose letter is not required to spell it. After the word has been spelled, the letter is returned to its original possessor. Indicate a spelling line for each team. Use a large sheet of paper and a dark crayon for recording the score. Use the words listed below.

Call a word. The players from each team who hold the needed letters rush to their spelling line, arrange themselves in the order in which the letters appear in the word, and hold the letters up in front of them. When one letter appears next to itself in a word, the player waves the letter back and forth to represent twin letters, for example, *l* in "propellers." In words like "airline," the player holding *i* stands between *a* and *r* and then hustles and stands between *l* and *n* to show he belongs in two places.

The first team to spell the word correctly scores three points. Give the other team one point for trying. Record the teams' scores after each word is spelled. The team first to score fifteen points wins the game.

Flight Talk words the teams could spell include:

aeronautic	velocity
aircraftsman	cargo
aircraftswoman	deplaning
air brake	flight kitchen
airway	gate pass
air speed	glide path
airline	instrument
altitude	pilot
automatic pilot	pressurization
propellers	stewardess
radar	terminal
scenic patterns	wheel brakes
wing span	flight

Red Flag Relay

Remind the players that from 1836 to 1896 the enforcement of the Red Flag Act retarded the development of mechanical vehicles in England. This Red Flag Act required all self-propelled vehicles to be preceded by a man carrying a red flag during the day and a white flag at night. It also limited speed to 4 miles an hour. As they participate, the drivers in the Red Flag Relay will sense something of the Englishmen's feeling about the Act.

Make a paper flag for each team by pasting a sheet of 8½ × 11-inch red and white paper back to back. Tack the reversible flag to a yardstick. Place a chair at a goal line and establish a starting line 15 feet from it. Have players select partners, form teams of five couples, and stand in double file formation behind the starting line. Let each couple decide who will be the flag-bearer and who will drive the steam road carriage of 1892. Give the flag-bearer his waving device.

On signal, the flag-bearer precedes the driver of the self-propelled vehicle and shows the red flag while the two are en route to the goal line. Since the vehicle is not allowed to go more than four miles an hour, assume that time has been consumed and the shades of night have fallen, so that on the return trip to the starting line the flag-bearer shows the white flag.

Before the couple goes to the end of the team, the flag-bearer gives the double flag to the next couple on the team who portrays the same role.

The relay continues until the five couples on one team complete the day and night trip. The team finishing first wins the relay.

Road Open

Have everyone sit in a circle except one person, "it," who stands in the center. Assign to each player, including "it," the name of a means of transportation of the past or present. Give "it" a list of the names of the means of transportation assigned to the players. "It" gives this list to each new "it" to use in weaving an imaginative tale.

"It" tells an exciting story about happenings on the road as the players travel in the various forms of transportation assigned to them. He does not mention the vehicle assigned to him. As "it" mentions any vehicle, the player assigned the word stands, turns around, and sits down. "It" may mention any of the words as frequently as he wishes.

At any time "it" may say, "Road open," and all the vehicles try out the open road by hurrying to another place in the circle. "It," also, seeks a place, but since there are places for all but one player, the player without a place becomes "it," and tells the next tale of the road. If "it" fails after two attempts to obtain a place, he selects another person to take his place.

Names of transportation means might include:

automobile	Hansom cab
bobsleigh	jinrikisha,
carriage	omnibus
caravan	prairie schooner
chariot	sedan chair
Conestoga wagon	shay
coach	stage coach
cutter	fringed-top surrey
electric car	truck
harmanaxa	

Captains of the Road

Explain to the players that many of the early settlers were familiar with moving freight by boat; hence the wagons they used to haul farm produce received nautical names, for example, "Mud Clipper," "Neptune Metamorphosed," and "Sailors' Misery." With the nautical influence, the driver was called "Captain." To keep a record of the progress of long distance "freighting," the Captain "cleared" at each town en route, and the newspaper reported that the nautically named wagon had passed through the town. The heaviest loads were moved after harvest time and in the spring, when the accumulation of flour, applejack, and cheese came to market. With a heavy load the Captain did well to make twenty miles a day.

On a piece of paper for each team draw two columns. Label one column, "Captain's Name" and the second, "Load." Write the words "Clearance Sheet" on the top of the paper. Place the clearance sheet and a pencil on a table at the goal line opposite each team. Establish a starting line 15 feet from the table at the goal line. Make a round label from cardboard for the Captain of each wagon. Print a nautical name on the captain's label for each team. Form teams of ten, and have the members of each team stand in a file behind the starting line. Give the first player on each team the captain's label for his imaginary wagon and a pin. Allow the team members time to think of ten different farm products or crafts from the pioneer homes which could have been transported in the wagons. Have each player select one item of which his load will be composed.

On signal, the first player of each team pins on his captain's label, dramatically drives his imaginary team to the first town, the goal, where he clears his load by writing his name and his load in the proper columns on the paper lying on the table at the goal line. As soon as the Captain completes the trip by returning to the starting line at 20 miles per day, he gives his Captain's label and pin to the next driver before going to the end of his team.

Play continues until one team's ten drivers clear their loads. All the Captains then shout the name of the team's wagon, "_____ arrived safely!"

Pioneer Loads. Play the same as Captains of the Road but allow all the teams to finish. In turn have the last Captain of each team return to the clearing table at the goal line and read the items that arrived in the group's load. The team with the most logical list wins the game.

Signs of the Road

Prepare enlarged copies of the highway signs on sheets of paper. Display these signs on a table, and cover them until it is time to play the game. Divide the group into teams of four. Have the players on each team sit so that they cannot see the table at any time from their places and cannot overhear one another. Have each team select a recorder. Give the recorder a sheet of 8½ × 11-inch paper and a pencil. (See Figure 9–3, page 208 for the signs.)

Uncover the signs. Have each team view in turn the signs of the road without discussing them with one another. After everyone has seen the signs, allow time for the teams to have their recorder list as many of the highway signs as the team members recall. Opposite each sign the recorder writes the meaning of the signs with the assistance of the team.

Call time and ask the team with the longest list of signs and their meanings to read it. If the list is correct, the team wins and is acclaimed a boon to safe driving.

Advantages

Provide two sheets of 8½ × 11-inch paper and a pencil for each team. Have players sit at tables in teams of four, a distance apart so that they do not overhear one another. Have each team select a recorder. Give the two sheets of paper and a pencil to the recorder.

On signal, each recorder writes briefly the advantages his team-mates decide that each of the following means of transportation affords: airplane, automobile, boat, bus, rocketship, and train. If necessary, the players can use the second sheets for reorganizing the lists.

After a designated time, ask the recorders to count the advantages on their lists. Have the recorder with the longest list of advantages for the six means of transportation read it. If the list is logical, his team wins the game.

HIGHWAY

A red light means *stop;* a yellow light means *proceed with caution;* and a green light means *go.* Other symbols vary somewhat from place to place. The following, usually painted on small signboards by the roadside, are widely used:

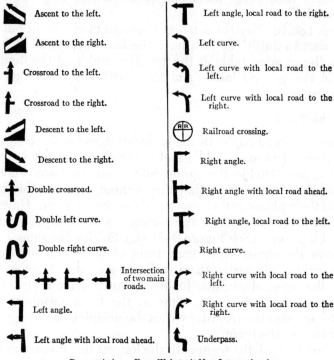

Ascent to the left.		Left angle, local road to the right.
Ascent to the right.		Left curve.
Crossroad to the left.		Left curve with local road to the left.
Crossroad to the right.		Left curve with local road to the right.
Descent to the left.		Railroad crossing.
Descent to the right.		Right angle.
Double crossroad.		Right angle with local road ahead.
Double left curve.		Right angle, local road to the left.
Double right curve.		Right curve.
Intersection of two main roads.		Right curve with local road to the left.
Left angle.		Right curve with local road to the right.
Left angle with local road ahead.		Underpass.

By permission. From Webster's New International
Dictionary, Second Edition
Copyright, 1934, 1939, 1945, 1950, 1953, 1954, 1957
by G. & C. Merriam Co.

FIGURE 9–3. Highway signs

Troupe on Tour

On a slip of paper for each team write one transportation idea to be dramatized. Form groups of six players. Give to each team one of the slips containing an activity associated with transportation. Allow each team to sit a distance from the other players, since the members decide together on the actions which best portray the activity. After a designated time, reassemble the group.

Have each group present its skit in turn while the others try to guess what activity or scene the actors are dramatizing. The team first to guess the activity being presented by the "troupe on tour" scores five points and earns the right to present the next dramatization or if this team has already performed, to select the next team to present a pantomime.

If no one guesses the title, the actors announce the theme of the skit and have the opportunity of selecting the next group of actors. The group having the highest score after all the skits have been presented wins the game.

Some activities or situations the troupes might pantomime include:

Launching Robert Fulton's steamboat, the *Clermont,* in 1807
A family on a trip in a house trailer on a Sunday afternoon
Tired drivers in an after-work traffic jam during a rainstorm
A child's first airplane trip
Boarding a crowded bus during the rush hours
Vacationists carrying loads of souvenirs and dashing after a train pulling out of the station
Passengers on the *Mayflower* on its two months' voyage to New England in 1620
Riding in a horse-drawn streetcar
A stage-coach driver paying toll at a hinged bar, the original turnpike in 1800
Launching of the first earth satellite
Riding in a rocket on the first trip to the moon

Creative Corral

Spontaneous fun rides high within the Creative Corral, as the party-goers unleash their imaginations in activities which stimulate their desire for self-expression.

The defroster Twin Artists, in which a player impersonating a kind of artist must locate another player impersonating the same kind of artist, fosters an artistic mood. After the defrosting process, which helps players meet one another, the socializers Stroke System, Staff and Clef, FACE in Three-Quarter Time, and Key-Line further assist by giving the players the opportunity to become better acquainted through team activities.

Follow the relays with the sense alerter Symbols, the creative fun maker Balletomane, and the brain teaser Dancing Letters. Then play one or several of the creative fun makers: Expressors, Sculptors, Draw-ers, Writers, Finger Painters, or Sketchers.

After the creative fun makers, select, according to the interests of the majority of the group, one or more of the following brain teasers: Orchestral Instruments, Composers, Creative Painters, or Novelists.

With creativity in high gear, climax the Creative Corral party with the game the Word's the Thing.

Supplies for the Creative Corral party include: paper, pencils, crayons, paper towels, items symbolic of various creative professions, water colors, water, paint brushes, small pans or old sauce dishes, drawing paper, some large flat pans, finger paint and paper, charcoal paper and pencils, cardboard, a large cloth or paper, a record player, and recordings of inspirational music.

Twin Artists

On duplicate slips of 3 × 5-inch paper write the names of creative professions with pantomime possibilities. Give a slip to each person. Be sure that both copies of each creative profession are distributed.

On signal, each person looks for an individual who is pantomiming the same creative profession that he is dramatically portraying. As soon as the twin artists locate one another, they are partners. Names of professions might include: actor or actress, cello player, clarinet player, dancer, costumer, designer, flutist, painter, photographer, sculptor, singer, violinist, weaver, or writer.

Stroke System

Players form circles of twenty players and face the center. The players of each circle count off by twos: ones face in, twos out. All players facing the center form Team 1; the players with their backs to the center form Team 2 in each circle. Provide a sheet of white 8½ × 11-inch paper mounted on a piece of heavy cardboard of the same size, and a bright-colored crayon for each team. Designate a starter for each team. Give him the crayon and paper.

On signal, the starter of each team makes one stroke on the paper with his crayon and passes the start of a design to the player on his right. In turn each person makes one stroke and passes the growing drawing and crayon to the next player. Continue the stroke system until all the players add a stroke. The winning team is the group that finishes first, but the miracle is the design drawn by the ten would-be artists. Allow the other groups to complete their designs. Ask the winning group to present its design, and have each group present its unique achievement in turn.

Staff and Clef. Play in the same manner as Stroke System, but with six players on each team. Have the first five players on each team draw on the paper one of the five lines of the musician's staff. The sixth and last player marks the clef 𝄞 on the staff. The first team to complete the staff and clef correctly wins the game.

Suggestion: Use the completed staff and clef in the games FACE in Three-Quarter Time and Key-Line.

FACE in Three-Quarter Time. Play in the same manner as Stroke System but with six players on each team. Ask the first four players to write *F, A, C, E* in the spaces of the staff. Beginning at the bottom of the staff, each player in turn writes one of the letters, for example, the first player writes, *F;* the second, *A,* until the word "FACE" appears in the four spaces of the staff. The fifth player writes *3* next to the clef, and the sixth writes *4* under the *3* to indicate ¾ time. The first team correctly to complete FACE in Three-Quarter Time wins the activity.

Key-Line. Play in the same manner as Stroke System but with six players on a team. Ask the first five players to write the letters of the lines of the staff. Beginning at the bottom line, the first player writes *e;* the second, *g;* third, *b;* fourth, *d;* fifth, *f.* The sixth player writes the key signature by placing a sharp, ♯, on the top line, *f.* The first team to complete labeling the lines and key correctly wins the game.

Symbols

On a table arrange items which symbolize some creative professions. Cover these items with a cloth until it is time to play the game. Provide a sheet of 8½ × 11-inch paper and a pencil for each player. Have the players sit so that they cannot see the display at any time from their places.

Remove the cover from the items. Call a few players at a time to come and observe the articles or pictures on the table. Ask the players to walk slowly by the symbols of creative professions and to observe the details without touching or discussing the items with one another. After all the players return to their places, give each a sheet of paper and a pencil and ask him to describe the symbols of the creative professions in as much detail as he can.

Items which symbolize creative professions might include: ballet dancer's slipper, artist's brushes, paints, photographer's camera or lights, charcoal pencil and paper, modeling clay, makeup or costume, typewriter, pen, pencil, paper, and reference book, musical instruments or pictures of musical instruments, programs for a play, concert, a television or radio program from a newspaper.

At the end of a designated time, read the list of symbols in detail, giving the color of the dancer's slippers, make of the typewriter, name of artist listed on the concert program, and other points of observation about the other items.

Each player gives himself two points for each correct observation. If players have made observations that are not on the list, ask them to state the points; if they are correct, allow the keen observers to score. The player with the highest score wins the game.

Balletomane

On a slip of paper for each group write some incident associated with the ballet which the players are to pantomime. Have players form groups of four. Give each group a slip, and allow time for the members to decide on an appropriate pantomime for the suggestion on the slip.

Call time and have each group present its pantomime in turn. The other groups, as balletomanes (ballet-lovers), attempt to guess what incident the pantomimers are portraying. The first group to guess correctly scores five points and has the honor of presenting its pantomime. If a group guesses correctly but has had a turn, it selects another group to present its pantomime. The performing group scores three points for its presentation, while the others except the correct guessers score one point for trying.

If the audience fails to guess the incident being pantomimed, the group announces the situation and selects the next group to pantomime. The performers score three points and everyone else, one point for trying. After everyone performs, the group with the most points is well on the way to becoming balletomanes.

Some incidents to write on the slips for the players to pantomime include:

An audience of balletomanes reacting to a flawless performance just completed by their favorite ballerina

A group waiting in a blizzard for gallery seats which are nearing a sellout

A balletomane victimizing, with his precious collection of pictures, programs, autographs, and clippings, a few friends who came only for a brief visit, and detaining them by a new spurt of enthusiasm for the ballet each time they make a move to leave

Cleaning house to the rhythm of the ballet (While the balletomanes are physically present to clean the house, in spirit they are at the ballet.)

Middle-aged balletomanes brushing up on technique after coming home from a splendid performance by a ballet company

Dancing Letters

Make two sets of alphabet cards, omitting W, X, and Y. Print one letter on each sheet of 8½ × 11-inch cardboard. Use a black crayon for making one set and a green one for the other set. Have players form two lines of fourteen and stand facing each other with 10 feet between the lines. Designate one line as Team 1, and give them the black letters; the other, as Team 2, with the green letters. Have the first player on each team give the vowels *a, e, i, o,* and *u* to the first five players and two consonants to each of the other players on the team.

Explain that when both consonants held by a player are needed in spelling a word, he gives one consonant to a player whose letter is not needed in spelling the word. Returning from the spelling line, the substitute player returns the letter to the individual. Indicate a spelling line for each team. Use a large sheet of paper and a dark crayon for recording the scores.

From the list which appears below, call one of the words. Each player whose letter is needed to spell the word hurries to the team's spelling line, stands in the order in which the letters appear in the word, and holds the letter in front of him.

When one letter appears next to itself in a word, the player waves the letter back and forth to represent twin letters, for example, *ll* in tarantella. In polonaise, the player who has *o* stands between *p* and *l* before he hustles to stand between *l* and *n* to show that his letter belongs in the two places.

The team first spelling the word correctly and holding the letters right side up in front of each player scores three points. Give the other team one point for trying. Record both scores. The team first to score fifteen points wins the Dancing Letters game.

Some words to spell include:

ballet	minuet
Charleston	morris dance
cotillion	polonaise
folk dance	quadrille
gavotte	polka
mazurka	rumba
square dance	Virginia reel
tango	tap dance
tarantella	waltz
jitterbug	bop
stomp	schottische

Expressors

To stimulate appreciation rather than negativism in creative endeavors, post signs in conspicuous places before the party:

SAY SOMETHING COMPLIMENTARY

TRY POSITIVE THINKING

FIND SOMETHING GOOD

For each player provide paper towels for wiping hands or paint brush, a water-color paint brush, drawing paper, and a small paint pan or old sauce dish for water. Divide the players into groups of four. For each group provide a table, chairs, water, and a water-color paint set. Protect the tops of the tables. Old wooden bread boards make excellent easels when drawing paper is thumbtacked to them. Provide soft inspirational music.

Allow time for the players to listen to the music and paint their impressions or feelings about the music. Without spoiling the fun, have the players be quiet enough so everyone can hear the music. Remind the dabbers in water colors that it is not necessary to draw particular objects. An individual can express his feelings through color or a series of designs that are meaningful to the creative artist.

After an allotted time, have each person write a title on his crea-tion. Provide space so each would-be artist can display his work (this lends a creative atmosphere to the party). Each person may keep the product of his creativity after the party.

Suggestion: Instead of restricting the players to water colors or one medium of expression, have a central supply table and allow the players to choose the medium they wish to use for expressing what the music means to them. Rather than having a series of creative activities as the ones which follow, conduct several at the same time and give the players a choice of medium.

Sculptors. Provide clay for each participant to use in modeling. Play the same as Expressors.

Draw-ers. Provide a large box of colored crayons for each group and a sheet of drawing paper for everyone. Play the same as Expressors.

Writers. Provide three sheets of 8½ × 11-inch paper and a pencil for each participant. Play the same as Expressors.

Finger Painters. Provide a large pan of water; red, blue, and yellow finger paints; four large sheets of finger-painting paper; and paper towels for each group. Be sure that the tops of the tables are well covered unless they are made of materials that are resistant to water and paint.

Have each player pass his sheet of paper through the water in the pan so that the paper is wet when he paints. For finger painting, the paper is flat on the table in front of the player. The painter may achieve better results by standing rather than sitting, for in addition to using his fingers to paint, he may decide to use his elbow, back of his hand, or palm to create different effects. Play the same as Expressors.

Sketchers. Provide charcoal paper and pencil for each player. Play the same as Expressors.

Orchestral Instruments

On several slips of 4 × 6-inch paper, write the first and last letters of the names of some of the instruments in an orchestra. Indicate the number of missing letters to be added by the players by using blanks, for example, "piccolo," p _ _ _ _ _ o. Divide the players into groups of four. Have each group sit at a table far enough away from the others so that they will not overhear one another. Have each group select a recorder. Give a pencil and a sheet of paper with the blanks to be filled in to each recorder.

Within a designated time, each recorder completes the names of the instruments in the orchestra with the assistance of the members of his group. After the allotted time, call time, and ask the recorder of the group having the longest list to read the names of the instruments in the orchestra. If the list is correct, his group wins the game.

Some names of instruments to use, with the proper arrangement of first and last letters and blanks, are given in the following:

Puzzle Form	Instrument
f _ _ _ e	flute
p _ _ _ _ _ o	piccolo
o _ _ e	oboe
E _ _ _ _ _ h h _ _ n	English horn
c _ _ _ _ _ _ t	clarinet
b _ _ _ _ _ n	bassoon
F _ _ _ _ h h _ _ n	French horn
t _ _ _ _ _ t	trumpet
c _ _ _ _ t	cornet
t _ _ _ _ _ _ e	trombone
t _ _ a	tuba
k _ _ _ _ _ _ _ _ m	kettledrum
b _ _ s d _ _ m	bass drum
g _ _ g	gong
t _ _ _ _ _ _ e	triangle
c _ _ _ _ _ s	cymbals
c _ _ _ _ _ _ _ s	castanets
t _ _ _ _ _ _ _ _ e	tambourine
x _ _ _ _ _ _ _ e	xylophone
t _ _ _ _ _ r b _ _ _ s	tubular bells
h _ _ p	harp
c _ _ _ _ _ a	celesta
v _ _ _ _ n	violin
v _ _ _ a	viola
c _ _ _ o	cello
d _ _ _ _ e b _ _ s	double bass

Composers. Use the names of composers. Play the same as Orchestral Instruments. Blanks and first and last letters of the names of composers to copy on the papers for the teams include:

Puzzle Form	Composer
B _ _ h	Bach
B _ _ _ _ s	Brahms
B _ _ _ _ _ _ _ n	Beethoven
B _ _ _ _ _ z	Berlioz
B _ _ _ _ _ n	Borodin
C _ _ _ _ n	Chopin
C _ _ _ _ _ _ r	Chabrier
d _ F _ _ _ a	de Falla
v _ n F _ _ _ _ w	von Flotow
F _ _ _ _ k	Franck
G _ _ _ g	Grieg
H _ _ _ _ l	Handel
H _ _ _ n	Haydn
M _ _ _ _ _ _ _ _ _ n	Mendelssohn
M _ _ _ _ t	Mozart
O _ _ _ _ _ _ _ h	Offenbach
R _ _ _ l	Ravel
R _ _ _ _ _ _ _ _ n	Rubinstein
S _ _ _ _ _ _ t	Schubert
S _ _ _ _ _ _ n	Schumann
S _ _ _ _ _ s	Strauss
S _ _ _ _ _ _ _ _ y	Stravinsky
T _ _ _ _ _ _ _ _ _ y	Tchaikovsky
W _ _ _ _ r	Wagner
V _ _ _ i	Verdi
R _ _ _ _ _ i	Rossini

Creative Painters. Use the names of painters. Play the same as Orchestral Instruments. Blanks and first and last letters of the names of painters to copy on the papers for the groups include:

Puzzle Form	Artist
C _ _ _ _ _ n	Chardin
G _ _ _ _ _ _ _ _ _ h	Gainsborough
H _ _ _ _ _ h	Hogarth
V _ n D _ _ e	Van Dyke
R _ _ _ _ s	Rubens
E _ G _ _ _ o	El Greco
R _ _ _ _ _ _ _ t	Rembrandt
M _ _ _ _ _ _ _ _ _ _ o	Michelangelo
T _ _ _ _ r	Turner
T _ _ _ _ n	Titian
V _ n G _ _ h	Van Gogh
W _ _ _ _ _ _ r	Whistler
P _ _ _ _ _ o	Picasso

Novelists. Use the names of novelists. Play the same as Orchestral Instruments. Blanks, first and last letters of the given and last names of some novelists to use on the papers for the groups include:

Puzzle Form	Novelist
A _ _ _ _ d B _ _ _ _ _ t	Arnold Bennett
W _ _ _ a C _ _ _ _ r	Willa Cather
T _ _ _ _ _ _ e D _ _ _ _ _ r	Theodore Dreiser
W _ _ _ _ _ m F _ _ _ _ _ _ r	William Faulkner
F. S _ _ _ t F _ _ _ _ _ _ _ _ d	F. Scott Fitzgerald
W _ _ _ _ _ m D _ _ n	William Dean Howells
H _ _ _ _ _ s	
A _ _ _ _ s H _ _ _ _ y	Aldous Huxley
H _ _ _ y J _ _ _ s	Henry James
J _ _ _ s J _ _ _ e	James Joyce
E _ _ _ _ t H _ _ _ _ _ _ _ y	Ernest Hemingway
S _ _ _ _ _ _ r L _ _ _ s	Sinclair Lewis
J _ _ k L _ _ _ _ n	Jack London
S _ _ _ _ _ _ t M _ _ _ _ _ m	Somerset Maugham
F _ _ _ k N _ _ _ _ s	Frank Norris
J _ _ n D _ s P _ _ _ _ s	John Dos Passos
U _ _ _ n S _ _ _ _ _ _ r	Upton Sinclair
M _ _ k T _ _ _ n	Mark Twain
E _ _ _ h W _ _ _ _ _ n	Edith Wharton
T _ _ _ _ s W _ _ _ e	Thomas Wolfe

Word's the Thing

Have the players form groups of ten or less. Give each group a different list of words. Provide each player with a sheet of paper and a pencil.

Allow the creative actors about ten minutes to prepare a play in which they must use every word that appears on their list. Each word must be used at least once in the play, but any can be used as frequently as the group decides. One person may tell the story while the others act, or several members of the group may have speaking parts.

After the allotted time, reassemble the group and in turn each acting ensemble presents its dramatization while the other players write the words they think they identify. After each presentation ask one of the actors to read the list of words assigned to his group. Have each player check his own paper. For each word that the viewing player identifies he scores two points. After all the groups have performed, each player adds his score. Have each acting group total the scores of all of its players. The group with the most points wins the acting and identifying game.

Some words to use on the lists include:

gardening	frugal	trade winds
building	tap dance	English terrier
privileges	baton	typewriter
document	sled	convertible
justified	dew	rhythm
veto	grandfather clock	design
hiking	Siberian Husky	waltz
singing	sculptor	opera
rights	gentle	sharp
rewards	pen	beat
erroneously	sedan	flat
shorthand	toe-hold	*largo* (slowly)
veterinarian	to do	*crescendo* (gradually
paint brush	dachshund	getting louder)
Dalmatian	long	*mesto* (sadly)
spotted	radio clock	*expressino*
sail boat	dynamite	(expressively)
wrist watch	artist	*legato* (smoothly)

Buttons Aglitter

With button-collecting ranking second only to stamp-collecting in the United States, the players have an opportunity to be introduced to a popular hobby and to have fun playing the games whose main supplies are buttons.

Since one of the highlights of the party is having each player make a Collector's Cloche—a buttony headdress in this creative fun maker—the opening defroster, Trading Buttons, has two functions: getting players to meet one another and acquiring buttons. The socializers—Prettiest Picker, Where's That Button?, and Pick Up the Buttons—also help in giving the individuals a chance to acquire more buttons in addition to helping them to become better acquainted. With the collection of these buttons the players make their buttony headdresses in Collector's Cloche. Everyone dons his showy headgear and wears it during the party. To stimulate the creative mood further, the players produce skits about the use of buttons in the Button Burlesque.

Provide a balance between active and quiet games by sandwiching the two brain teasers—Begins with Button and What's in a Button?—between the socializers Beauty's Bracelet; Buttonholing; Sew, Brother, Sew; Watch Your Buttons; and Box the Buttons.

Box the Buttons is suggested for the final activity for the party to insure that everyone has a chance to be well enough acquainted so that he will enjoy the fun of the game even if he may not be successful in boxing the buttons.

In addition to an assortment of buttons the supplies used in the party include: a cardboard with the outline of a man's coat with a lapel buttonhole, several old clean men's shirts with five buttonholes and corresponding buttons, paste, thread, needles, crepe and writing paper, and pencils.

Trading Buttons

Ask each guest to bring five pretty buttons to the party. Provide an assortment of different kinds of buttons as extras so that the players can locate five buttons made from five different materials. Inform the players that they are acquiring a new hobby, Trading Buttons. Have the players form teams of five.

On signal, each player trades buttons until he possesses five buttons made from five different materials. The team members may help one another, and the first team having its five members each show the leader five buttons made from five different materials wins the button-trading activity.

Each member of the winning team takes some of the extra buttons from the leader and trades with the members of the other teams until everyone in each group acquires five buttons made of different materials.

Reassemble the players when everyone has five buttons made of five different materials. They can use these later in the game Collector's Cloche (see page 221).

Prettiest Picker

Place five attractive buttons in a pile on a table in line with each team. Players form teams of five and stand in single files behind the starting line, which is 15 feet from the goal.

On signal and from the starting line, the first player dashes to the table (goal), picks the prettiest button, puts it on his head, clasps both hands behind his back and hurries back to the starting line. If the button falls off, the player replaces it on his head and continues more cautiously to the starting line. As soon as he touches the hand of the next player, he goes to the end of the file. Play continues until one team is first to have each player back in place with the prettiest button he has selected. The winning team states in unison, "We have the prettiest buttons."

Suggestion: Each player can add the prettiest button to his collection to be used in the game Collector's Cloche (see page 221).

Where's That Button?

Provide two duplicate buttons for each player. Use four different duplicate buttons for each team. If the old button box does not furnish the needed buttons, secure several cards of buttons from a notions department. Hide one duplicate button for each player under chairs or in other places to which a wayward button is apt to roll.

Players form teams of four. Call the teams together and tell them to imagine they are leaving the house when a button pops off. A duplicate of the button each player supposedly lost is hidden in the room. To refresh his memory, give each player a duplicate of the button he is to find. Give different duplicate buttons to each member of each team.

On signal, each player looks for the lost button, the duplicate of which he holds in his hand. As soon as a player finds his duplicate button, he may help the other members of his team find their buttons. The first team to show four buttons and their duplicates to the leader wins the game. Each player keeps the buttons to use in Collector's Cloche (see page 221).

Pick Up the Buttons

Provide a 3 × 5-inch box containing twenty-four buttons and a table and four chairs for each team. Divide the players into teams of four, and have each team sit at a table. Give a piece of 3 × 5-inch paper and a pencil to each player.

On signal, the first player upsets the button box by turning it over the buttons. He then takes the box off the buttons and tries to pick up a button without moving any other button. The player keeps any buttons he acquires without disturbing the others. Each player's turn continues until he disturbs a button in the pile as he attempts to pick a button. If he moves a button, the next player has a turn.

If all the buttons have been picked up before the end of the five-minute round, each player writes on his score card the number of buttons he has picked up and returns them to the box. The next player shakes the box, upsets it on the buttons, removes the box, and tries to pick a button without disturbing the pile. Play continues for the designated time.

Call time after five minutes of play. Ask the players to count their buttons and record on the score cards the number they have picked from the pile. At each table the player with the highest score wins the game and receives four buttons; second highest score, three buttons; third, two buttons; and fourth, one button. The players add the buttons they win in Pick Up the Buttons to their button collection to use in the Collector's Cloche game described below.

Collector's Cloche

Players form groups of four, and each group sits at a table. Provide four different-color 12 × 18-inch strips of crepe paper for each table. Also place a spool of thread, four darning needles, and a supply of paste on each table. Have each player bring all his buttons to adorn the bell-shaped Collector's Cloche.

On signal, have the players at each table select a partner, for whom they will make a Collector's Cloche. Let each player select the colored crepe paper for the hat which his partner will create. Each would-be milliner then runs basting stitches 3 inches from the 18-inch side of the crepe paper. Have the cloche-makers tie the unsewed side together about 2 inches from the top and paste the 12-inch ends together.

Let the model, for whom the cloche is being made, turn up the brim of the cloche at the line of the basting stitches. The model stretches the crepe paper hat by trying it on for size, then returns the hat to the would-be milliner, who sews the model's buttons in the most becoming locations on the hat. With ceremony, each cloche-maker presents his creation to his partner, who wears the Collector's Cloche for better or for worse.

Suggestion: The quantity and variety of buttons will increase if the Collector's Cloche is made after playing the Trading Buttons game, in which the player needs all his buttons, and the games in which he can add to his button collection, for example: Where's That Button?, Prettiest Picker, and Pick Up the Buttons.

Button Burlesque

On a slip of 4 × 6-inch paper for each group write one use of buttons. Divide the players into groups of six. Give to each group one of the slips containing a use of buttons to be dramatized. Players may use mimicry of the actions of the characters and their use of buttons. Button burlesques may be portrayed through dances, original songs, or caricatures.

Allow each group to gather a distance from the other players and to decide on an appropriate presentation for portraying the use of buttons as suggested on its slip. After a designated time, reassemble the group.

Each group presents its button burlesque in turn while the other teams try to guess which use of buttons is being portrayed. The team first guessing the correct title of the burlesque scores five points and gains the right to present the next dramatization. If the correct guessers have already performed, they instead select the next group to present a burlesque. If no one guesses the title of the burlesque, the actors announce the title and have the honor of selecting the next team to dramatize a way to use buttons. Bestow the title "Best Burlesque Guessers" on the team having the highest score after all the groups have had a turn.

Some possible button burlesques include:

Ancient Chinese wearing buttons on their hats as a sign of rank
People wearing different political party buttons meeting the day before a Presidential election
Young girl admiring the buttons on the uniform of her newly enlisted marine
Kindergarteners helping each other button raincoats on the first day of school
Morning scene when mother did not sew the button on father's suit, although he had reminded her of it the night before
Greeks and Romans using buttons as fasteners before the tenth century
Sixteenth century citizens wearing magnificent buttons as decorations

Beauty's Bracelet

Players form circles of twenty players and face the center. The members of each circle count off by twos. The Number 1's face in, they are Team 1; the Number 2's face out, they are Team 2. Designate a starter for each team, and provide him with six buttons with holes large enough to pass elastic thread through and a 12-inch piece of elastic thread (the kind sometimes used for hat elastics; it is available in notions departments).

On signal, the starter begins passing the elastic thread around the circle by giving it to the player on his right, who sends it to the next person on the team. Each player continues to pass the elastic thread to his neighbor until it reaches the last player, who stands to the left of the starter. Immediately after passing the elastic thread the starter passes each button, one at a time. As soon as the last player receives the elastic thread he ties a knot at the end of the thread. The last player threads the buttons on the elastic thread as he receives them. As soon as he strings the sixth button on the thread, he ties the ends of the elastic thread together, puts the bracelet on his wrist, and raises his arm shouting, "Beauty's bracelet is ready." Have each team select a beauty to wear the bracelet created by the team.

Buttonholing

Explain to the players that "Buttonholing" of voters began in earnest in the 1892 political campaign, when celluloid buttons with tabs to be folded into the lapel buttonhole were first used. Getting eligible voters to use their constitutional right to vote inspires the Buttonholing game.

Draw the outline of a man's suit coat, with a line to indicate a lapel buttonhole, on a 12 × 24-inch piece of cardboard for each team. Mark a snapping line across the bottom of the cardboard 12 inches from the lapel buttonhole. Paint "Vote" on one large button for each team. On the top of a table at the goal line, which is opposite the starting line 10 feet away, place the lapel buttonhole drawing, a pencil, and a score card for each team. Have players form teams of five and stand in files behind the starting line in relay formation. Give a "Vote" button to the first player on each team.

On signal, the first player hustles to the table to try to snap the "Vote" button from the snapping line to the lapel buttonhole on the drawing. Each player who snaps the "Vote" button to the lapel buttonhole writes a score of five on the team's score card. He records a consolation score of one for trying if he does not buttonhole the prospective voter.

Vote buttonholing continues, with each player passing the "Vote" button on to the next contestant as he returns to the starting line on his way to the end of the line. In turn each member of the team takes the button, hustles to the diagram, and tries his luck at Buttonholing. After all the members participate, the last player adds the score for the team, and the group with the highest score wins the game.

Begins with Button

Players form couples. Give each couple a sheet of 8½ × 11-inch paper and a pencil. Have the couples sit so that they do not overhear one another.

On signal, each couple writes all the names they can think of beginning with the word "button," for example: "buttonhole stitch" and "buttonmold." After an allotted time, have the couple with the longest list read the words beginning with "button" and give the definitions of the words. The couple with the longest correct list of words they can define win the game.

Some words beginning with "button" and their definitions are:

Word	Definition
button aster	herb
button balance	an assay balance having magnifying lenses for reading the graduations when weighing beads of silver or gold
buttonbur	the cocklebur
buttonbush	a shrub with globular flower heads

Word	Definition
button cactus	a small globe-shaped cactus of Texas and adjacent Mexico which has edible fruit
button chrysanthemum	any of a group of garden chrysanthemums with numerous small heads
button clover	an annual European forage plant, with greenish-yellow flowers
button ear	a dog's ear which falls forward and hides the inside
buttoned	fastened with buttons, adorned with buttons
buttoner	a person who buttons or an item which buttons
button flower	tropical tree or shrub
buttonhead rivet	a bolt with head almost hemispherical in form
buttonhole	an opening for a button, to hold by the buttonhole, to delay one through conversation, to use the buttonhole stitch, to make finished openings for buttons
buttonholer	a person who makes finished openings for buttons
buttonhole stitch	a closely worked loop stitch used to make a firm finish on the edge of material
buttonhook	an item which enables one to draw buttons through buttonholes
buttonmold	a disk to be made into a button by covering with cloth or other material
button sage	black sage
button shoe	a shoe having buttons for fastening
button snakeroot	a plant with long spikes and rounded button-like heads of flowers
button snakeweed	a spiny plant with thistlelike heads of flowers
button stick	a strip of brass which is slotted so that it fits over a row of buttons and enables a person to polish the buttons without soiling the cloth of a military blouse
button strike	a device used by a union to force the members' payment of dues and to prevent the employment of workers who do not possess union buttons
button thistle	the bull thistle
button tree	a shrub or tree with buttonlike fruits
buttonweed	a troublesome weed with buttonlike flowers and fruit
button willow	the buttonbush
buttonwood	the plane tree
buttonwood shrub	the buttonbush

Sew, Brother, Sew

For each team obtain a worn but clean man's shirt with five buttonholes. Remove all the buttons from each shirt, but keep the buttons or obtain five others which fit the buttonholes. Secure a spool of brightly colored thread and a large-eyed needle for each team. Place a straight-backed chair at the goal line opposite each team. Have five couples in relay formation behind the starting line 10 feet from the chair at the goal line. Give the sewing supplies to the boy and the shirt to the girl of each first couple.

On signal, the first couple of each team hurries to the chair at the goal line. The girl puts the shirt around the back of the chair and holds it in place so that the boy can sew the button in the right place. Either partner may thread the needle, but the boy must sew on the button without assistance except verbal suggestions. As soon as the boy sews on the button, the girl takes the shirt from the chair; and the boy picks up the sewing supplies. As the couple rushes to the starting line, the girl buttons the shirt. If the boy drops any of the supplies, the two must stop while he picks up the item before proceeding. Before going to the end of the line, the girl gives the shirt to the next girl and the boy gives his sewing supplies to the next sewer. As the couple hastens to the goal, the girl unbuttons the shirt. Play continues until the boys of each couple sew the five buttons in the correct places. The first team to have the buttons on the shirt and have the girl of the last couple hold up the buttoned shirt wins the game.

What's in a Button?

Collect materials that are used to make buttons. Arrange the display on a table and cover the items with a cloth until it is time to play the game. Give a sheet of 4×6-inch paper and a pencil to each player. Provide chairs for everyone. Be sure the seated players cannot see the items on the table at any time.

Uncover the display of materials for making buttons. On signal, small groups of players observe the items without talking to one another. After everyone has a chance to view the items, each player writes on his paper as many of the items as he can remember. After an allotted time, have the player with the longest list read it. The person with the longest correct list wins the observation game.

Some materials used to make buttons include:

bone	leather
composition	metal
coin	nuts
fabric	paper
fur	pearl
glass	plastic
horn	porcelain
ivory	wood
jewels	

Watch Your Buttons

Provide two large unbreakable buttons for each team. Draw a goal line, and 12 feet from it indicate a starting line. Players stand in files behind the starting line. Give two buttons to the first player on each team.

On signal, the first player places one button on each shoulder and proceeds to the goal line. If a button falls, the player stops, spanks the button, and replaces it on his shoulder. Continue with each player carrying the buttons on his shoulders to the goal line and back to the starting line, giving them to the next player, and going to the end of the line. The team wins the game when it is first to have all its players complete the shoulder button-carrying relay.

Box the Buttons

Provide a chair, three unbreakable buttons, and a box approximately 4×6 inches for each team. Mark a throwing line on the floor. At the goal line, 6 feet from the throwing line, place a box on a chair in line with each team. Players form teams of six and stand in relay formation behind the throwing line. Have each team appoint one player to record the scores for the team members. Give a piece of 3×5-inch paper and a pencil to the scorekeeper on each team. Give three buttons to the first player of each team.

On signal, the first player on each team tosses one button at a time to the box. For each button he gets in he scores five points for his team. Only boxed buttons count. In addition to taking his turn trying to Box the Buttons, the scorekeeper records the score for the team. Each player tosses the buttons in turn and goes to the end of his team. After each player has had a turn, the scorekeeper adds the score, and the team having the highest score wins the game.

Do-It-Together

While advertisements concerning the upkeep of a home frequently stress the do-it-yourself aspect, in the Do-It-Together party the social instinct adds to the fun as the players attempt house hunting, painting, repairing, and landscaping.

Players first meet one another in the defroster, Floor Plans, in which they match the plans for houses. Then they find the exterior of the future home in the socializer, the Dream House Relay.

Scarcely have they moved into the new house when in the brain teaser, Home for Sale, they compose an advertisement to sell the dwelling.

In another defroster, House Hunting, new couples pair up by matching the advertisement with the exterior and floor plan of the house. Doing home repairs follows in the socializers—Laying Linoleum, Speedy Painters, and Nuts to You—and in the creative activity, Screen Patching. In the brain teaser, Regal Neatness, the players select the Queen and King of Neatness to reign in the Land of Do-It-Together.

Depending upon the interest of the players, choose from the three socializers Neighborly Borrowing, Time To Paint, and Let's Start a Garden, the Lawn Planting Relay; and the sense alerters the Fix-It Hand Tools or Paint-Up Time Supplies.

For another group activity select the hose fixers' No More Leaks; for individual performance, the Hose Mending Race. No doubt anyone having done home repairing has experienced a version of the socializer Unexpected Guests, which precedes the creative final activity, Handy Folks at Work.

The supplies for the huge undertaking of moving into one house, selling it, finding another, and settling down to keeping the home and equipment in repair include: magazine pictures of floor plans and exteriors of houses, the real estate section of a local newspaper, small boxes and cartons, some sticks, nuts and bolts, supplies for painting, pieces of old screening, some hand and gardening tools, pieces of old hose, friction tape, and paper and pencils.

Floor Plans

For every two players cut out a floor plan of a house. Mount each plan on a piece of lightweight cardboard and number each one on the back. Cut each floor plan in half in a zigzag manner. Put all of the left halves of the plans in one box and the right halves in another box.

Give each player one half of a plan, perhaps the left for boys and the right for girls. Make certain to distribute both halves of a plan, but not consecutively. On signal, each player seeks the person having the other half of his home plan. The players who piece the halves of the plan together are partners for the Dream House Relay and Home for Sale.

Dream House Relay

Cut out the pictures of the house exteriors for the plans used in Floor Plans. Mount the pictures on lightweight cardboard and number them on the back to correspond with their floor plans. Arrange a table to resemble a real estate display of houses, with "For Sale" signs and brightly colored paper pennants thumbtacked to small sticks attached to the rear and sides of the table. Display the exterior views of the homes for which the players already have the floor plans. The players keep the same partners and floor plans. They form teams of five couples and each team stands in double file behind the starting line, which is located 10 feet from the table or goal.

On signal, the first couple of each team hurries to the real estate display to find the exterior of the house for which they have the floor plans. They may look at the numbers which appear on the back of their floor plans and the pictures of exteriors. As soon as the couple finds the exterior of the house, the two hurry back to the starting line, shake hands with the couple next in line, and go to the end of the line.

Play continues until one team is first to finish, with all couples back in place and possessing the correct exteriors for their floor plans. The players shout in unison, "We have found our Dream Houses," to indicate their victory.

Have the couples keep the floor plans and exterior views of the houses to use in Home for Sale.

Home For Sale

The players keep the same partners and use the floor plans and the exteriors of the houses acquired in the Dream House Relay. Partners sit at tables. Give each couple a sheet of 8½ × 11-inch paper, a pencil, a paper clip, and the real estate classified section of a local newspaper to use for a reference in formulating an advertisement.

On signal, each couple scans some of the advertisements in the local paper, studies the floor plan and the exterior of their home, and then writes an ad telling of the good points of the home. Following the style of the advertisements in the newspaper, the twosome creates an advertisement that is bound to catch a prospective home buyer.

After an allotted time call the writing to a halt. Ask one of the members of each couple in turn to read its advertisement. When each couple has presented its real estate copy, ask the group to decide which advertisement had the most sales appeal.

Have each couple clip its floor plan and exterior picture together and collect them with the advertisements to use in House Hunting.

House Hunting

Put the advertisements written in Home for Sale in one box and place the clipped-together exteriors and floor plans in another box. Give one advertisement to each boy, and an exterior and floor plan to every girl. If boys or girls are outnumbered, give half the players the advertisements and the others the pictures and floor plans.

On signal, all of the players having advertisements try to locate the player with the plan and exterior picture of the home advertised. When the homes and their advertisements get together, the players are partners for succeeding games.

Laying Linoleum

For each couple cut from magazines a picture of a room with linoleum (or asphalt tile) floor covering. Mount each picture on lightweight cardboard. Cut the section of the picture having the floor covering into six zigzag pieces. Hide five pieces of each picture in easily accessible places so that the players will not need to open drawers or move or stand on furniture to find them. Players are in couples. Give each couple one of the remaining pieces of the pictured linoleum.

On signal, each couple look for the other pieces of the linoleum of which they have a sample. The first couple to find the five other pieces and assemble their linoleum floor wins the game.

Speedy Painters

For each team of five couples provide two clean paint cans with wire handles, two clean paint brushes, and an old sheet or other large piece of material to be used for a drop cloth. Place a chair at the goal line 15 feet from each relay team's starting line. Each team of five couples stands in double file behind its starting line.

Give the supplies to the first couple on each team. On signal, the couple hurries to the goal line, one member of the twosome carrying the two paint cans and the other carrying the brushes and the drop cloth. When they reach the chair, which marks the spot for the paint job, they cover the floor with the drop cloth and place the paint cans on it. Each player makes a few brush strokes with one of the brushes. Then, each picking up the supplies which he carried to the goal, the couple hurry back to the starting line and give the supplies to the next couple before going to the end of the line.

The imaginary painting continues until all of the five couples on some team complete all of the steps in the speedy painting and are acclaimed "Speediest Painters."

Nuts to You

Fit together a nut and bolt for each player. Have a variety of sizes for each team. If old nuts and bolts are used, be sure they are clean and the threads are not stripped. Players form teams of six and stand in relay formation behind the starting line. Place a chair at the goal line 15 feet from each team's starting line. On the chair for each team place a pile of six sets of matching nuts and bolts which have been separated.

On signal, the first player of each team hurries to the goal line, searches for a matching nut and bolt in the pile, and assembles the two. Then he hurries back to the starting line, gives his assembled nut and bolt to the next player, and goes to the end of his line. The second player, carrying the first player's nut and bolt, repeats the process and returns to hand both his and the first player's nut and bolt assembly to the third player.

Play continues in this way with each player giving one more nut and bolt assembly to the next player than he received. When the last player has assembled the final set and returned to his place, he holds up the six pairs of nuts and bolts assembled by his team. The first team to indicate in this way that it has finished wins the relay.

Screen Patching

Give each couple a piece of screening (either plastic or wire) with a hole in it, a patch slightly larger than the hole, and a strand of wire or plastic. Couples sit at table. Give a newspaper to each couple to cover the top of the table.

On signal, each couple places the patch on the screening and uses the strand of wire or plastic to fasten the patch in place. The boy maneuvers the wire while the girl holds the patch. The first couple holding up a completed screen patch wins the title "Speedy Patchers."

Regal Neatness

Use this activity after Screen Patching. Have thumbtacks and a yardstick available. Give a slip of 2 × 2-inch paper and a pencil to each couple. Ask the couples to write on their slips "Candidates for Queen and King of Neatness" and their names, and to attach the slip to their patched screening.

Display the screens on a table and let the players select the neatest patch. Roll the screening of the winners around the yardstick and attach it with thumbtacks. Give this "scepter" to the Queen and King of Neatness to use as they reign in the Land of Do-It-Together.

Neighborly Borrowing

Provide for each team of ten players a small carton containing a hammer, a screwdriver, ten nails, ten nuts and bolts, and a sheet of sandpaper. Players form teams of ten, and each team stands in a circle. Designate a starter for each team and give him the carton of equipment.

On signal, the starter of each group dumps the items on the floor in front of him and passes the empty carton to his neighbor on the right. Then he passes, one at a time, the ten nails, ten nuts and bolts, the sheet of sandpaper, hammer, and screwdriver to his neighbor on the right, who is in a borrowing mood. Passing continues with each person "lending" the items to the neighbor on his right, who is equally anxious to borrow. If a player drops an item, he must pick it up and send it on its way before he passes the next article on to his neighbor.

As soon as the last player receives the carton he places it on the floor in front of him and places in it the other items when they come to him. He must note carefully the items he places in the box, for as soon as he receives the last item he shouts, "Thanks neighbors," to indicate his team has finished. The first team to have all the items back in the carton wins the game.

Time To Paint. Wrap the following items in a large sheet or other cloth (dropcloth): clean paint can which has been filled with rocks and the cover replaced, clean paint roller and pan, slacks to wear while painting, small paint brush, and a bar of paint-removing soap. Play the same as Neighborly Borrowing.

Suggestion: Many of these same supplies can be used in the game Unexpected Guests.

Let's Start a Garden. Place the following gardening equipment in a large garden basket: shovel, spading fork, trowel, hand seeder, ball of garden twine, package of seeds, clean dry hose, pruning shears, and a bag labeled "Fertilizer" but containing rags. Play the same as Neighborly Borrowing.

Lawn Planting Relay

Establish a goal line and 20 feet from it indicate a starting line. Players form teams of nine, stand in relay formation behind the starting line, and number off consecutively. Tell the teams that each has recently moved into the Dream House, but it has no lawn.

The teams must perform the steps in building a lawn after the land has been graded and the top soil replaced.

In the relay, each member of the team will pantomime a different step in the process. For example, player Number 1 gathers samples of soil for testing; Number 2 spreads the fertilizer; 3 rolls the ground; 4 removes weeds; 5 sows the seed; 6 covers the seeds lightly with soil by using a brush broom; 7 sprinkles the lawn lightly; 8 mows the lawn; and 9 removes the grass clippings.

On signal, the first player of each team begins pantomiming his assigned activity to the end of his team's "lawn" (the goal line) and back. When he reaches the starting line again he touches the extended hand of the second player, to allow him to begin his work, and goes to the end of his line. In turn the players build up the lawn. When a team has completed its lawn by pantomiming all the steps, the players sit down to relax after the strenuous activity. The first team to thus indicate that their work is finished wins the game.

Fix-It Hand Tools

On a table arrange some hand tools needed in the home workshop, for example:

adjustable cutting pliers	adjustable wrench
screwdrivers	pipe wrench
medium mill file	plumber's force pump
brad awl	3- or 4-inch C clamp
rubber tape	claw hammer
friction tape	carpenter's axe
1-inch wood chisel	cross saw
glue	keyhole saw
sandpaper	6-foot steel tape
jack plane	try square
brace and assorted bits	pocket knife
pump-type oil can	putty knife

Cover the items. Have a sheet of 8½ × 11-inch paper for each couple.

Players pair off and sit facing away from the table. Remove the cover from the table and ask a few couples at a time to come and look at the hand tools display and try to remember what tools are shown. The couples walk slowly past the tools, observe, and silently return to their places. After everyone has viewed the tools, give a sheet of paper and a pencil to each couple to record the names of the tools they remember seeing.

After a reasonable length of time, state the names of the tools which were displayed and let each couple check their own paper. The couple with the longest correct list wins the game.

Paint-Up Time Supplies. Display some supplies needed to paint the exterior of a frame house; then play the same as Fix-It Hand Tools. Some supplies which might be used are:

dropcloth	scraper
stepladder	wire brush
plank	dusting brush
calking gun	putty
calking compound	turpentine
aluminum foil	paint
scraping knife	paint brushes
extension ladder	linseed oil

No More Leaks

Prepare a 2-foot piece of old rubber hose for each group of five by making five different cuts in the hose without cutting through the hose. Have a 6-inch piece of black friction tape for each player.

Players form teams of five and stand in single files. Give a piece of hose to the first player of each team, and to every player distribute a piece of black friction tape 6 inches long.

On signal, each player in turn mends one cut in the hose. As soon as the player puts the tape in place, he passes the hose to the player behind him. The first team to display five neat patches wins the relay.

Hose Mending Race. Players sit in a circle. Give each player a piece of hose 2 inches long with one cut in it and a piece of friction tape 6 inches long.

On signal, each player mends his piece of hose. The winner is the player who first presents a neat hose patch.

Unexpected Guests

Collect duplicate painting supplies for each team (see list). Behind the goal line scatter each team's paint supplies. Ten feet from the goal line establish a starting line. Players stand in teams of eight in relay formation behind the starting line.

Everything is set for redecorating the living room when the doorbell rings. (Ring the doorbell or other bell or chimes for a starting signal.) The third cousins from Fuzzyville are at the door.

When the doorbell rings, the first player hurries to the goal line, grabs the dropcloth, returns to the starting line, places the cloth to the side of the team so that the players do not step on it, and then goes to the end of his line. Play continues with each player picking

up one item at the goal line, placing it on the dropcloth, and then
going to the end of the line. The first team to secure all of the items
from the goal line and place them in the dropcloth wins the game.
Before announcing the winner ring the doorbell frantically to show
the impatience of the unexpected guests.

Painting supplies used for this game might include:

> an old sheet (for the drop cloth)
> an empty paint can cleaned and filled with rocks and the cover replaced
> clean paint rag
> clean roller
> clean pan
> large cloth or sheet for covering furniture
> small paint brush
> stick for stirring the paint
> gallon can labeled "Turpentine"

Suggestion: Many of these supplies can be used in the game
Neighborly Borrowing.

Handy Folks At Work

For each group write on a slip of 3 × 5-inch paper an activity in
which handy folks might engage. Players form groups of six. Give
each group one of the slips and tell them that all of the group
members must take part in pantomiming the activity. All members
of the group may perform the same action, or each may show a
different interpretation of the assigned activity. Allow time for the
players to decide on the actions for their skits.

Call on one of the groups to present its version of the assigned
activity. The other groups try to guess what the handy folks are
doing. If a team correctly guesses the activity portrayed, they are
the next actors. If they have had a turn, they may choose the next
handy folks to dramatize their assigned activity. If no one guesses
the title or action of the activity, the actors announce the title and
ask another group to present its handy workers.

Some activities which have pantomime possibilities are:

> painting the interior of a house
> varnishing a floor with someone stranded in the middle
> making and hanging drapes
> putting on second-floor storm windows on a cold windy day
> repairing the roof after a wind storm
> building a garage
> re-upholstering a chair
> repairing the plumbing
> building an outdoor fireplace
> removing the finish and refinishing furniture

Thrifty Tips

With everyone familiar with the problems of saving money, the party opens with the defroster Franklin's Quips, or words of wisdom for making and retaining a bit of the green. Franklin's mirthful remarks afford a good defroster and party-opener because they bring smiles out of a universal problem.

Many an individual would like to be a horticulturist who nurtures Money Trees successfully. In the socializer Money Trees the players are one step ahead, for they have the opportunity to pick bills designed for the occasion which range in value from $1 to $1000.

To prevent the magic of the Money Trees from upsetting the players' economic senses, the Flight of a Dollar gives the participants a chance to see what happens to the green vagabond from one pay day to another. After seeing how fast the dollar flies, the players go creative in Thrifty Advertising, designing a pictorial advertisement which is used in the guessing game Thrifty Advertising Display, which follows on page 238.

What to use in lieu of cash is the basis of the socializer Barter Relay, and the sense alerter Substitutes for Cash. In the next socializer, For a Rainy Day, the players go through the motions of depositing money in the bank. However, fair weather had better prevail, for the money is imitation.

Honest Abe Lincoln inspires the players in the brain teaser Penny Wise as they closely scrutinize a penny to find the answers to a series of designated questions. In the next brain tickler, Between Paydays, the players try to add a humorous twist to ways to save between those special occasions. While in a thrifty mood, each couple tries to write the longest list of words associated with thrift in the mental enticer Thrifty Twosome.

In the concluding creative game, Economy, the players' pantomimes bring them back to the world of dollars and sense as they dramatically present ways to save money.

For all these Thrifty Tips only the following supplies are needed: imitation money, paper, pencils, crayons, several rubber-type dollars, small wrapped cakes, pairs of inexpensive or available sandals or slippers, items used as media of exchange, several Lincoln pennies, imitation monthly paychecks, and pins. A detailed description of the supplies is listed at the beginning of each game.

Franklin's Quips

Prepare the players by explaining that Benjamin Franklin popularized a common sense philosophy from his personal belief in the advantages of industry and thrift. Many of Franklin's quips are familiar American proverbs. The players can discover the reason Franklin's sayings have lived as they reunite them in this game.

Write each of the Benjamin Franklin quips on a separate slip of paper. Cut each slip in two pieces as shown in the suggestions. Provide half a slip for each player. Put all the first halves in one box, the second halves in another. Be sure to distribute both halves of each quotation. Give each player a pin and half a quotation.

On signal, each player seeks the person having the other half of the thrifty quip. When the two halves of Franklin's quips meet, each player pins on his half, and they are partners.

Some of Franklin's quips which can be used and a good place to split them are given in the following list:

If you would be wealthy,/think of saving as well as of getting.
Beware of little expenses;/a small leak will sink a great ship.
Buy what thou hast no need of,/and ere long thou shalt sell thy necessities.
Wise men learn by others' harms;/fools scarcely by their own.
If you would know the value of money,/go and try to borrow some.
Laziness travels so slowly/that poverty overtakes him.
He that hath a trade/hath an estate.
Industry pays debts,/while despair increases them.
One today is worth two tomorrows;/have you something to do tomorrow?
   Do it today.
Employ thy time well/if thou meanest to gain leisure.
Trouble springs from idleness/and grievous toil from needless ease.
Keep thy shop/and thy shop will keep thee.
Not to oversee workmen/is to leave them your purse open.
He that idly loses five shillings' worth of time/loses five shillings and might
   as prudently throw five shillings into the sea.
'Tis as truly folly for the poor to ape the rich/as for the frog to swell in
   order to equal the ox.

Money Trees

Make duplicate fake money for each team. Make more bills than there are players for each team. Include some $1, $5, $10, $20, $500, and $1000 bills for each team. For each team draw a tree with many branches on a large piece of paper about 60 × 24 inches in size. Mount the drawing of the tree on cardboard, and thumbtack the fake money to the branches. Establish a goal line, and 12 feet from it indicate a starting line. Place the mounted money trees against a wall at the goal line. Have the players form teams and stand behind the starting line in single file formation and face the team's money tree.

On signal, the first player hurries to the money tree and takes the highest denomination bill without dropping the thumbtack or disturbing the money tree. He returns to the starting line, touches the extended hand of the second player, and goes to the end of his team. If a player drops a thumbtack, he must pick it up before continuing.

Continue having each player pick the highest bill off the money tree until everyone has a turn. As soon as the last player returns to the team, ask each team to add the total money picked by its members. The first team to have the most money wins the title of the "best money tree pickers."

Flight of a Dollar

Players form teams of ten. Ask each team to form a circle facing the center. Give one player on each team a real or play-type dollar bill. Since between paydays a dollar passes through the hands of people in varied vocations in exchange for products or services, let each member of every team pretend he represents his favorite trade or profession while playing the Flight of a Dollar.

On signal, the holder of the dollar bill starts passing it around the community circle of persons in varied vocations. Each player passes the dollar to the next person until the starter holds it again. He shouts, "One," and sends it around the circle again. After each flight of the dollar, the starter announces the number of the circuit completed until he receives the dollar the tenth time, when he shouts, "Payday," to indicate his team has won the game.

Thrifty Advertising

Have four players sit at each table. Give a sheet of paper and a pencil to each player. Provide each group with a box of crayons.

Have each group of four decide to represent a company for whose product they will design a pictorial advertisement. Each member of the team draws a design, or all the members make a composite design unless the team prefers that one member make the drawing for the advertisement using the suggestions of the others. Tell the players to use no words, only drawings, to stimulate interest in the chosen product.

Ask each group to label all the designs on the back: "To Sell _____" (name of the product). Collect the artistic advertisements after a designated time for exhibition in the Thrifty Advertising Display game.

Thrifty Advertising Display

Write a number on the lower right corner of each of the designs made in the Thrifty Advertising game. Arrange the drawings as if in an art institute exhibition. Give each player a sheet of paper and a pencil, and count the number of entries in the Thrifty Advertising Display. On the left-hand side of his paper have each player write the numbers of the advertising entries beginning with number one.

On signal, each player visits the display and writes opposite each number the product he thinks the advertisement is trying to sell. After an allotted time, read from the back of the advertisement the article the would-be commercial artists planned to sell. Have each player check his own list. The person guessing all or most of the products suggested by the artistic advertisers wins the game.

Barter Relay

Provide a small wrapped cake for each team. Place a pair of sandals or inexpensive slippers on a chair at the goal line directly in line with each team. Have teams of ten stand in file formation behind a starting line, which should be 12 feet from the chair at the goal line. Give a cake to the first player on each team. Explain briefly to the group the process of bartering.

On signal, the first player, representing a baker, rushes to the chair at the goal line to exchange his cake for a supposedly needed pair of sandals. He takes the sandals to the second player and goes to the end of his team. The second player takes the sandals to the chair and barters them for the cake. Continue with each player bartering the cake and sandals by exchanging them at the chair on the goal line and giving them to the next player before going to the end of the line. The team first to finish bartering and having the cake in the most nearly perfect condition wins the relay.

Substitutes for Cash

On a table arrange items which have been used at different times as media of exchange (see page 239). Cover these items with a cloth until it is time to play the game. Give a sheet of 4×6-inch paper and a pencil to each player. Seat the players so that they cannot see the items on display.

Remove the cover from the items. Call a few players at a time to come and look at the articles or pictures on the table. Have the players walk slowly passed the media of exchange on display, observe, and return to their places without discussing the items.

Ask the players to write the names of as many items as they can remember seeing after everyone has had a turn observing the display. At the end of the allotted time, read the list of substitutes for cash which has been on exhibition. Let each player check his own list. The player with the longest correct list wins the game.

Some items which have been used as media of exchange are beads and other ornaments, cigarettes, copper, coffee, furs, gold, ivory, shells, silver, stones, tobacco, oxen, and sheep (use pictures).

For a Rainy Day

Make duplicate denominations of fake money for the nine players on each team. Add the amount of the nine bills; use the correct total to check the winning team's answer. Form teams of ten. Select a bank cashier for each team. He sits at a table at the goal line facing the file of nine players on his team. The first player stands directly in front of the cashier's table. Give a pencil and a sheet of paper to each cashier. Give the first player on each team a set of the fake money to distribute to the members of his team.

On signal, the first player presents his fake money to the cashier, who records the amount of the deposit while the player goes to the end of the line. Continue with each player depositing his fake money and going to the end of the line. As soon as the last deposit is made, the cashier adds the deposits and announces the total. The first cashier to announce the correct total wins the game for his team.

Penny Wise

Have the players sit at tables. Give each a Lincoln penny, a sheet of paper, and a pencil. Have each player write on the left side of his paper the items he is to try to find on a Lincoln penny as given in the suggestions below. Omit the answers. Remind the players that the answers must be found on the Lincoln penny.

On signal, each player tries to see the relationships of what he observes on the Lincoln penny and the list on his paper. He writes his conjectures on the right side of his paper. After an allotted time, call a halt to the game and read the answers given in the suggestions. The players check their own papers. The individual with the most correct answers wins the game and receives the huge prize: one Lincoln penny.

Some of the items and the answers the players try to find by scrutinizing a Lincoln penny include:

Item	Answer
The name of a song	"America"
A privilege	Liberty
A small animal	Hare (hair)

Item	Answer
A quantity of Indian corn	Ear
Part of a hill	Brow
Something denoting self	I (eye)
Part of a door	Lock (of hair)
A foreign fruit	Date
What ships sail on	Sea (*C*)
A perfume	Scent (cent)
A Chinese beverage	Tea (*T*)
A term for marriages	United (States)
Part of a plant	Leaf
A religious edifice	Temple
A messenger	One sent (cent)
A method of voting	Ayes and noes (eyes and nose)

Between Paydays

Have the players sit at tables in groups of four. Each team selects one person for a recorder. Provide each group with a monthly pay check for the same amount. Give one pencil and two sheets of 8½ × 11-inch paper to each group.

On signal, each group tries to decide upon the most humorous plan for the thrifty spending of the monthly pay check. The recorder jots down the members' suggestions on one sheet of paper. Have each group select one member to read the plan. If necessary, the recorder and spokesman may copy the Between Paydays ideas on the second sheet of paper.

At the end of a designated time, call the planning to a halt. Ask the spokesman for the group to read the group's humorous yet thrifty ideas for spending the pay check. Allow the groups to decide which list is the best.

Thrifty Twosome

Players form couples and sit at tables. For each couple provide a sheet of paper and a pencil. Have the couples sit so that they do not overhear one another.

On signal, each couple writes all the words about thrift that come to mind. After an allotted time, have the couple with the longest list read the words associated with thrift. If the associations with thrift are logical, this couple becomes the "thrifty twosome."

Economy

On one slip of 3 × 5-inch paper for each team write the name of one way to save money, for example: buying bargains, purchasing in large quantities, making over clothes, making and using a budget, paying cash for purchases, and refraining from tapping the piggy bank. Have players form teams of four. Separate the teams so that they can discuss ways to add comedy to the economy pantomimes without being heard by the other teams. Give one slip of economy suggestions to each team.

Allow time for the teams to discuss the actions to pantomime ways to save money. At the end of an allotted time, each team has a turn at making its economy presentation while the other teams try to guess which thrift suggestion is being portrayed. The team that first guesses the correct title of the economy pantomime scores five points, the performing team one point. If no one guesses the title of the pantomime, the group announces the title and has the honor of selecting the next team to present its pantomime. At the end of the economy presentation the team with the most points is awarded the title of being "the most thrifty-minded."

Tell-Tale

Ears, as well as eyes, play a part in the players' enjoyment of the games in this party. The participants are exposed to forms of communication ranging from television and the telephone to signaling and the messenger on foot.

Discovering the name of which hero or heroine is pinned on his or her back gives the player an excuse for approaching others in the defroster Heroes and Heroines. Three socializers ranging from the Simplified Reporting of a story to the Wigwag (one of the earliest forms of communication) and the Pony Express help the players to have a variety of fun.

The sense alerter Sense It? challenges the players' realization of the senses which are used in the various forms of communication. In the socializer Signaling, the players engage in an early device employed to convey messages.

Using the local telephone book in the brain teaser Names and Numbers, Please! brings the party to the home town. Insert the socializer Cleft Relay before the brain teaser Morse Code.

A dramatic relay and socializer, Come Here!, permits the players to take part in the early history of the telephone before engaging in the final creative fun makers, Communications' Cast or Mercury's Messengers.

The supplies for the party include: paper, cardboard, pencils, boxes, men's white handkerchiefs or cloth that size, sticks, small tacks or thumbtacks, pins, music with a galloping rhythm, a record player, shopping bags with handles, envelopes or folded newspaper, strips of cloth and some square pieces, small baskets, unbreakable barrel-shaped glasses, cup hooks, telephone books, current stories from the local newspapers, and a copy of the Morse code. For detailed descriptions of the supplies see the formation and preparation which precedes each activity.

Heroes and Heroines

Secure two small boxes. Label one "Heroes" and the other "Heroines." Have stick pins available. Give each player a slip of paper and a pencil. Have each girl write the name of a television or movie hero on her slip of paper, and ask every boy to write the name of a feminine star on his slip. Collect the girls' slips and place them in the box labeled "Heroes"; place the boys in the heroines' box. Distribute a pin to everyone, a hero's label to each girl, and a heroine's name to every boy. Without disclosing the name of the celebrity, ask the girls to pin their slips on the back of a boy's clothing; the boys pin their slips on the back of a girl's clothing.

On signal, the players scatter. Each player, in his attempt to establish his identity, approaches other individuals and asks them questions which they can answer with "Yes" or "No." When a player guesses the identity of the person whose name appears on the back of his clothing, he requests the person giving him the last clue to remove the label. He pins it on the front of his clothing. Ask the first boy and girl who establish their identity to report to the leader. Play continues until everyone guesses whom he supposedly represents. Then announce the names of the winners, who were the first couple to establish their identity.

Simplified Reporting

For each team cut out a current story from a newspaper. Mount each story on lightweight cardboard and cut it into five pieces. Hide the pieces from each story about the room in places accessible enough that the players do not need to open drawers, move items, or stand on furniture to find them. Players form teams of five, and each team sits at a table.

On signal, each team sets forth to find a story. As a player finds a piece of a story, he brings it to the team's table, and the players try to match the parts together. If a part does not match, the finder rehides the piece where he found it and continues his search. The first team to find five parts of a story and piece them together correctly wins the Simplified Reporting game.

Wigwag

Provide two improvised flags for each team. With small tacks attach a man's white handkerchief or a piece of material that size to a yardstick. Mark a goal line, and 12 feet from it indicate a starting line. Players stand in files behind the starting line. Give two flags to the first player on each team. Tell the players that they are using wigwagging, an early form of signaling in which waving the flag to the left denotes a dash, to the right a dot. In this game, however, the message is very simple: dash, dash, dash.

On signal, the first player hurries to the goal, faces his team, gives the message "dash, dash, dash" by waving the flag in his left hand to the left three times. He merely holds the other flag in his right hand. On completing the signaling the player hurries back to his team, gives the two flags to the next player, and goes to the end of the file.

The relay continues with each player wigwagging the same message. If he drops the flags en route to and from the goal, he must stop and pick them up before proceeding. When he drops a flag or waves it to the right instead of the left, or uses the wrong flag, he must do over his three left wigwags. The team first to have all its players correctly wigwag and return to their starting positions wins the game.

Pony Express

Explain to the players that they are to relive the days of the Old West. Through two thousand miles of wilderness, the pony express riders carried the mail from St. Joseph, Missouri, the western end of the telegraph line, to Sacramento, California, in 1860 and 1861. Riding one pony about 10 miles between stations, the riders brought in the mail in eight days, which was much quicker than by ship, wagon train, or stage coach, which had previously carried the mail. At certain stations, riders as well as ponies were exchanged. When replacements were not available, however, the riders continued on their route, since the mail had to arrive on time if the pony express rider expected to maintain a good record. In the game Pony Express the players take the roles of both the riders and the ponies, as they gallop along the lonely, dangerous road to carry the mail to the waiting relief rider.

Provide music with a galloping rhythm to play while the players ride along their routes. Have either a pianist or record player available. Establish two starting lines 20 feet apart. Players form teams of eight and number off consecutively. The even numbers of each team stand consecutively in a file behind one starting line, and the odd numbers facing them stand consecutively in a file behind the other starting line in shuffle relay formation.

For each team secure a large shopping bag with handles to use for a mail bag and a piece of clean cloth, 6 inches wide and 44 inches long. Partially fill each bag with envelopes to represent the mail. In lieu of the envelopes use folded newspapers. Give the cloth and the mail bag to the first player on each team. Start the music.

On signal, the first player on each team quickly ties the cloth around his waist to hold the handles of the mail bag at his side. Playing the roles of both the rider and the pony, the mail carrier, with the mail bag securely in place, mounts his imaginative pony and starts galloping toward the opposite starting line, the relief station. As soon as he arrives, he hurriedly unties the cloth and gives it and the mail bag containing the precious cargo to the Number 2 player on his team before he goes to the end of the file. Number 2 carries the mail to Number 3 on his team.

The pony express riders continue carrying the mail from the odd numbered players to the even numbered ones and from the even numbered to the odd numbered players, until all eight players have taken a turn. The first team to complete the shuffle relay and shout, "Pony Express arrives in Sacramento, California," wins the relay.

Sense It?

Make a list of some of the means of communication and the sense or senses an individual must employ in receiving them. Players sit in a circle and face the center. Select "it," who stands in the center of the circle, and give him the suggested list.

"It" approaches one of the players in the group and states the name of a means of communication. Before "it" counts to ten the player must point to his eyes, ears, or both, depending upon the senses involved in receiving the form of communication. If the player responds correctly before "it" reaches the count of ten, "it" moves on to another player and tries to catch him. If the player fails to respond correctly, he exchanges places with "it." The outgoing "it" gives the list to the incoming one. When "it" fails to catch a player after three attempts, he selects someone to take his place and joins the group.

The following list names several different means of communication under the sense or senses they employ:

Eyes	*Ears*	*Eyes and Ears*
Wigwagging	Telephone	Television
Smoke signals	Radio	Sound movies

Eyes	Ears	Eyes and Ears
Heliograph (reflection of sun's rays in a mirror)	Morse code	Illustrated lectures
	Sonorous sound	Radar
	Phonograph records	Commercials
Fires or lights on hill-tops	Tape recordings	Sermons
	Conversation	Concerts
Carrier pigeons	Commercials	Recitals
Letters	Drum signals	Plays
Books	Siren	Operas
Magazines	Chimes	Ballets
Newspapers	Bells	Operettas
Silent movies	Clocks	Musical comedies
Photographs	Air-raid siren	Demonstrations
Advertising		

Signaling

In some communities the workmen building a home follow the custom of hoisting a barrel to the roof on its completion to indicate to the new home owners that they expect a meal. Using a barrel for a device to secure attention is not restricted to the men's desire for a free meal, for during the American Revolution the hoisting of a barrel on a stick was a method used for signaling. In addition, these early Americans used a basket and a flag on the stick to indicate other signals. Whether one, both, or none of these items appeared on the stick depended on the message being sent and the meaning of the prearranged signals. Even the bare stick was a significant signal.

In the following game the players try some of the early American techniques of signaling.

For each team of four players provide a stick 3 feet long, a piece of cloth 6-inches square, a small basket, an unbreakable barrel-shaped water glass, and three cup hooks. Fasten the first two hooks 6 inches from the top of the stick and 6 inches apart. Place the third hook 3 inches from the one above it. Pin or sew a piece of tape on the two ends of the cloth or flag to make a loop at the two ends. Tie a piece of tape on the basket, and leave a loop for fastening it on a cup hook. Establish a goal line, and 20 feet away indicate a starting line.

Players form groups of four and stand in files behind the starting line. Give the stick to the first player, the barrel-shaped glass to the second, the basket to the third, and the flag to the fourth.

On signal, the first player of each team hastens to the goal line, turns and faces his team, holds the stick aloft, makes a circle motion with it, and hurries back to his team, where he gives the stick to the second player and goes to the end of the file. The second player takes the stick, places the barrel-shaped glass on the tip of it, and hurries to the goal. He turns, holds the stick bearing the imitation barrel aloft, and, to signal, raises and lowers the stick and barrel twice. Then he hustles back to the team, gives the stick and barrel to the third player, and goes to the end of his team. The third player takes the stick, hangs the basket on the third hook from the top, hurries to the goal, turns, moves the stick containing the barrel and basket twice to the left and twice to the right, and then returns to the starting line, where he gives the signaling device to the fourth player. The fourth player adds the flag on the top two hooks of the stick and is off to the goal, where he turns to face the team, moves the stick forward and back four times before heading for the starting line, where he goes to the end of the file. He holds up the stick, and he and the other members of the team shout in unison, "Our signals helped us to win." The first team to complete the action and announce its success wins the signaling activity.

If during the game any of the items fall, the player must replace them before proceeding to his signaling post or returning to his team.

Names and Numbers, Please!

Provide a local classified telephone directory for each team. Players sit in groups of six a distance apart so that the teams do not overhear one another. Have each group select a recorder. Give a sheet of paper and a pencil to each recorder.

On signal, each team glances through the classified directory, as the members seek the names of various types of companies and institutions engaged in communications (the transfer of thoughts and messages). The team members must dictate to the recorder the exact name and telephone number of the company or institution.

After an allotted time, call a halt to the search, and ask the recorder with the longest list to read his teams' names and phone numbers. Use a directory to check the answers. If the list is correct, the team wins the Names and Numbers, Please! game.

Some of the types of businesses and institutions engaged in communications include:

Advertising agencies	Post office
Bookbinders	Phonograph dealers
Book sellers	Phonograph records dealers
Letter companies	Publishing houses
Libraries	Radio manufacturing
Magazine publishers	Radio repairing
Magazine sellers	Radio stations
Newspaper printers	Recording equipment and supplies

Recording instruments
Recording studios
Schools
Telegraph companies
Telephone answering service

Telephone apparatus
Telephone company
Television broadcasting stations
Television dealers
Television repairing

Cleft Relay

Before the days of democracy a lowly servant carried the mail in a cleft of a long stick so that he would not defile either the message or the person to whom he delivered the mail by touching it. While the servant was delivering the letter, the pole was useful in helping him to vault ditches and streams.

Players form circles of twenty and face the center. The members of each circle count off by twos; the Number 1's become Team 1 and the 2's become Team 2 and face out. Provide each team with a sturdy stick 1 yard long. Make a cut or cleft in each stick 1 foot from the top to hold a letter. Insert a letter in the cleft of each team's stick. Designate a starter for each team, and give him the stick with the cleft holding the letter.

On signal, the starter of each team passes the letter in the cleft of the stick to the player on his right, who sends it on to the next person on his team.

Each person continues in turn to pass the letter in the cleft of the stick to his neighbor until it reaches the last player who stands to the left of the starter. As soon as he receives the letter, he raises the stick and the players on the team shout in unison, "Letter received undefiled."

Morse Code

Players unfamiliar with the Morse code can benefit by a brief explanation of its purpose. Samuel F. B. Morse demonstrated the practicality of transmitting messages over wire by sending a message from Washington, D.C., to Baltimore in 1844. The Morse code is a telegraphic alphabet using the dot, a very brief depression of the telegraph key, and the dash, lasting three times as long as the dot. The time between letters is as long as one dash, and between words as long as two dashes.

On a sheet of 34 × 44-inch paper mounted on cardboard enlarge a copy of the letters of the Morse code as shown under Morse alphabet or code in *Webster's New International Dictionary,* Second Edition. On the Morse code poster include the definitions of dots and dashes as given in the dictionary. Players sit at tables in groups of four so that they can easily read the Morse code alphabet. Have the person who will tap the Morse code practice before the party.

Give a sheet of 8½ × 11-inch paper and a pencil to each player. Have the code sender sit at a table near the code poster and give him a pencil with an eraser to tap the dots and dashes.

On signal, the sender slowly taps out a message. The players watch the enlarged Morse code and write the letters as they are tapped, or the players may write the dots and dashes as they are tapped, watching for the spaces of time between letters and words, and write the letters after the message is completed.

After each short message is completed, allow time for the four members of each group to compare their respective messages and decide on the correct one. Ask one member of each group to read the message the players decided is the correct one. If the message is correct, the group scores five points. All the groups unable to decipher the code score one point for trying. The first group to score fifteen points wins the message-sending game.

Some simple messages to have the players decipher include: "Have fun," "Keep smiling," "Tell-Tale party," "Morse code used," "Try again," "It works," and "Thanks to Morse."

Come Here!

Explain that on March 10, 1876, the first complete sentence was heard on the experimental telephone when Alexander Graham Bell called his assistant and said, "Watson, come here; I want you." Repeating the same words, Mr. Bell made the first transcontinental telephone call linking San Francisco to New York on January 25, 1915. In the game Come Here! the players relive a part of the history of one form of communication as they impersonate both Mr. Bell in making the first transcontinental telephone call and Mr. Watson receiving it.

For each team make two cardboard signs about 25 × 6 inches in size and imprint "San Francisco" on one sign for each team and "New York" on the other sign. Place a table at the goal line for each team and use Scotch tape or masking tape to attach the New York card to it. On the side of the table place a chair. Establish a starting line 15 feet from it and then place a chair for each team directly in line with the table. Fasten the San Francisco card to the chair at the starting line. Players stand in files of six behind the starting line opposite their team's table.

On signal, the first player of each team hurries from San Francisco to New York to impersonate Mr. Bell making the first transcontinental telephone call. He sits on the chair beside the table at the goal line, pantomimes using the 1915 telephone, and says, "Watson, come here; I want you," and then rises and stands behind the table. The next player on each team impersonates Mr. Watson, who receives the message in San Francisco; but unlike the historical event, he dashes for New York, the goal line, as soon as Mr. Bell completes the message. Arriving at the goal he repeats the actions of the first player.

Each player continues playing the dual role of Mr. Bell and Mr. Watson until one team is first to complete the action. The first team to have the last player join the other members in New York and impersonate Mr. Bell (although in his case there is no player in San Francisco to respond) wins the game.

Communications' Cast

On a slip of 4 × 6-inch paper for each group write the name of one means of communication, for example, smoke signal, heliograph, fire or light, telephone, radio, television, book, newspaper, magazine, or letter.

Players form groups of six. Give one of the slips to each group. All members of a group must participate in pantomiming the means of communication even if this necessitates having some of the players duplicate the actions of another player in their group. Allow each group to gather a distance from the others and to decide on the best way to present the assigned means of communication. After an allotted time reassemble the pantomimers.

Call on the first group to present its pantomime while the others try to guess the means of communication being depicted. The first group to guess the method of communicating scores five points and has the honor of selecting the next group to perform. If the successful guessers have not performed, they may select themselves. If no one guesses the method being depicted in pantomime, the actors announce the title, and everyone including the performing group scores one point for trying. The group also has the honor of selecting the next performers. The team with the highest score at the conclusion of the pantomiming wins the game.

Mercury's Messengers. Play the same as Communications' Cast with the exception of writing on each group's slip one way of sending messages.

Some of the methods of sending messages might include:

In 3800 b.c.	Runners carrying important messages
In 1000 b.c.	Dispatching and receiving messages by carrier pigeons
In 1464	Wearing court clothes, a hat with a plume, and carrying the king's mail

In 1851	Sending a letter from New York to San Francisco through the Isthmus of Panama and requiring three months
In 1915	The first airmail service between New York, Philadelphia, and Washington, D.C.
Modern times	A train slowing up slightly in a small town to pick up mail from a special hook by the tracks
	A rural carrier driving on the side of his car nearest the rural mail boxes along the roadway
	Helicopter service between the airport, main post office, and suburban post offices
	Mail man with a cart to deliver mail in the urban areas

Everybody's Birthday

Since everyone has a birthday, each individual has something in common with the other persons at a party even if he does not know anyone. To help the individuals to meet one another, begin the party with the defroster Signs of the Zodiac, a considerably different kind of defroster, which gives the players a reason for talking with one another. Continue with the defroster Each His Own, so that the players find the other persons born under the same zodiac sign.

Follow with Creative Cards, in which each player makes a card for his secret pal, who acquires the original birthday card in the socializer Happy Birthday Relay. Have the players use their birthday cards again in the brain teaser Card Shop.

Whether to include one or all of the four seasonal relays—Winter Shivers, Spring Sprouts, Autumn Shuffle, and Summer Swims—depends on the group and the seasons of the year during which most of the players celebrate their birthdays. The birth dates are disclosed in the first defroster, Signs of the Zodiac.

Receiving a gift is one of the hopes of the birthday celebrant, and the sense alerter Presents fulfills this desire, but it requires the players to guess the contents of the packages. If the social thermometer still registers low, use the defroster Ditto Daters, and either Piecers of Greetings or Rhyme Matchers.

Next to a present the famous symbol of the birthday is a cake, so in the creative Cake Capers each player frosts his own miniature delight, a cupcake, which he consumes during refreshments.

Participating in the Zodiac Symbols, the final socializer, should

help even the most retiring individual to forget himself as he joins
the others in the search for the twelve signs of the zodiac. The
sense alerter Birthday Gems and the creative activity Flower of
the Month conclude Everybody's Birthday.

Before the party provide the following supplies, listed in detail
before each game: cardboard, paper, pencils, crayons, paste, scissors,
old magazines, old birthday cards, extra presents for those who forget to bring them, colored pictures of birthday gems, a cupcake for
each player, and icing supplies.

Signs of the Zodiac

Provide twelve sheets of 8½ × 11-inch paper and twelve pencils
on tables near the entrance to the room. Head each sheet with the
name of a sign of the zodiac and the inclusive dates (see below).

As each player arrives have him sign the sheet headed by the
zodiac sign under which he was born. Have several assistants near
the signs of the zodiac sheets to welcome the individuals and ask
the birthday, not the year, of each person and provide him with the
correct sheet to sign. Have a slip of 3 × 5-inch paper for each
player. Print the name of one of the signs of the zodiac on each
slip. Make extra slips for each of the twelve signs. Give each player
a slip bearing the name of the sign under which he was born, a pin,
a pencil, and a sheet of 8½ × 11-inch paper. Ask each player to
write his name, the month, and day of his birthday on the slip.
(These birthdays can be used in the game Ditto Daters.)

On signal, the players move around the room and try to acquire
as many signatures of persons and the names of the zodiac signs
under which the individuals were born as possible within a designated time.

Take the sheets on which the players signed their names when
they arrived at the party, and tabulate the number of persons born
under each sign of the zodiac. After a designated time, reassemble
the players and ask each person to count and record the number of
persons he found who were born under each of the twelve signs.
Read the results of the tabulation of the sheets signed as the players
arrived. The player whose totals are exactly the same or the nearest
wins the game.

Names of signs of the zodiac, with dates, are as follows:

Aries, the Ram: March 21–April 19
Taurus, the Bull: April 20–May 20
Gemini, the Twins: May 21–June 21
Cancer, the Crab: June 22–July 22
Leo, the Lion: July 23–August 22
Virgo, the Virgin: August 23–September 22

Libra, the Scales: September 23–October 23
Scorpius, the Scorpion: October 24–November 21
Sagittarius, the Archer: November 22–December 21
Capricornus, the Sea Goat: December 22–January 19
Aquarius, the Water Bearer: January 20–February 18
Pisces, the Fishes: February 19–March 20

Each His Own

Make an enlarged copy of the names and symbols of the zodiac on a sheet of paper about 34 × 44 inches. Mount the paper on cardboard the same size, and place it on a central table. Provide pencils also. Use the labels the players are wearing from the Signs of the Zodiac game (see page 251), or provide each player with a 3 × 5-inch slip of paper bearing the name of the zodiac sign under which he was born and a pin.

On signal, the players are off to locate Each His Own—all the other players born under the same sign. When the players can find no other players born under the same sign, they reassemble at the table. Using a pencil, each player draws the symbol of the zodiac on the label he is wearing. He may copy the symbol from the large replica which is on the table.

Delay announcing the winning group until each player wears a label bearing his zodiac symbol. The first group to gather all players born under the same sign and to wear the symbol on their labels wins the Each His Own game.

Suggestion: Save the chart of the zodiac signs and symbols for use in the Zodiac Symbols game.

Creative Cards

For every four players provide old magazines with colored advertisements and a box of crayons, paste, and scissors on a table. For each player have a chair at a table, a sheet of 8½ × 11-inch paper, and a slip of 3 × 5-inch paper. Players sit at the tables. Each player writes on the smaller paper his name, one hobby, and the day and the month that he was born. Collect the slips, mix them, and let each player pick a slip. He may return his own if he draws it and pick a second time. The name which each player draws is his Secret Pal, for whom he will make a birthday card.

On signal, each player selects a picture from the magazines or draws a picture to use in making the birthday card. Each player may use the hobby and season of the year in the good wishes he chooses to extend on the card for his Secret Pal. Ask each card designer to write his Secret Pal's name on the front of the birthday card masterpiece. After a designated time, collect the cards.

Suggestion: Save the birthday cards for use in the Happy Birthday Relay and the Card Shop games.

Happy Birthday Relay

Place the cards made in the Creative Cards game (see page 252) on a long table at the front of the room. Be sure that there is a birthday card for each participant. Use the table for a goal for the teams. Establish a starting line 10 feet from the goal line. Have the players form teams and stand in single files behind the starting line.

On signal, the first player of each team hurries to the table at the goal line, takes the card bearing his name, turns, hustles to the starting line, touches the extended hand of the next person, and goes to the end of his team.

Play continues with each player claiming his birthday card made by his Secret Pal. The winning team is the group that is first to have all its members in place with their birthday cards. The players wave the cards overhead to indicate they have finished.

Card Shop

Display the cards made in the Creative Cards game (see page 252) as if they were in a shop. Attach a number with a paper clip to each card. Players are sitting. Give each player a piece of paper approximately 4¼ × 5½ inches and a pencil. Ask each player to write the following classifications on the left-hand side of his paper: funniest, most clever, most beautiful, most colorful, most original, and most appropriate for the occasion.

On signal, each player visits the card shop to determine which cards he thinks fit into the categories on the left-hand side of his paper. Ask each player to write the number of the card he thinks is best in each classification. When everyone has returned to his place after visiting the card shop, read each classification, and ask the players to state the numbers of the cards they rated as the best for each category. The card receiving the most votes wins the acclaim of the players for being the best in its category. Hold up each winning card so that all the players can admire it. Let each Secret Pal again acquire his handmade birthday card.

Winter Shivers

Explain to the players that since everyone was born during a season as well as on a particular day, birth celebrations could well last a season rather than a day. To help everyone picture some of the possibilities of season-long birth celebrations, the following games allow the players to perform some activity associated with the seasons of the year.

Place a chair at the goal line in front of each team, and establish a starting line 20 feet from it. Divide the players into teams, and have them stand in files behind the starting line.

On signal, the first player of each team pulls his imaginary coat around him and hurries to and from the goal in supposedly the worst blizzard since 1888. Play continues with each player in turn braving the supposed blizzard, to and from the goal, touching the extended hand of the next player on his team, and going to the end of the file. The first team to have all its members pantomime a walk in the blizzard and be back in place wins the game.

Spring Sprouts. Play the same as Winter Shivers with the exception of having each player halt five times on his way to the goal and pretend he is planting a seedling. Between the starting and goal lines ahead of each team, draw five circles at various intervals, or place five cardboard disks on the floor.

On signal, the players hustle to each circle, stop, kneel, pretend to plant a seedling, pat the ground around it, proceed to the goal, and hurry back to the starting line.

Summer Swims. Play the same as Winter Shivers with the exception of having each player use his arms to pretend he is swimming as he proceeds to and from the goal.

Autumn Shuffle. Play the same as Winter Shivers with the exception of having each player pretend he is shuffling through fallen leaves as he proceeds to and from the goal.

Presents

Have each player bring a wrapped unboxed birthday present for a Secret Pal attending Everybody's Birthday party. Use the names of the Secret Pals drawn in the Creative Card game for the recipients of the gifts. Arrange the gifts on a large table at the front of the room. Have several clever but inexpensive wrapped gifts on hand to sell to players who forget to bring a gift. Number the gifts consecutively, beginning with number one. Make the numbers readable, but do not spoil the gift wrapping. Players sit so they can see the gifts and the numbers on them. Give each player a sheet of paper and a pencil, and ask him to write the numbers of the gifts in a column on the left-hand side of the paper, beginning with number one.

On signal, each player guesses what is in each package by looking at the package from where he sits. Each player writes each guess opposite the number of the package on his sheet. After an allotted time, have the players walk by the gifts on the display table and place the Secret Pals' names on the presents. Each player should put the name of the Secret Pal on the present which he brought. If a person cannot recognize his gift, he may place the Secret Pal's name on a similar looking gift which does not have a name.

After everyone returns to his place and a present is labeled for each player, hold up the gift labeled with number one and call the name of the Secret Pal on the present. The Secret Pal claims his gift, opens it, and displays it as each player checks his guess for that particular package. Each player who has guessed the contents of the package correctly gives himself one point. Proceed in the same manner with package number two, and so on, until each player has received a gift.

Verification or contradiction of guesses continues as each player in turn shows his gift and calls on the person with the next number until all gifts have been viewed. The players then add their scores. While the one with the highest scores wins the game, everyone has a present.

Piecers of Greetings

For every two players cut the illustrated part of an old birthday card in half in a zigzag manner. Put the first half of each card in one box; the second half in another. Assemble the players and give half a birthday card to each player. Be sure to distribute both halves of the cards but not consecutively.

On signal, each player tries to find the person holding the other half of the birthday card. When the two players find one another and piece the card together, the individuals are partners.

Rhyme Matchers. Cut the verse section of each card in half. Each player seeks the person having the other half of the rhyme. Play the same as Piecers of Greetings.

Ditto Daters

Have the players wear the labels used in the Signs of the Zodiac game. Ask them to add the date to the labels if they are not already on them.

On signal, each player looks for the other players having a birthday on the same day of any month; for example, all players having a birthday on the eighth of any month look for one another. After a designated time, ask each ditto-dater group to join hands and count its members. Have the largest group come to the front of the room. If it is so that all of them celebrate their birthday on the same day, the members are the winning Ditto Daters. The other players sing "Happy ditto dates to you" to the tune of "Happy Birthday." In place of the person's name in the "Happy Birthday" song say, "dear dittos."

Cake Capers

Provide enough table space so that each player can frost a cupcake. Cover the tops of the tables. On each table put a dish containing white frosting, food coloring, a spoon, knife, cake decorating tube, and waxed paper. Players sit at the tables. Give each player the following: a small piece of paper, a pencil, a cupcake, a small paper plate, two paper napkins, an apron or its substitute, a large clean dishtowel.

On signal, each player begins decorating a birthday cupcake. Allow time for the more skilled to achieve a virtual work of art but not so much time that the unskilled decorator becomes bored. At the end of the allotted time, have each player transfer his cupcake from the waxed paper to the paper plate. Have each player write his name on the slip of paper and place it with his decorated birthday cupcake.

Place the decorated birthday cupcakes on a table for everyone to admire. Allow the players to decide on the most "birthday-like decorated cupcake." The winner has the honor of helping to serve the birthday cupcakes.

Suggestion: Use the decorated cupcakes for part of the party refreshments.

Zodiac Symbols

On sets of twelve 3 × 5-inch slips of paper of a different color for each team, draw the twelve zodiac symbols. Have also one extra slip of each color. Leave this slip blank. On a table for each team place this blank slip as a sample of the color of the set of symbols the team is to find. Place the sets around the room so that they can be found without opening drawers, moving items, or standing on furniture. Players form teams of four, and each team gathers near its table. On signal, each team looks at the sample colored slip on the table and goes in search of the twelve zodiac symbols which appear on the slips of the corresponding color. The first team to find the twelve symbols on the slips of the team's color and to arrange the symbols in their correct order wins the game.

Suggestion: The enlarged copy of signs and symbols of the zodiac made in Each His Own may be used for checking the order of the symbols.

Birthday Gems

Provide a table at the front of the room. Obtain colored pictures of the twelve gems representing the months of the year (see below). *Webster's New International Dictionary* (unabridged) displays a page of gems including the birthday gems. Cover the pictures until it is time to play the game.

Have the players form teams of four. Each team sits a distance from the other units so that the players cannot overhear one another. Have each team select a birthday gem expert to act as recorder for the team. Give each recorder a pencil and a sheet of paper with the months of the year written in a column on the left-hand side of the paper, or request the recorder to write the names of the months.

Uncover the pictures of the birthday gems. Ask the members of one team at a time to view the pictures, try to select the twelve birthday gems, and return to their places without discussing the gems with one another. After everyone views the gems and is in place, the birthday gem expert of each team records a birthday gem opposite each month of the year as the members of the group suggest the gems.

After a designated time, read the teams' lists. The team naming all or most of the gems correctly wins the game. The birthday gems include:

January—garnet
February—amethyst
March—bloodstone
April—diamond
May—emerald
June—pearl
July—ruby
August—sardonyx
September—sapphire
October—opal
November—topaz
December—turquoise

Flower of the Month

Write the name of a flower of the month on a slip of paper for each team (see list). Have the players sit in teams of six so that they do not overhear the plans for the pantomimes of the names of the flowers. Allow time for each group to decide which action to use in pantomiming the name of the flower on its slip. All the members must participate by using actions, gestures, impromptu conversation, or facial expressions to convey the name of the flower of the month.

On signal, each team takes a turn presenting a charade by dramatizing the name of the assigned flower of the month by syllables, by words, or by both. One player on the team reveals which system of pantomiming is being used.

The team first to guess the correct title of the charade being presented scores five points and gains the right to present the next pantomime or select the next group if the members have already had a turn. If the team knows the month the flower officially designates, an additional point is scored. If the flower is not guessed by the time all the syllables or words are presented, the actors repeat the complete dramatization with no breaks between words or syllables. If no one guesses the name of the flower, the actors announce it and select the next team to present a charade. After everyone has presented its dramatization, the team with the highest score wins the Flower of the Month game.

Suggestions: Since less than twelve teams will participate in most instances, the flowers are listed according to their pantomiming possibilities. In some of the names the syllables take a creative turn to improve this possibility.

Flower	*Charade Possibility*	*Month*
Larkspur	*lark*—a songbird	July
	spur—part of a cowboy boot; urging someone to go to work	
Honeysuckle	*honey*—bees; putting a spread on bread	June
	suck—drinking through a straw	
	ell—dining area; letter of the alphabet; overhead railroad	
Violet	*vie*—a contest	February
	oh—exclamation	
	let—permitting, renting	
Gladiolus	*glad*—showing happiness	August
	iol—yodeling (in the mountains)	
	us—pointing at self and other member or members	
Carnation	*car*—driving an auto	January
	neigh—sound of a horse	
	shun—person avoiding someone or something; driver deciding to pass a hitchhiker by	
Jonquil	*John*—a man's name	March
	quill—writing with a quill pen	

Flower	Charade Possibility	Month
Lily of the Valley	*lily*—buying mother an Easter gift *off*—falling from a cliff *the*—pointing out an object *valley*—mountains and valleys	May
Cosmos	*cause*—talking about the reason why *moss*—feeling at the base of a tree	October
Sweet Pea	*sweet*—putting sugar in tea; eating a candy bar *pea*—shelling peas	April
Narcissus	*nar*—the word "no" with a twang *sis*—brief for sister *us*—pointing at self and other player or players	December
Aster	*Asked her*—an old-fashioned proposal	September
Chrysanthemum	*Chris*—talking about a boy named Christopher *ant*—anthills; ants crawling *he*—pointing at a boy *mum*—showing silence	November

Time's Afleeting

In the Time's Afleeting party the theme develops through a variety of concepts of time, so the leader may select the defroster he decides best for his group: Noting Notes, an up-the-scale game; Varied Tempo, a rhythmic partner finder; or the historical Time Tellers. If the leader wishes to use all three defrosters at the beginning of the party, he may use them in the given order.

Continue with several of the socializers—Change of Shifts, Finding a Year, Yearly Happening, and Unusual Year—and one of the relays, Father Time and Head Saves Heels. Then give the party-goers an opportunity to test their memory power by thinking of words they associate with time in the brain teaser Time Associators. In International Date Line, another workout for the mental processes, the players have a chance to cross the date line and discover how to gain or lose a day. Other brain teasers to include are Telling Time and Saving Time.

To conclude the party in the dramatic vein select one or more games from the creative fun makers: Troupe Time, Last Minutes, Clocks, and Headlines.

A detailed description of the required supplies appears before each activity. In general, the items needed to play the games are white and colored paper, pencils, several old sheets, some lengths of rope, a few trays loaded with unbreakable items, thumbtacks, maps showing the section of the world crossed by the International Date Line, simple devices used to tell time before the invention of clocks, and timely headlines from local newspapers.

Noting the Notes

Draw musical notes of different time values (whole notes, half notes, etc.) or cut them from old sheet music. Paste one kind of note on two 3 × 5-inch slips of paper (for example, a quarter note on two slips, an eighth note on two slips). Make a slip for each player. Place one slip of each kind in a box and the duplicate in another container. If the group is large, one kind of note may be used on more than two slips, but make the same number of slips for each kind of note.

Distribute one slip to each person. On signal, each player tries to find the other player holding the slip with the kind of note he possesses. When the two meet, they are partners. The first two players matching the notes win the game. Continue playing until everyone has a partner.

Varied Tempo. Write on duplicate slips musical terms for tempo. Players are to move in the tempo written on their slips and search for others enacting the same tempo. Some terms which might be used are:

Presto—very fast
Vivace—lively
Andante—moderate speed
Largo—very slow and stately
Accelerando—increase speed gradually
Ritardando—decrease speed gradually

Play the same as Noting the Notes.

Time Tellers. Write on duplicate slips the name of a time-telling device. Play the same as Noting the Notes. Some time-telling devices might be:

time candles	sundial
hourglass	clock
burning knotted ropes	watch

Change of Shifts

Players sit in a circle and count off by threes. The 1's form Shift 1; the 2's, Shift 2; and the 3's, Shift 3. Select one person to be "it."

"It" stands in the center of the circle and says, for example, "Shift 1 and Shift 2 change!" The players in the two shifts called must find new places, while "it" tries to secure one of the momentarily vacant seats. If "it" succeeds, the player without a place becomes "it." If "it" fails to secure a place, he returns to the center of the circle and calls two other numbers: "Shift 2 and Shift 3 change!" or "Shift 1 and Shift 3 change!" If after three attempts "it" fails to secure a place, he selects someone to take his place.

Finding a Year

Write each of the twenty-four Japanese names for months (see below) on a separate slip of 3×5-inch paper. On twenty-four separate slips of another color write the twelve Dutch names and the twelve Navaho names of months (see below). Make duplicate sets of twenty-four slips, each set in a different color, for each extra team if there will be more than two. Before the game hide the slips in places where they are partially visible so that players will not need to move anything, open drawers, or stand on furniture to find them.

Players form teams of about twelve players. Designate a table as home base for each team where it will assemble the year after finding all its slips. Give each team a blank slip of the color it is searching for.

On signal, the members of each team look for the slips of the color of their sample. As soon as a team has found all twenty-four slips the members arrange them in the correct order at their home base. The first team to correctly arrange all the months wins the game. Suggest that the winners help the other players find their missing months so that everyone may add a year.

The names of the months to use are the following:

JAPANESE *

In Japanese, each of our months is divided into two.

| *January* | *July* |
| Little Cold | Little Heat |

| *January* | *July* |
| Great Cold | Great Heat |

* From P. W. Wilson, *The Romance of the Calendar* (New York: W. W. Norton & Co., Inc., 1937), p. 57. Copyright, 1937, by P. W. Wilson.

February Rise of Spring	*August* Rise of Autumn
February Rain Water	*August* Limit of Heat
March Awakening of Insects	*September* White Dew
March Vernal Equinox	*September* Autumn Equinox
April Clear and Bright	*October* Cold Dew
April Cereal Rain	*October* Frost Fall
May Rise of Summer	*November* Rise of Winter
May Little Filling	*November* Little Snow
June Grain in the Ear	*December* Great Snow
June Summer Solstice	*December* Great Cold

DUTCH **

January Snowing Month	*July* Harvest Month
February Rainy Month	*August* Heat Month
March Windy Month	*September* Fruitful Month
April Budding Month	*October* Vintage Month
May Flowering Month	*November* Foggy Month
June Meadows Month	*December* Freezing Month

** *Ibid.*

NAVAHO *

| January | July |
| Melting Snow (probably) | The Big Sugar Cane |

| February | August |
| Eaglets | Light Ripening |

	September
March	Harvest, the Great Ripe
(meaning is obscure)	

	October
April	Ghaji "back to back"
Short Corn	White of winter and yellow of summer meet. Turning backs to one another, one advances, the other retraces its steps.

| May | |
| Tall Corn | |

| June | November |
| Month of Planting | Light or Slender Wind |

December
Much or Big Wind

Unusual Year. Prepare four sets of twelve 3 × 5-inch slips, all the same color. On each slip of one set write one of the Dutch names of the months; on each slip of the second set write one of the Navaho names; and on each slip of the third set write both of the Japanese names for one month (see pages 261–62). On each slip of the fourth set write one of the Roman names for the months (see below). Hide the slips as for Finding a Year.

Players form four teams and each team selects a captain to stand at the team's table and assemble the year. Each group is to find slips to make one year which may be any combination of Japanese, Dutch, Navaho, and Roman names as long as it has all twelve months, January through December.

On signal, the players begin the search for the slips. When a player finds a slip he hurries to the team's table and gives it to the captain, who places it in its correct position in the year. If the slip names a month the team already has, the player must return it to the place where he found it before seeking one of the missing months.

Hunting for the months continues until one team completes its year. If the months are in the correct order, the team wins the game.

* Material about the Navaho months of the year obtained from *Ethnologic Dictionary of the Navaho Language,* written and published by the Franciscan Fathers, St. Michael's, Arizona, 1910.

The Roman names of the months and a brief note about their meaning which can be used are as follows:

January
Derived from the double-faced god, Janus, who gazed back at the old year and forward to the coming one

February
From the Roman religious festival, Februa, held on February 15, a day of purification and dedication

March
From Mars, god of war and protector of the fields

April
Associated with the Latin *aperire*, "to open"; and the opening of flowers

May
From Maia, goddess of increase and growth

June
Derived from Junius, name of a Roman family

July
Named for Julius Caesar

August
Named for Augustus Caesar, first Roman emperor

September
Septem, Roman number 7

October
Octo, Roman number 8

November
Novem, Roman number 9

December
Decem, Roman number 10

Yearly Happening

For each team make four sets of twelve 3 × 5-inch slips. On one set for each team write the Dutch names for the months; on the second set write the Navaho names; on the third, the Roman names; and on the fourth, the Japanese names, putting both Japanese names for one of our months on the same slip (see pages 261–62 and 264). Place a table for each team at the goal line and on each table place the team's four sets of slips face down. Indicate a starting line 15 feet from the goal.

Players form teams of twelve and stand in files behind the starting line. Beginning with *January* for the first player, each player on every team is assigned a month of the year, the twelfth player being *December*.

On signal, the *January* of each team hurries to his team's table and finds the slips bearing the Dutch, the Japanese, the Navaho, and the Roman names for his month. The player who finds them and returns to his place first scores three points for his team. All others score one point for trying. Play continues with the players finding the slips and returning to their places as quickly as possible in order to score. The team with the highest score when the teams have completed their years wins the game.

Father Time

For each team prepare a Father Time costume. In the middle of an old sheet cut a slit large enough to slip over the player's head, and provide a soft rope a yard and a half long. Establish the goal line and 20 feet from it indicate a starting line. Players form teams and stand in single files behind the starting line. Give the Father Time costume to the first player on each team.

On signal, the first player on each team slips into his robe (the sheet), ties the rope around his waist, and pretends that he is carrying a scythe. Each player moves on noiseless feet to the goal and back, cutting time with his imaginary scythe. Returning to the starting line he removes his costume, gives it to the next person, and goes to the end of the line.

The Father Time relay continues with the players impersonating the old gentleman. The efficiency and speed with which Father Time's scythe cuts time determines the winning team, for the first group to have all of its costumed Father Times make the complete trip wins the relay.

Head Saves Heels

For each team provide a tray loaded with more unbreakable items than can easily be carried on it. Establish a goal line and 20 feet from it indicate a starting line. Players form teams and stand in single files behind the starting line. Give a loaded tray to the first person on each team.

On signal, the first player on each team carries the tray cautiously to the goal line and back, hands the loaded tray to the next player, and goes to the end of his line. If a player drops any items, he must stop, put the tray on the floor, replace the item, and proceed on his round trip to and from the goal. The team which is first to finish, because its players have saved time by using their heads and proceeding carefully, wins the game.

Time Associators

Prepare a list of words having some relation to time (see list). Players form groups of four and sit at tables, each group separated from the others so they do not overhear one another. Have each group select a recorder. Give each player a sheet of 8½ × 11-inch paper and a pencil. Distribute an extra sheet of paper to each recorder.

Slowly read the list of words that are related to time and have everyone write the word that he associates with each. After reading the entire list, ask the players in each group to confer and select from each individual's words the time associators that are not duplicated in the group. The recorder makes a composite list of these words.

Ask the recorder with the longest list to read it. If the associations with the given words are logical, the group wins the title of "Best Time Associators."

Some of the words to include in the list of words having some relationship to time include:

Minute	Eternity
Moment	Hour
Day	Opportunity
Year	Perpetuity
Calendar	Century
Clock	Week
Rhythm	Month
Watch	Second

International Date Line

For each team of five players make a map of the world showing the meridian 180°, the Arctic Circle, Tropic of Cancer, Equator, Tropic of Capricorn, and the Anarctic Circle. Also indicate Alaska, the Aleutian Islands, the Hawaiian Islands, New Zealand, and Australia on the maps. Mount the maps on cardboard and place a map on a table opposite each relay team. Establish a starting line 10 feet from the tables or goal line. Players stand in file in teams of five behind the starting line. Give five thumbtacks to the first player on each team to distribute to his teammates.

Remind the players that one can gain or lose a day, depending upon whether he crosses the International Date Line from the east or the west. By locating the meridian of 180° the players will re-establish the line selected by mariners as the place for "changing dates."

On signal, the first player of each team hurries to the map at the goal and places his thumbtack at the place where the International Date Line crosses the Arctic Circle. Returning to the starting line, he touches the extended hand of the next player before going to the end of the line.

In turn each player hustles to the map and places his thumbtack where the date line crosses each of the following: Tropic of Cancer, Equator, Tropic of Capricorn, and the Anarctic Circle. The winning team is the fivesome which first correctly places its thumbtacks along the International Date Line.

Telling Time

On a table arrange some devices that were used for telling time before the manufacture of clocks; for example:

alarm candle	—A shoe is tied to a pin stuck in the candle. When the candle burned to the pin, the shoe dropped and awakened the sleeper.
six time candles	—Each candle is 12 inches long and 3 inches wide, with alternating 3-inch wide strips of black and white. The candles burned 3 inches in an hour, so when six candles had burned, twenty-four hours had passed. (In lieu of 3-inch wide candles use ones that are readily available.)
lamp wick knotted at intervals	—The passage of time was indicated by the number of knots which had burned.
egg timer	—A small sandglass.
sun dial	—If a sun dial is not available, draw one on a flat surface; mark the twelve hours and indicate the gnomon or style which casts a shadow on the dial, showing the time of day.

Cover the display until time to play the game.

Players form groups of four which sit in separate parts of the room facing away from the table. Have each group select a recorder; give him a sheet of 8½ × 11-inch paper and a pencil.

Uncover the display. Ask each group in turn to pass the table and observe the time-tellers. Players may not discuss the items. After everyone has observed the display, ask the recorders to write on the sheets of paper their group's version of how time was told by using the displayed devices.

After an allotted time call the recorders to the display table. Have each recorder in turn tell his group's ideas about how each device was used. For correct explanation the group scores five points. All other groups having the same answer also score five points. All others score one point for trying. The team with the highest score wins the game.

Saving Time

Players form teams of four which sit at separate tables so that they cannot overhear each other. Ask each team to select a recorder. Give the recorders pencils and sheets of 8½ × 11-inch paper.

On signal, each team begins thinking of ways of saving time. Suggest that the players try to think of different and unusual methods, for the team with the most original ideas will win. The recorder for each team writes down his team's ideas.

Give the signal to stop and have each recorder read his list of time-savers. For each idea that everyone agrees is possible the team scores. If no other team thought of it, the idea scores five points. If two teams have the same idea, each scores four points; three teams with the same method each score three points; four teams with identical ideas score two points each; and if more than four thought of it, each scores one point. The team with the highest score after all ideas have been read wins the contest.

Troupe Time

On a 3×5-inch slip for each team write the name of a time of the day or year which the team is to dramatize—for example, bedtime, coffee time, seeding time, harvest time, blossom time, winter time, and vacation time. Players form groups of six in separate areas so that they cannot overhear one another. Give each group one of the Troupe Time slips. Allow time for each group to decide on the best way to present its dramatization. All the members of a group must participate. If the players write a brief play, one person may read the lines while the others pantomime the action. Some groups may decide to use impromptu conversation, and others may use pantomime entirely to portray the time of the day or year. The method of presentation is the group's choice. At the end of the allotted time reassemble the groups.

Call on the first group to present its dramatization. All of the other groups try to guess the time of day or year being depicted. The first group to guess scores five points and has the honor of being next to perform. If the group has had a turn, it may select another group to present its dramatization. If no one guesses what is being depicted, the actors announce it, choose the group to perform next, and everyone, including the performing group, scores one point for trying. The team having the highest score after all groups have presented their skits wins.

Last Minutes. Play the same as Troupe Time except have each group dramatize one of the following situations.

Mother, father, four-year-old son, and six-year-old daughter are ready to leave grandmother's home when they discover that their dog is missing. Everyone, including grandmother, combs the neighborhood and shouts frantically for an hour before Flighty is found and put in the family car. Amidst panting, farewells are finally made.

An elderly lady wants a special kind of material for a dress for her three-year-old granddaughter. Dozens of bolts are draped across the counter, but grandmother and the three-year-old cannot get together on their selection. It is a minute before closing time and the clerk has a date. The other clerks and the store manager are trying to put the bolts away, but an elderly lady and a three-year-old at odds in selecting material can make it difficult.

Office employees the last ten minutes before quitting time, with the boss gone for the day.

A family at breakfast with everyone due at work or school at a different time.

One teacher is trying to assist the last four children in a kindergarten class in getting bundled up for the trip home through a snowstorm. However, the four youngsters insist the outer attire is not being put on "like mother does it."

Four hungry children and mother are waiting dinner for father, who is usually late because of a last-minute job at the office but insists that the family dine together.

Clocks. Play the same as Troupe Time. Have each group present a scene in which a certain kind of clock plays an important role. Some kinds of clocks to assign are: grandfather clock, radio-alarm clock, loud-ticking shrill-belled clock, timer clock on a cooking range, banjo clock, and cuckoo clock.

Headlines. Play the same as Troupe Time except have each group dramatize a timely headline from a current newspaper.

South of the Equator

Crossing the equator means a world of fun for the partygoers, from the time they all get acquainted to the finale when they dramatize some incidents associated with the tropics.

To start developing a friendly feeling use one or both of the defrosters, Country Match and Casual Meeting. The socializer, Map Making, acquaints the players with the countries south of the equator. Next, the brain teaser, South Bound, helps the players pack for the trip.

Arriving south of the equator the players participate in the activities of the native people and the animals in the socializers Going to Market and Kangaroo Hoppers.

Even during a brief stay, visitors acquire impressions of their surroundings, so in the brain teaser, Tropical Thoughts, the players list what they associate with the tropics. In the socializer, Trade Winds, the players discover the significance of currents of air, as they attempt to blow an object into the opposing team's territory.

Choose between the brain teasers Warm Words, Touring, and

Southern Itinerary before the players test their senses in the sense alerter, Aromas and Textures, and compete in the culminating creative fun maker, Tropical Troupes.

The supplies required for the trip south of the equator include paper, pencils, boxes, maps or copies of the southern hemisphere, bushel baskets, vegetables, trays containing unbreakable items which are substitutes for actual native crafts, table tennis balls, and tropical products that are easily obtained.

Country Match

For every two players make duplicate 3 × 5-inch slips with the name of a country south of the equator (see page 274 for suggestions). Put one slip of each set in one box and the duplicates in another. Assemble the players and give one slip to each player, slips from one box to boys and from the other to girls, if there are the same number of each. Be sure to distribute both slips of each set, but not consecutively.

On signal, each player tries to find the person holding the slip with the same name as his. When the two players find one another, they are partners for some of the subsequent games.

Casual Meeting. On duplicate slips for every two players write the names of cities and towns south of the equator (see page 274 for suggestions). The players casually meet in the towns or cities named on their slips. Play the same as Country Match.

Map Making

Obtain or make for each team a map of the world south of the equator. See that the names of countries and boundaries show on the maps. Mount the maps on light-weight cardboard. Carefully cut each country out of the map, leaving the boundaries so the players can reassemble it. Before the party place the cut-out countries in partially visible places so the players will not have to open drawers, move items, or stand on furniture to find them.

Players form teams of five and sit at separate tables. Place a map from which the countries have been removed on each team's table.

On signal, the players search for the hidden countries. As each player finds a country, he returns to his team's table and tries to fit the piece into the team's map. If he finds a piece which the team already has located, he must return it to the original hiding place.

The first team having all of the countries south of the equator fitted into their map calls, "We're south of the equator." If the map is correctly reassembled, the team wins the game.

South Bound

Have players form two teams, which sit facing one another. Designate one as Team 1, the other as Team 2. Give the last player on each team a sheet of 8½ × 11-inch paper and a pencil for keeping score. Have a watch or clock.

Name a letter of the alphabet, for example C. Allow the first player on Team 1 just 10 seconds to name some item beginning with that letter that he wishes to take with him on his trip south of the equator. He may say "camera," or an object modified by a word beginning with the letter C, such as "colored film." If the player responds correctly, he scores one point, which the scorekeeper for his team records. Play continues with the first player on Team 2 attempting to name another article beginning with the same letter. The teams alternate in this way, each player naming an article which has not been named previously. If one player cannot answer in the allotted time, the next player on the other team has a chance. If he is successful, play proceeds. If he is not, give the players another letter of the alphabet to use and continue until all members of both teams have had a turn. The team with the highest score wins the game.

Some of the items the players may wish to take with them include:

A—apparel, aspirin, airmail envelopes
B—books, binoculars, blouse, bathing suit
H—hat, housecoat, handkerchief, halter
M—manicure set, money, makeup, medicine, magazines
P—pen, pants, pajamas, purse
S—shirt, stockings, socks, sweater, suitcase, suit, shaving supplies, shorts, stationery, sun hat, sun suit, sun glasses, swimming trunks

Going to Market

Provide a half-bushel basket for each team and fill it almost to the top with crumpled paper. On top put some vegetables, such as a cabbage, potatoes, onions, and carrots or beets with tops. Secure unbreakable plastic dishes or other items to represent native ware and put some of them on a large tray for each team. Place a chair at the goal line 20 feet from each team's starting line.

Have players form teams of five couples each and stand in double file behind the starting line. Give a basket to the first boy on each team and a tray containing supposed native dishes to the first girl.

On signal, the boy places the basket on his shoulder and the girl places the tray on her head, each holding the burden with one hand.

The couple then carries its wares to market, the chair at the goal. Going around the chair, the couple heads back to the starting line, where they give the items to the next couple before going to the end of the team. Going to market and returning continues until one team wins the relay by being first to have all five couples complete the round trip.

Kangaroo Hoppers

Have the players stand in teams of ten in single files behind the starting line. Place a chair at the goal line 15 feet from each team's starting line.

On signal, the first player on each team assumes the kangaroo's standing position and hops to the goal, circles the chair, and hops back to the starting line where he touches the front paw (hand) of the next kangaroo before going to the end of his line.

Play continues with the players of each team hopping to and from the goal in kangaroo style. The first team to finish with all members in their original places are the "Champion Kangaroo Hoppers" and wins the game.

Tropical Thoughts

Couples sit at tables where they cannot be overheard by others. For each couple provide a sheet of 8½ × 11-inch paper and a pencil.

On signal, each couple writes all of the thoughts that they associate with a trip to the tropics. After a designated time have the couple with the longest list read the twosome's "tropical thoughts." If the associations with the tropics are logical, the couple wins the game.

Some associations with a trip to the tropics might be:

new foods	throwing away the snow shovel
tree-ripened fruits daily	skidless driving in the winter
basking in the sun on a beach	luxurious growth
cool clothes	several crops in a year
permanent sun tan	islands
no heating bills	South Sea island music

Trade Winds

Provide a table and a table tennis ball for every four players. Have extra balls available for replacements. Print the word "Equator" in the center of an area 12 inches wide in the middle of each table. One couple stands at one end of its table and the other couple stands at the opposite end. One couple is the northern hemisphere and the other is the southern hemisphere. One player of each couple is captain and the other is scorekeeper.

Explain to the players that the trade winds which blow toward the equator are deflected by the rotation of the earth, but in this game the breath of the players in the northern and the southern hemispheres sends objects over the equator.

On signal, one of the captains at each table places the table tennis ball on the word "Equator." Immediately both couples blow at the ball in an attempt to keep it away from their hemisphere. Each time the ball is blown out of the equator area into one of the hemispheres, the couple which blew it there scores five points, and one of the captains replaces the ball on the word "Equator."

Play continues with both couples trying to keep the ball away from their hemisphere. Whenever the ball goes off the table, one of the captains replaces it on the word "Equator" and the human trade winds continue to blow. The first team to score twenty-five points wins the game.

Warm Words

Make a set of alphabet cards for each team on 8½ × 11-inch cardboard, printing each letter on a separate card. Use different colored crayons for making each set. Have a large sheet of paper and a dark crayon for recording scores.

Players form teams of about 12 players which stand about 10 feet apart. Indicate a spelling line for each team. Give a set of letters to each team, but do not distribute the letters J, K, V, W, X, and Z in any set. Give the vowels (A, E, I, O, and U) to the first five players on each team and distribute the consonants equally among the rest of the players. Explain that if any player holds two or more consonants which appear in the word to be spelled, he gives one card to a player whose letters are not needed in that word. When the substitute returns from the spelling line he returns the card to the original holder.

Call a word (see suggestions p. 274), and the players from each team who hold the letters appearing in the word rush to their spelling line, arrange themselves in order to spell the word, and hold up their letters in front of them. When one letter appears twice consecutively in a word, for example R in "torrid," the player waves his card back and forth to represent twin letters. If a letter appears two or three times separately, for example A in "alpaca," the player hurries between the places where the letter belongs.

The team which is first to line up in the correct order with the letters held right side up in front of the players scores three points. Give the other team one point for trying and record both scores. The team which first scores fifteen points wins the contest.

Some words to include in the speedy spelling are:

alpaca	hot	parched
arid	Indian Ocean	sultry
coconut	island	superb scenery
desert	llama	tortoise shell
equator	lush	torrid
gorgeous	magnificent	tropics
heat	palm	Tropic of Capricorn
hibiscus	papaya	tropical medicine

Touring. Play the same as Warm Words except use all of the letters of the alphabet.

Some names which might be used in this game are:

Adelaide	Melbourne	Port Elizabeth
Sucre	Perth	Tananarive
Asuncion	Sydney	Johannesburg
Buenos Aires	Dunedin	Benquela
La Paz	Wellington	Punta Arenas
Lima	Hobart	Valparaiso
Montevideo	Quito	Chacabuco
Brisbane	Guayaquil	Palembang
Canberra	Port Stanley	Soerabaja
Rio de Janeiro	Capetown	Timaru

Southern Itinerary. Play the same as Warm Words except use all of the letters of the alphabet.

Some of the countries to include are:

Australia	Bolivia	Chile
Paraguay	Peru	New Zealand
Argentina	Uruguay	Madagascar
Tasmania	Brazil	Ecuador

Aromas and Textures

Collect some samples of foods and products of the tropics which the players will attempt to identify by either smell or touch (see suggestions p. 275). Place each sample in an old saucer or small paper plate and place the samples on a table. Cover the items with a cloth so the players will not see them. Obtain a roll of paper toweling for blindfolds and two paper clips to fasten each blindfold on the players.

The players form teams of ten and each team selects a recorder. Seat the teams with their backs to the table of samples so that no one can see the table at any time. Have the players blindfold each other and give each player two paper napkins. Uncover the table.

Lead the first two players on each team to the table. Pick up each sample and tell the players to touch or smell it and try to identify it to themselves without a word. The players are led back to their places and try to remember the items they identified. When they are back in place they may remove their blindfolds.

Continue leading players, two from each team at a time, to the table of samples. After everyone has had a turn the teams gather in separate parts of the room. Give each recorder a sheet of paper and a pencil and ask him to write down the items the members of his team have identified. After a reasonable length of time ask the recorder of the team with the longest list to read it. Show the items as they are identified. If all the items are correct, the team wins the game, and its members are acclaimed the "Best Sniffers and Feelers."

Samples of tropical products might include:

To Smell	To Touch
banana slices	avocado
butter	coconut (whole)
coffee	coal
cacao bean or cocoa	cotton
cinnamon	maize—corn
cloves	kapok
chili peppers	lead
ginger	lumber (piece of wood)
mustard seed	mango (whole)
orange slices	pineapple (whole)
paprika	rubber
red pepper	silver
tea	sugar
tapioca (made from Cassava)	sweet potato
tobacco	wool

Tropical Troupes

Players form groups of six. On a slip of 4 × 6-inch paper for each group write an incident associated with the tropics which has dramatic possibilities (see suggestions p. 276). Give a slip to each troupe and allow the players time to decide how they wish to dramatize the incident. The players pantomime the action and may not use any English words. If the language of another country may be logically used, any player who speaks the language may employ it in the skit. The linguist must quickly teach the necessary words to the other members of his troupe, for everyone in the group must participate.

At the end of a designated time each troupe presents its skit. While one group performs, the other troupes try to guess the incident which is being dramatized. When the members of a group correctly guess the incident, they are the next performers. If they have had a turn they choose the next troupe to dramatize. If no one guesses the incident, the actors disclose the incident and choose another troupe to appear.

Some incidents which might be associated with the tropics include:

> Peddlers selling tangarines strung on a raffia cord.
> Picking papaya, limes, grapefruit, and oranges from trees in the dooryard.
> Making tropical cocoa by boiling ground roasted cacao beans with ground maize and chili peppers.
> Christopher Columbus and his crew tasting pineapple for the first time.
> Spanish and Portuguese sailors carrying the slips and crowns of pineapple to distant lands.
> Tourists visiting a native market and wanting to buy articles but unable to speak the language.
> Trip from Australia to Europe in 1840 bringing the first living pair of talking shell parakeets or budgereegahs.
> Modern Robinson Crusoes shipwrecked on an island south of the equator.
> Establishing an observation station in the tropics in observance of the International Geophysical Year.
> Victorious Olympic teams returning from Australia.
> Tourists unable to speak the native language trying to understand the rate of exchange as they buy tickets for the next side trip south of the equator.
> Sitting on the floor eating fish cooked in coconut milk, sweet potatoes, and ripe papaya drenched in lime juice in a tropical island home.
> Walking on a trail cut through coconut trees on a plantation and encountering many strange creatures.

Special Occasions Calendar*

January

1	New Year's Day
1	Paul Revere, 1735, leading silversmith of New England and an American Revolutionary patriot
3	Cicero, 106 B.C., great Roman orator, philosopher, and politician
7	Gregory XIII (Ugo Buoncompagni), 1502, pope who changed the calendar to the form now in use
11	Alexander Hamilton, 1757, American lawyer and statesman
14	Albert Schweitzer, 1875, philosopher, theologian, physician, musician, and author of *Reverence for Life*
17	Benjamin Franklin, 1706, American statesman, scientist, printer, and writer
18	Daniel Webster, 1782, American statesman, orator, and lawyer
19	Robert E. Lee, 1807, American Confederate general
24	Gold discovered in California, 1848

* See pages 276–80.

25 Robert Burns, 1759, Scottish poet
27 Mozart, 1756, Austrian composer
31 Schubert, 1797, Austrian composer

NOTE 1: Date for celebrating Arbor Day varies in different states and countries depending upon their climate. Bird Day is frequently celebrated on the same day as Arbor Day.

NOTE 2: The exact date of the founding of the YWCA is unknown. In 1855 the Honorable Mrs. Arthur Kinnaird opened the General Female Training Institute in London and Miss Emma Robarts started the first prayer union. These two groups came together in 1877 in London under the name YWCA.

February

2 Groundhog Day
7 Charles Dickens, 1812, English novelist
8 Boy Scouts of America incorporated in Washington, D.C., 1910
11 Thomas A. Edison, 1847, American electrician and inventor
12 Abraham Lincoln, 1809, sixteenth president of the United States
12 Charles Darwin, 1809, English naturalist
14 St. Valentine's Day
22 George Washington, 1732, American general and first president of the United States
22 Sir Robert Baden-Powell, 1857, British soldier and founder of the Boy Scouts
22 James Russell Lowell, 1819, American poet, essayist, and diplomat
23 Handel, 1685, German composer
26 Buffalo Bill (William Frederick Cody), 1845, American plainsman, army scout, and organizer of Buffalo Bill's Wild West Shows
27 Henry W. Longfellow, 1807, American poet
29 Leap Year

March

3 Alexander Graham Bell, 1847, inventor of the telephone
6 Michelangelo, 1470, Italian painter and sculptor
7 Luther Burbank, 1849, American naturalist and plant breeder who developed new varieties of flowers and vegetables
8 Andrew Carnegie, 1835, Scottish-American steel manufacturer and philanthropist; founded in 1889 his first free public library in Braddock, near Pittsburgh, Pa.
17 St. Patrick's Day
21 First day of spring

NOTE: The earliest possible date for Easter is March 24; the latest, April 25.

April

1 All Fools' Day
3 First Pony Express riders between Sacramento and St. Joseph, Missouri, 1860
3 Washington Irving, 1783, American essayist, novelist, and historian
3 John Burroughs, 1837, American naturalist and author
6 R. E. Peary, 1856, discovered the North Pole, 1909

7   Walter Camp, 1859, called "Father of American Football," also known for his daily-dozen exercises

12   *Tatler,* famous newspaper of Addison and Steele, and forerunner of the modern magazine, first appeared in 1709

13   Thomas Jefferson, 1743, author of the Declaration of Independence, third president of the United States

18   Paul Revere's Ride, 1775

19   Five Ringling brothers: Charles, Otto, Albert, Alfred, and John started a traveling wagon show, the Ringling Brothers Circus, which merged in 1907 with the troupe of Barnum and Bailey and became the largest and most famed American circus

23   William Shakespeare, 1564, English poet and dramatist

23   Joseph M. Turner, 1775, English landscape painter

24   The *Boston News Letter,* America's first newspaper, published in Boston

27   Ulysses S. Grant, 1822, American general and eighteenth president of the United States

May

1   May Day

4   John J. Audubon, 1785, American ornithologist, artist, and scientist

9   Richard E. Byrd, 1898, American aviator and explorer, flew to the North Pole, 1926; South Pole, 1929

12   Florence Nightingale, 1820, English army nurse, hospital reformer, and philanthropist, known as "the Lady with the Lamp"

15   First air mail service, 1918

21   Charles A. Lindbergh, 1902, American aviator, flew over the Atlantic Ocean, 1927

21   American Association of the Red Cross founded, 1881

25   Ralph Waldo Emerson, 1803, American essayist, poet, philosopher

30   Memorial or Decoration Day

NOTE: The second Sunday of May is Mother's Day.

June

3   Jefferson Davis, 1808, President of the Confederate States of America, 1861–1865

14   Flag Day, anniversary of adoption of the Stars and Stripes as the official national flag in 1777

14   Harriet Beecher Stowe, 1811, American author

21   First day of summer, longest day of the year

21   Daniel Carter Beard, 1850, American illustrator, naturalist, and one of the founders of the Boy Scouts of America

24   Henry Ward Beecher, 1813, American pulpit orator and lecturer

28   Johannes Gutenberg first used movable type for printing

NOTE: The third Sunday of June is Father's Day.

July

1   Dominion Day in Canada

4   Independence Day

4   Nathaniel Hawthorne, 1804, American novelist and story writer

5   P. T. Barnum, 1810, American showman
6   John Paul Jones, 1747, American naval officer, born in Scotland
12   Julius Caesar, 100 B.C., Roman general, statesman, and writer
15   Rembrandt van Rijn, 1606, Dutch painter

August

6   Alfred Tennyson, 1809, English poet
9   Izaak Walton, 1593, English writer: author of *The Compleat Angler* or *The Contemplative Man's Recreation*—first edition, 1653
11   Fulton's steamboat, *Clermont*, launched in 1807
15   Sir Walter Scott, 1771, Scottish novelist and poet
17   David Crockett, 1786, American pioneer and politician
28   Johann Wolfgang von Goethe, 1749, German author
29   Oliver Wendell Holmes, 1809, American physician, poet, essayist, and novelist

September

2   Albert G. Spalding, 1850, one of the developers of modern baseball
4   Start of self-service restaurants, 1885, forerunner of the cafeteria
6   Jane Addams, 1860, American social worker, founded Hull House in Chicago, one of the first social settlements in the United States
6   Lafayette Day, Marquis de Lafayette, 1757, French general and statesman who served in America
13   John J. Pershing, 1860, American general
15   James Fenimore Cooper, 1789, American novelist
16   Pilgrims sailed from England, 1620
16   Mexico, Independence Day, 1821
17   Constitution Day, 1787
23   First day of autumn
26   First American gymnasium started, 1825
NOTE: Labor Day is the first Monday of September.

October

7   James Whitcomb Riley, 1853, American lyric poet
11   Sir George Williams, 1821, English businessman, originator of YMCA in 1844
12   Columbus Day
15   Virgil, 70 B.C., Roman poet
27   Theodore Roosevelt, 1858, twenty-sixth president of the United States
31   Halloween
31   Juliette Gordon Low, 1860, founder of Girl Scouts in the United States

November

2   Daniel Boone, 1735, American explorer and colonizer
11   Veterans' Day, formerly Armistice Day, 1918
13   Robert Louis Stevenson, 1850, Scottish novelist and poet
NOTE: Thanksgiving Day is celebrated on the fourth Thursday of November.

December

6	Saint Nicholas, patron saint of children
9	John Milton, 1608, English poet
14	Amundsen reached the South Pole, 1911
16	Beethoven, 1770, Prussian composer
17	John Greenleaf Whittier, 1807, American poet
17	Wright Brothers' first airplane flight, 1903
21	First day of winter, shortest day of the year
24	Kit (Christopher) Carson, 1809, American frontiersman
25	Christmas
27	Louis Pasteur, 1822, French chemist
28	Woodrow Wilson, 1856, twenty-eighth president of the United States
29	William E. Gladstone, 1809, English statesman, premier
30	Rudyard Kipling, 1865, English poet, novelist, story writer
31	New Year's Eve

ROTATIVE

review

PARTY

FUN MAKERS

CONTENTS

Rotative parties fulfill one of the aims of social recreation—that of having everyone participate. In the rotative party plan several different simple games are in progress at the same time in designated areas. With the players forming groups of four, each unit plays one game for five minutes and then on signal moves on to the next activity. During the course of the party each group plays all of the games that have been planned.

Rotative parties should not be confused with progressive parties. While the setup for the games is similar for both types of parties, the philosophy behind them is quite different. In the rotative party all of the players move on to another activity after five minutes of play; in the progressive plan the two highest scorers move to the next game, and the two low scorers remain to repeat the activity. The progressive system penalizes the losers and thus is contrary to the philosophy of social recreation. Being stranded at the same game for a portion of the party is embarrassing for some and becomes boring to all. The rotative plan keeps everyone in a good frame of mind, for win or lose each person moves on to another game and has a try at something new.

Careful planning is necessary if the rotative party is to be fully successful. Several points must be kept in mind in handling the preliminary arrangements and directing the play:

Games. All activities must be simple, easy to understand, and require no previous practice. With the participants playing a game for five minutes, adding up scores, and then moving on to a new game, everyone must be able to swing into an activity with a minimum of directions. Complicated activities result in confusion and spoil the fun.

The games in this chapter are all easy to learn and to play. They require inexpensive equipment which can be readily obtained or easily made. The pattern for all the games is the same; that is, they all require the participant to handle an object in order to score points: to toss, slide, bounce, catch, snap, roll, pick up, remove, or drop an object in a specified manner and get it to a designated place. To aid the selection of activities, the games are grouped in categories in the list which precedes this chapter.

Equipment. Have all equipment and supplies ready to use. Set up each game where it is to be played before the group arrives.

Draw the diagrams and other markings necessary for playing the game.

Preparation. Each game must be numbered. Mark the number on a large cardboard and place it where it is clearly visible to the players—on the wall above the game area, fastened to the table on which the game is played, or on an easel or music stand.

Score Cards. Before the party, prepare a score card for each group of four (see illustration). Each score card gives the number of the game which the group is to start with. If a group's card tells it to start playing game Number 8, its second game is Number 9 and its third is Number 10. It then proceeds to game Number 1 and progresses until it has played game Number 7, which completes the group's circuit of ten games.

ROTATIVE PARTY

Start Play at Game Number 8

Number Game	Janet Hall	Bill Nye	Betty Gie	Joe Dodd	Total
1					
2					
3					
4					
5					
6					
7					
8					
9					
10					
Total					

Groups and Captains. When the players arrive, divide them into groups of four and ask each team to select a captain. Give the captain the score card and a pencil. He is responsible for marking the scores for each member of his team and the team's total score for each game, as well as the final scores at the completion of the activities. The captain is also responsible for seeing that the members of his group are ready to rotate from one activity to another and that they get there quickly.

Playing the Games. As soon as each team has its score card, ask the captain to direct the members to the game at which it starts. Play does not start until the "Go" signal is given.

Allow players to go into action for five minutes; then give the signal to stop, and everyone must halt. Allow a few minutes for recording scores and moving to the next activity. With everyone in place give the signal to start the next game.

Scoring. Players score points as indicated in the description of each game.

If the players play rapidly during the time allowed for each game, they have more opportunity to chalk up a score than if they play leisurely. As soon as the members of a foursome complete a round of play, they immediately start over again and continue until the stop signal is given. The players in each group must compete in order, and in no case should a team be allowed to have its best player participate more often than the others in order to score more points for the team.

Games Committee. For a really successful rotative party, have a Games Committee. Station one committee member at each activity. He checks that supplies and equipment are ready for each group, re-marks chalk diagrams or lines that may have been erased during play, explains the game briefly to the group, gets the game under way, watches that it is played correctly and fairly, sees that players stop when the signal is given, and assists the captain with tallying scores if necessary.

If it is impossible to have a committee member stationed at each game, post a set of typed rules at each game. Before the party starts explain every activity to the captains. Make several persons who are not captains responsible for making sure that equipment and supplies are always ready, for re-marking diagrams and other lines if necessary, and for checking that the rules of the games are easily available to the players.

TOSSERS

Chair Quoits

Place the seat of a chair on the seat of a standing chair so that the legs of the top chair are up. Mark a throwing line on the floor 5 feet from the chairs. Obtain four rope quoits or round gaskets.

On signal, one of the foursome takes the four quoits and stands behind the throwing line. Tossing the quoits one at a time, he attempts to put a ring around each leg of the chair. He scores one point for each ringer and three additional points if he rings all four legs. Each player in turn tosses four quoits. As soon as all four have tossed, a second round begins, until the signal to stop is given.

Ring Toss

To prepare a scoring board, secure a scrap piece of wood about 18 inches wide and 24 inches long and at least ½-inch thick. Drive eleven nails into the board, spaced as shown in Figure 10–1 and tilted upward at a slight angle. Allow the nails to extend from the board at least 2½ inches. Number each nail as shown in the illustration.

Hang the board on a wall, or prop it on a table so that it is at an angle. Mark a throwing line about 6 feet from the board. Secure a dozen fruit jar rings or round gaskets about 3 inches in diameter.

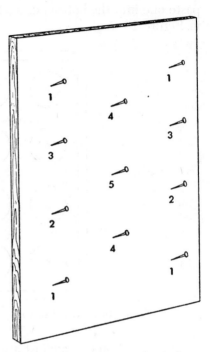

Each player takes three rings. In turn, each player stands at the throwing line for three attempts to ring the nails. Scores are determined by the numbers marked under the nails.

FIGURE 10–1. Scoring board for Ring Toss

Circle the Nail

Make a target by driving a nail into a piece of scrap wood approximately 6 inches square and 1 inch thick so that the nail extends out of the wood about 2½ inches. Place the target on a table and mark a throwing line on the floor 6 feet from the table. Secure four fruit jar rubbers or round gaskets.

In turn, each of the four players stands behind the throwing line and tosses a ring at the target. Ringers score three points; the two rings lying closest to the nail score two points each.

Clothespin Toss

Using a 1-inch lid of a cardboard box, approximately 12 × 12 inches, place it on a table. Cut a small hole, just large enough to hold a clothespin securely, in each corner and one in the center. Insert a clothespin in each opening. Mark a throwing line 6 feet from the table. Secure five fruit jar rubbers or round gaskets.

On signal, each player in turn stands behind the throwing line and tosses five rings, one at a time, and attempts to ring the clothespins. Each ringer scores two points. For ringing all five clothespins a player scores three additional points.

Muffin Pan Toss

Secure a muffin pan and twelve washers the size of a penny. Cut out twelve disks from a sheet of cardboard. Number the disks and paste one into the bottom of each compartment of the pan as shown in Figure 10–2.

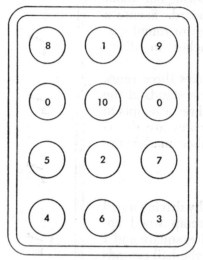

FIGURE 10–2. Labeled scoring compartments for Muffin Pan Toss

Set a book on end against a wall and lean the pan against it with the top edge of the pan resting on the top of the book so that it rests at an angle. Mark a throwing line 8 feet from the muffin pan.

In turn, each player stands behind the throwing line and tosses three washers, one at a time, at the muffin pan. The player scores the points designated by the numbers in the compartments in which he has tossed his washers.

Washer Pitch

Draw on the floor, or on a piece of heavy cardboard placed on the floor, a target consisting of three concentric circles: one 8, one 16, and one 24 inches in diameter. Number the smallest circle "3"; the middle circle "2"; and the largest circle "1." Mark a throwing line 8 feet from the target. Secure a dozen washers, 3 inches in diameter.

In turn every member of the group stands behind the throwing line and tosses three washers, one at a time, at the target. Players score the points marked in the circle in which the greater portion of the washer rests.

Rubber Heel Toss

On the floor draw the diagram shown in Figure 10–3. Label the scoring areas as indicated in the illustration. Mark a throwing line 10 feet from the diagram. Secure three rubber heels.

From behind the throwing line, each player in turn tosses the three heels, one at a time, at the scoring area. Players score according to the number in the area where the heel falls. Heels resting on a line score no points.

Beanbag Throw

Use either of the plans shown in Figure 10–4 to make a bean-board. For the plan at the left the board is 24 inches long and 18 inches wide. Use a piece of wood ¼-inch thick or a piece of heavy cardboard. Cut three round holes in it: the upper one 4 inches in diameter; the middle one, 5 inches; and the lower one, 6 inches. The upper hole counts three points; the middle, two; and the lower, one. Mark the score under the holes. For the plan at the right the board is 24 inches wide and 30 inches long. Cut five triangular holes, varying in size from 4 to 8 inches in the positions illustrated.

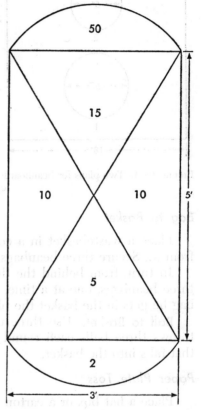

FIGURE 10–3. Labeled scoring sections for playing area for Rubber Heel Toss

Mark the score above the holes as shown. Place the board at a 45-degree angle and mark a throwing line 8 feet from the board. Secure three beanbags.

The players take turns in tossing three beanbags from behind the throwing line. Tossers score according to the holes in which the beanbags fall. Any beanbags lying on the board score no points for the tosser.

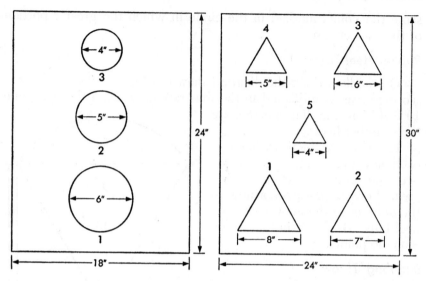

FIGURE 10–4. Two plans for beanboards with scoring values for circular and triangular openings

Bag to Basket

Place a wastebasket in a corner. Mark a throwing line 10 feet from it. Secure three beanbags.

In turn, from behind the throwing line each player throws the three beanbags, one at a time, at the wastebasket. For each beanbag he gets in the basket the player scores one point.

Ball to Basket. Use three tennis or rubber balls. Each player throws three balls each round and scores one point for each ball that falls into the basket.

Paper Plate Toss

Place a hat box or a carton about the same size as a hat box on the floor. Mark a throwing line 6 feet from the container. Have a dozen paper plates.

Standing behind the throwing line, each player has three paper plates every round to try to toss in the container. For each successful toss the player scores one point.

Peanut Target Throw

Place a round dishpan or container on the floor. In it put a bowl 9 inches in diameter. In the bowl place a metal measuring cup. Draw a throwing line 6 feet from the target. Have twelve peanuts and some extras on hand (in the tossing the shells might break, and frequently many of the peanuts reach another target—the players' mouths).

From behind the throwing line each player tosses three peanuts each turn. For any peanuts which land in the cup he scores four points; in the bowl, three points; and in the dishpan, two.

Cards in the Hat

Place a man's hat on the floor 5 feet from a chair. Divide a deck of playing cards into four stacks of thirteen cards each.

In turn each player sits on the chair facing the hat. Holding a stack of thirteen cards in his left hand he places his right elbow on his right knee and attempts to flip the cards into the hat with his right hand, one at a time. The cards are flipped with the wrist, not thrown.

For each card he gets into the hat, the player scores one point. Cards on the brim do not count, but they may be knocked in the hat by subsequent cards.

Feed the Elephant

Secure a large funnel. Place the funnel (elephant's mouth) on a table so that it faces the throwing line which is six feet from the table. Have twelve peanuts and some extras on hand.

In turn, from behind the throwing line each player tosses his three peanuts, one at a time, to the target. For each peanut that goes into the elephant's mouth the player scores two points. Peanuts that touch any part of the opening of the funnel count one point.

Bottle Top Toss

On the floor draw a target of five circles as shown in Figure 10–5. Make each circle 10 inches in diameter. Mark the score in the areas as illustrated. Indicate a throwing line 6 feet from the target. Secure twenty bottle tops or buttons.

In turn, from behind the throwing line each player tosses, one at a time, five bottle tops. He scores according to the areas in which the tops rest. If a top rests in more than one scoring area, the player takes the score from that in which most of the top rests.

False Alarm

Hang a bell in the center of a wire clothes hanger which has been shaped into a circle. Suspend the hanger from the ceiling, so that it is about 5 feet from the floor. Secure three tennis balls.

Each player in turn throws three tennis balls and attempts to put each one through the circle without ringing the bell hanging in the center of it. For each successful throw the player scores one point. If a player rings the bell, it is a false alarm, and he scores no points.

Circle Toss. Use shuttlecocks instead of tennis balls and eliminate the bell. For each successful throw through the circle the player scores a point.

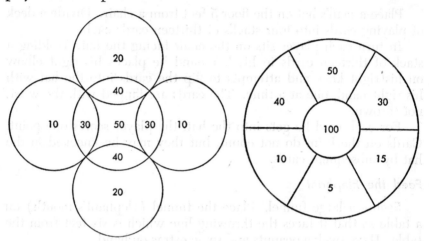

FIGURE 10–5. Target and scoring areas for Bottle Top Toss

FIGURE 10–6. Target and scoring areas for Shuttlecock Target Toss

Shuttlecock Target Toss

Draw a large circle on the floor and mark out the scoring areas as shown in Figure 10–6. Mark a throwing line 9 feet from the circle. Secure three shuttlecocks.

In turn each player stands behind the throwing line and tries to toss his three shuttlecocks, one at a time, into the scoring areas.

PROPELLERS

Miniature Shuffleboard

On the floor draw the diagram shown in Figure 10–7. The large square is 36 × 36 inches. Mark off and label the scoring area as illustrated. Establish a throwing line 8 feet from the diagram. Secure eight table coasters which will slide on the floor.

Two players participate at a time; each person has four coasters. Standing behind the throwing line, the two players alternate in sliding the coasters into the scoring area. As soon as they have played their eight coasters, each counts his score and the next twosome goes into action. For each coaster which lands in the "10 off" area the player must subtract ten points from his total score. If a coaster rests on a line, the score is taken from the area in which most of the coaster has come to rest.

Disk Quoits

Draw three concentric circles on the floor, respectively 6, 12, and 18 inches in diameter. Write the number 4 in the inner circle, 3 in the next circle, and 2 in the outer one. Mark a throwing line 8 feet from the diagram. Secure three table coasters which will slide on a floor.

In turn each player stands behind the line and slides the three coasters, one at a time, into the scoring area. For any coasters that rest in the inner circle the player scores four points; in the next circle, three; and in the outer one, two. If a coaster rests in two circles, the player takes the score from the circle in which most of the coaster rests.

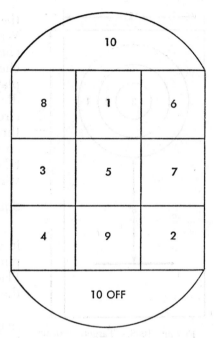

FIGURE 10–7. Playing area for Miniature Shuffleboard with labeled scoring sections

Calendar Slide

On the top of a table draw the calendar of a month containing thirty-one days. Four feet from the diagram mark a starting line on the table. Secure three checkers.

The first player in the foursome slides a checker from behind the starting line toward the scoring area. The score is the date of the square in which the checker stops. Everyone has three chances each round. If a checker rests in two squares, the score is the date in which the largest part of the checker rests.

Checker Snap

On a cardboard 12-inches wide and 24-inches long draw three concentric circles as illustrated in Figure 10–8. Make the circles

3, 6, and 9 inches in diameter, respectively. Number the smallest circle 3, the middle circle 2, and the largest circle 1, for scoring purposes. Mark a snapping line 8 inches from the outer circle. Place the card on a table. Secure three checkers.

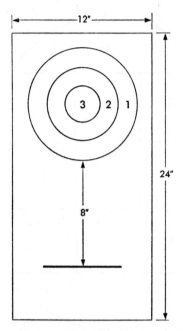

In turn, each player places one of the checkers on the snapping line. With one of his fingers he snaps the checker toward the target. If the checker stops in the center circle, the player scores three points; in the middle circle, two points; in the outer circle, one point. Each player snaps three checkers each round. If a checker rests in two circles, the player takes the score from the circle in which most of the checker rests.

Figure 10–8. Target, scoring areas, and snapping line for Checker Snap

Square Stops

Place four checkers 4 inches apart in a square on a table. Mark a snapping line 12 inches from the checkers. Place another checker directly behind the line.

In turn, each player attempts to snap the checker behind the line with his finger so that it stops inside the square created by the four checkers without displacing any of them. For each success the player scores five points. If the checkers rest partly in the square, the player scores three points. When a player displaces one of the four checkers, he scores no points and must replace the checkers.

Golf Tee Tenpins

On a table draw circles for ten golf tees in the triangular placement used in bowling (see Figure 10–9). Place a tee, top down, in each circle. Mark a starting line 12 inches from the point of the triangle. Secure two buttons, ½ inch in diameter, which can slide over a smooth surface.

In turn, each player places one of the buttons on the starting line and snaps it with a finger, attempting to knock down the tees. Another group member sets up the fallen tees after each attempt. Each player snaps two buttons every turn. Each upset counts one

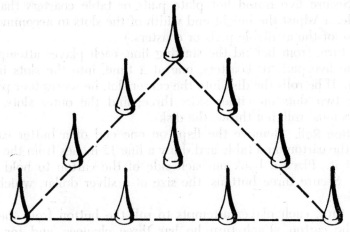

FIGURE 10-9. Placement of tees for Golf Tee Tenpins

point. If the player knocks all tees down at one time, he scores ten points and gets an additional five points for the complete knock-down.

Table Shuffleboard

On a table draw a diagram similar to the one illustrated in Figure 10-7, page 291, except have each small square measure 6 inches; thus the diagram will be 18-inches wide. Twenty-four inches from the drawing mark a snapping line. Secure eight bottle tops.

Two players participate at a time. Each person has four bottle tops, and the players alternate in snapping them from the snapping line. Play and score the same as Miniature Shuffleboard (see page 290).

Box the Checker

Secure three checkers and a small box, approximately 2-inches square and 1-inch deep. Remove one-half of the bottom of the box. Place the box on a table with the bottom up, the open end toward a snapping line drawn 18-inches away.

Each player in turn places one of the checkers on the snapping line and snaps the checker with his finger, attempting to get the checker into the box. The player snaps three checkers each round of play, and scores one point for each checker he boxes.

Disk Roll

In the side of a large carton cut five upright slots 1-inch wide and 2-inches apart. Draw a starting line 6 feet from this side of the box. Secure five round hot plate pads or table coasters that are rollable. (Adjust the height and width of the slots to accommodate the size of the available pads or coasters.)

In turn, from behind the starting line, each player attempts to roll the five pads or coasters, one at a time, into the slots in the carton. If he rolls the disk into the center slot, he scores four points; in the two slots on either side, three; and the outer slots, two. Players must roll, not throw, the disks.

Button Roll. Remove the flaps on one end of a butter carton. Place the carton on a table and draw a line 12 inches from the open end of it. Place a book on each side of the carton to hold it in place. Secure three buttons, the size of a silver dollar, which can be rolled.

In turn, each player attempts to roll the button from the line into the carton. Each turn he has three chances, and for each successful roll he scores one point.

Egg Roll

Place a round gasket of 4-inch diameter on a table. Mark a line 3 feet from the gasket. Secure a rubber or hard-boiled egg.

In turn, from behind the line, each player rolls the egg toward the gasket in an endeavor to get it in the ring. If he succeeds, the player scores one point.

Table Tennis Ball Roll

Place a quart milk carton on the floor. Mark a line 12 feet from the carton. Secure four table tennis balls.

Standing behind the line, each player in turn rolls one ball each turn and attempts to hit the carton. For each hit the player scores one point. If no one hits the carton in one round, the player whose ball rests nearest the carton scores a point.

Cootie

On each side of a small cube of wood print one of the following letters: *B, H, L, A, E, T*. These letters represent parts of a cootie. *B* represents the body; *H*, the head; *L*, leg; *A*, antenna; *E*, eye; and *T*, tail. Secure a metal cup and have a sheet of paper and pencil for each participant.

Each player takes turns in rolling the cube from the cup. When a player rolls the letter *B*, he draws an oblong figure on his paper to represent the body of the Cootie and is entitled to another roll. If he rolls *L* (leg), *H* (head), or *T* (tail), he adds that part of the body to the Cootie. If he rolls any of the letters representing these parts before he rolls *B* (body), he cannot add them. If he rolls *E* (eye) or *A* (antenna) before he rolls *H* (head), he cannot add them. Whenever the player rolls a letter that he can use in the construction of the Cootie, he has another turn.

Play continues until the stop signal or until someone completes the Cootie (see Figure 10–10), which has six legs, two eyes, two antennae, one body, a head, and a tail. For a complete Cootie a

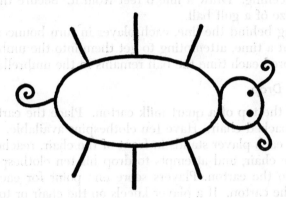

FIGURE 10–10. Drawing of a cootie, showing parts used in Cootie

player scores thirteen points, one for each part. Players having incomplete Cooties score one point for each part of the body that they have drawn. If someone completes a Cootie before the five-minute signal, the group starts the game again.

BOUNCERS AND CATCHERS

Wastebasket Bounce

Place a wastebasket in a corner. Mark a line about 9 feet from the basket. Secure three rubber or tennis balls.

In turn each player steps to the line and bounces one of the three balls on the floor and attempts to get it into the basket. For each successful basket he scores a point. He has three chances each round of play.

Table Tennis Bounceball

Place an egg carton with twelve compartments on the floor. Mark a line 5 feet from the carton. Only three table tennis balls are used by the players, but have extras on hand.

Standing behind the line each player in turn bounces a table tennis ball on the floor and attempts to get it into one of the compartments of the carton. The player scores a point for each ball that remains in the carton. Each player has three chances during every round.

Umbrella Bounceball

Open an old umbrella and brace it on the floor with its handle facing the ceiling. Draw a line 6 feet from it. Secure three rubber balls the size of a golf ball.

Standing behind the line, each player in turn bounces the three balls, one at a time, attempting to get them into the umbrella. One point is scored each time the ball remains in the umbrella.

Clothespin Drop

Cut off the top of a quart milk carton. Place the carton behind a straight-backed chair. Have ten clothespins available.

In turn each player stands in front of the chair, reaches over the back of the chair, and attempts to drop his ten clothespins, one at a time, into the carton. Players score one point for each pin that goes into the carton. If a player kneels on the chair or touches it at any time while he drops the clothespins, he forfeits one attempt to score.

Card Drop

Place an old hat on the floor behind a straight-backed chair. Secure forty playing cards or forty pieces of cardboard the size of a playing card.

Each player holds ten cards. The first person stands in front of the chair, reaches over, and attempts to drop his cards, one at a time, into the hat. For each card that he drops into the hat the player scores one point. If a player kneels on the chair or touches it any time while he drops his cards, he forfeits one attempt to score.

Beany Vase Drop

Place an old vase on the floor behind a straight-backed chair. Secure forty navy beans, ten for each player, and a small reserve supply.

In turn, each player stands in front of the chair, reaches over, and attempts to drop ten beans, one at a time, into the vase behind the chair. One point is scored for each success. Players may not touch the chair. If they do, they forfeit one attempt to score.

Teaspoon Flip

Put an unbreakable tumbler on a table and beside it place two teaspoons with the handle of one overlapping the handle end of the other about an inch.

In turn, each player strikes the bowl of the bottom spoon with his fist, flipping the top spoon, which he tries to catch in the tumbler. While the spoon is briefly in the air, the player must manipulate the tumbler quickly so that he can catch the spoon. For each successful catch he scores one point.

Funnel Ball

Obtain a funnel and a small rubber ball.

In turn each player bounces the ball from a designated area on the floor to a wall and attempts to catch it in the funnel on the rebound. Each player has three tries. He scores one point for each catch he makes.

Ring Catch

Obtain two pieces of broom handle, each 36 inches long, and twelve round gaskets, 4 inches in diameter. Draw two parallel lines 9 feet apart on the floor.

Standing behind one of the two lines two of the players (catchers) hold the broom handles. Facing them and standing behind the opposite line each of the other two players (tossers) has six round gaskets. The first tosser throws one of the gaskets to the first catcher, who attempts to catch the ring on his broom handle. Catchers may move forward to catch the ring, but the throwers must remain behind their line. For each successful catch the player scores one point.

After the first pair of players has finished its six attempts, the second twosome goes into action. After the twelve rings have been tossed, the tossers and catchers change places and equipment.

PICK-UPS

Egg Pick-Up

On a table place a rubber or hard-boiled egg, an egg cup, and a wooden mixing spoon.

Placing one hand behind his back, the first player attempts to pick up the egg with the wooden mixing spoon and deposit it in the egg cup without tipping the container. Each player scores one point for each successful egg pick-up and deposit.

Navy Bean Shift

Place a small bowl of navy beans, a paper plate, and some toothpicks on a table.

In turn, each player takes one toothpick in each hand and attempts to pick up a navy bean from the bowl with the two toothpicks. He must transfer the bean to the paper plate. Each player is allowed five attempts. He scores one point for each bean that he picks up and deposits on the plate.

Toothpick Jackstraws

On a table drop a handful of round toothpicks in a heap. Place a tweezer on the table.

In turn, each player takes the tweezer and attempts to remove one toothpick at a time without disturbing any of the other toothpicks. If he moves any toothpick other than the one he is trying to secure, he loses his turn and the next member of the foursome has a chance. One point is scored for each toothpick that is removed successfully.

If all of the toothpicks are removed before the stop signal, one of the players holds the toothpicks a few inches above the table and drops them. Play continues in the same manner.

Coin Balance

Supply a quarter and a card 3-inches square.

In turn, each player places the card on the end of the left forefinger (or right forefinger if he is left-handed) and puts the quarter on the card. With his other hand the player tries to carefully remove the card without upsetting the coin, and balance the coin on his finger. If he succeeds he scores a point.

PART III

OUTDOOR
SOCIAL
GAMES

PICNIC
FUN MAKERS

CONTENTS

Good food and plenty of it is an essential to a successful picnic, but it is far from the whole picture of a successful day in the out-of-doors. Picnics require activities—a carefully planned and skillfully directed program of activities which arouse enthusiasm and interest. The secret of success is planning activities that are appropriate for the group, the place, and the occasion.

Committees

To achieve a successful picnic it is essential that a number of committees share the responsibility: General, Grounds, Publicity, Transportation, Prizes, Finance, Hospitality, Refreshments, and Program. The General Committee, composed of the chairmen of the other picnic committees, coordinates the plans for the affair. The recreation leader usually appoints the chairmen. He may act as chairman for the General Committee or suggest that the group elect a person to this position. In brief, the duties of the other committees follow:

Grounds Committee: Locates and arranges for the use of the picnic grounds. In selecting a place for the picnic, the committee should be sure that it has ample level space for the activities, shelter in case of rain, cooking facilities (if needed), toilet facilities, shade, parking space, and containers for litter.

Publicity Committee: Informs potential picnickers of the date, time, place, activities, and cost. If everyone furnishes his own lunch, the picnickers should be notified whether or not beverages, ice cream, or other treats will be provided.

Depending upon the group to be reached, the Publicity Committee may use fliers, posters, skits, postals, house organs, newspapers, displays, motion pictures or photographs of previous picnics, or other media to advertise the event.

Transportation Committee: Arranges transportation to the picnic —bus, private car, train, or boat. This group works closely with the publicity committee. If transportation is to be mainly by private car, this committee's main assignment is to determine who needs and who can provide rides. Secure the home addresses of those needing and giving rides so that the committee can pair up persons who live in the same vicinity. Try to have those with space in their cars take the initiative and invite the others, as some people hesitate to bother someone to take them.

Private cars transporting guest passengers are liable to damages in case of injuries. Members of the transportation committee should call this fact to the attention of those who offer to use other private cars for the affair.

Prizes Committee: Plans for and purchases prizes. This committee first checks with the General Committee to find out how much may be spent for prizes and obtains the money from the Finance Committee. The Prizes Committee works closely with the Program Committee. Prizes should be provided for as many of the events as possible, but avoid expensive items and money prizes. Prizes should serve merely as a pleasant token for having won an event. The awards should occur at a "ceremony" at the end of the game period.

Since young children do not understand the competitive aspect of play or realize that prizes go only to the few who win, have a small gift for every child.

Finance Committee: Arranges for funds and pays bills for the picnic. Contributions may be collected from the picnickers, tickets may be sold, or there may be a fund provided for the affair.

Hospitality Committee: Greets and introduces picnickers. This committee should provide get-acquainted labels and distribute these at "registration" tables. Have crayons for writing names and pins for attaching labels. Use some of the Defrosters in Chapter 2 to assist picnic participants in meeting others.

Suggest that children under sixteen write their ages on the get-acquainted labels; this helps the Program Committee to maneuver players into various age groups for the games.

Refreshments Committee: Arranges for the food. Depending upon the situation, as well as the group, picnickers may bring their own food and use outdoor grills, or food may be purchased from the place where the picnic is held. For some affairs, this committee arranges for a caterer to provide the food, which the members of the committee, or the caterers serve.

Program Committee: Plans a schedule of activities. This committee secures equipment and supplies for the games and has everything in readiness, including personnel for the events, so that the activities can proceed without any delay.

Because of the range of ages in many picnic groups and the variety of activities, it is important to have a staff of dependable, adjustable, well-informed individuals to help with the games. Some should be assigned as directors of games and others as judges, and certain parents may be chosen as helpers for the activities for the little children. The committee should explain beforehand exactly what each director of games and each parent is to do. The group of judges should assist the individuals conducting the games. In contests, relays, races, or other events in which it helps to have more than one set of eyes to decide on the winners, several judges should be assigned to strategic places.

If possible the Program Committee should secure the use of a loudspeaker system to assemble the groups for games, to inform individuals about the program, and to make other needed announcements.

In planning the program of games the following age groupings should be considered:

Smallest fry (ages 2 through 5)
Ages 6 and 7
Ages 8 and 9
Ages 10 through 12
Ages 13 through 15
Over 15
Adults

While both sexes participate together in some events, there should be several separate events for boys and girls of about ten and older.

Since it is better to have a program of games that is as lively as the participants than one that stretches out so that the group becomes bored, plan the activities so that the various age groups perform at the same time in different designated areas. Prepare a special area for the smallest fry. A quiet comfortable place away from the noise and distractions of other activities affords a good setting.

Activities

Games for the very young at a picnic frequently result in bewilderment, frustration, and tears because the activities are not geared to a child's level. To prevent the picnic from being "rained out" for children from two through five, provide noncompetitive activities in which everyone participates at his own level of performance.

Some of the supplies needed to pave the way for fun for the children include: 24 × 18-inch drawing paper; large crayons; modeling clay; clean, discarded "grown-up" clothes for a dress-up parade; puzzles with large pieces which are easily handled and assembled; paste, blunt scissors, magazine pictures of children and familiar activities, and scrapbooks which become treasures to take home; and some colorfully illustrated children's books.

In conducting activities for the very young, remember that their interest span is short, so include a variety of fun makers. Have someone prepared to read or tell a few simple short stories. Remember, children of this age enjoy stories built around them, about people they know like the postman or the deliveryman, about animals, and about everyday happenings with which they are familiar.

For a special treat and probable conclusion to their activities, plan a treasure hunt. Use wrapped candy as clues along a path. Have one parent accompany each group of five children. At the end of the trail hide a box containing a small toy for each child which he can enjoy using immediately. The four- and five-year-old children will also enjoy the Candy Scramble and the Candy Sucker Search. (See page 306.)

To aid the program leaders in selecting activities for older picnickers, the games and events are grouped in this chapter as Hide and Seekers, Contests, Relay Eventers, and Race Eventers. The list preceding the chapter alphabetizes the activities within each category.

The supplies and equipment necessary to conduct the activities are easy to acquire and transport. They range from various items of clothing to kitchen utensils and hardware. Many games can be played with picnic supplies—paper bags, cups, plates, and napkins. Some are of the crayon and paper variety. A few require items such as baskets (or cartons), tires, brooms, umbrellas, folded chairs, tin cans, and pails. The Program Committee's problem is not necessarily to secure the "props," but rather to accumulate all supplies and equipment for the relays, races, and contests and have them available in the right place at the right moment.

HIDE AND SEEKERS

Little Treasures

Cut ten 2 × 2-inch slips of colored paper. On each slip write the name of a prize. Hide the slips in various places on the picnic grounds. Conceal them so that only one corner of the slip is in view.

Assemble the group and announce that the first slip is hidden, for example, "within twenty feet of the flag pole," or some other obvious landmark to give the players a lead. The group scatters as everyone seeks the first slip. When a player finds the slip, reassemble the group and announce that the second slip is, for example, "within fifteen feet of first base on the baseball diamond."

Continue until all ten slips have been found. The winners then present their slips and claim their treasures.

Watermelon Tree

Before the group arrives place a watermelon in a burlap bag and
hide it in a tree within the picnic area. Do not place the watermelon higher than 10 feet from the ground. Hide it carefully, but
so that it can be seen clearly from some angle.

As the picnickers assemble announce something such as the
following:

There is a very rare tree on the grounds. It is most unusual and cannot
be found anywhere else in the world. This tree has the ability to grow a watermelon! Another striking thing is that the watermelon grows on the tree in a
burlap sack. To add to its wonder the watermelon grows in plain sight not
higher than 10 feet from the ground. To be accommodating, this remarkable
tree has produced a watermelon in time for the picnic.

Anyone who can find the tree bearing the watermelon should report the
phenomenon to Mr. _____. The prize to the first one who locates the
watermelon tree is, of course, the watermelon. But even more important, the
winner will be recognized as the person who has seen the most unusual tree
in the world!

Lucky Spot

Select in advance some place in the picnic area that will be the
lucky spot.

Announce to the picnickers that there is a lucky spot on the
grounds and that some time during the picnic a signal will sound.
When the signal is given, everyone must stand still, and the person
standing on or nearest the spot will win a prize.

To maintain interest hold the signal until near the end of the
picnic.

Candy Sucker Search

Within a designated area insert candy suckers in the grass so
that the tops of them are clearly visible.

Assemble the children. Tell the group that candy suckers are
hiding and waiting for the children to find them.

On signal the children search for the suckers. At the end of a
designated time call a halt to the hunt and assemble the searchers.
Distribute suckers to the children who were unable to find any.

Candy Scramble

Players stand in a line facing the leader, who is about 30 feet
away. Give each child a small paper bag. From a basket the leader
scatters wrapped pieces of candy over the area. On signal, the chil-

dren run forward and gather as many pieces of candy as they can within a designated time.

Keep the group of scramblers small, for it gives everyone more opportunity to get some of the candy. In addition, it lessens the possibility of injury among the excited children.

Have extra candy on hand for anyone who does not pick up any.

CONTESTS

How Many?

At some central location on the picnic grounds place a container full of small objects on a table. Contestants try to guess the number of objects in the container—perhaps beans in a bottle, wrapped candy in a jar, peanuts (in the shell) in a plastic bag, chicken feed (candy corn) in a plastic bag, or nails in a jar.

Station several members of the Hospitality or Program Committee at the table with large sheets of paper and some pencils. Each person wishing to enter the guessing contest gives his name and states his guess to a committee member, who writes it on the paper.

At a previously designated time the lists of names and guesses are given to the Program Committee chairman, who is the only one who knows the actual number of objects in the container. The person whose guess is most nearly correct wins the contest. The prize? The object of the guessing.

How Much? Have contestants guess the weight of an object such as a watermelon, a cake, a basket of fruit, a dozen paper plates. Again, the prize is the object of the guessing.

Potato Knockabout

Players stand within a designated area. Give each player a potato and a tablespoon. Request everyone to place the potato on his spoon.

On signal, each player attempts to knock the potatoes from the spoons of the other contestants. At the same time he tries to guard his own potato and keep it from getting upset. Players may twist and turn to avoid having their potatoes knocked about, but they may not use their hands to protect or hold them. Anyone who does so is out of the game.

A contestant is eliminated from the knockabout when his potato is grounded. The last player with the potato still on his spoon wins the contest.

Snatching Tails

Give each participant a strip of white cloth 2 yards long and 2 inches wide and a strip of colored cloth 24 inches long and 2 inches wide. Request each player to tie the strip of white cloth securely around his waist. In the back of this have him hang his strip of colored cloth as a tail.

Each person is to snatch as many tails as he can, while twisting and turning to prevent other players from snatching his tail. A player may not hold his tail with his hands, sit down, or do anything that makes it impossible for the others to get the tail if they are quick.

Any player who loses his tail is out of the game. When the signal to stop is given, the player who is still in the game and has snatched the most tails wins the tail-snatching contest.

Hats Off!

Mark off an area in which the players must remain during the activity. Give each player a paper bag to wear on his head like a hat.

On signal, each player attempts to knock off the other participants' hats with his hands. At the same time he is on guard to try to keep his own hat from being knocked off, but he may not touch his own hat with his hands. If a player loses his hat, he picks it up and joins the spectators. The last person left with a hat wins.

Suggestion: Have this contest follow the Hats On! relay (see page 312), so that players will already have "hats" on their heads.

Calling Junior or Sis

Contestants (adults) stand in a single line facing a committee of judges. Give each judge a paper and pencil.

In turn, each contestant announces his own name (which the judges record) and then pretends that he or she is calling Junior or Sis home to dinner. The judges select the winner on the basis of effectiveness and humor in trying to get Junior or Sis to dash for home.

Calling Mom or Dad. In turn the contestants (boys and girls) pretend to call Mom or Dad at bedtime. Each wants a last-minute reprieve from going to sleep by asking for water or a snack, or by suddenly developing a pain that requires their parents' immediate attention.

The call that the committee agrees would make any Mom or Dad "come arunning" wins the contest.

Paper Plate Sail

Secure at least a dozen paper plates—more if there will be more than twelve contestants on a team. Mark a throwing line.

Players form teams, and one team stands along the throwing line. Give each member of the participating team a paper plate. In turn each player tosses his paper plate. After every member of the team has a chance to sail his paper plate, put a marker at the farthest edge of the paper plate which went the greatest distance. Have several members of the team pick up the plates. Another team then toes the throwing line, each participant with a paper plate. In turn, each player sails his paper plate. Mark the place where the farthest plate landed and ask several members of the team to pick up the plates.

The team whose marker is the greatest distance from the throwing line wins the contest.

RELAY EVENTERS

Picnic on the Spot

Secure a folding chair, an old umbrella, and a picnic basket for each team. Mark a starting line and indicate a goal line 50 feet from it.

Players form teams and stand in single files behind the starting line. Give the first player of each team a folded chair, an umbrella, and a picnic basket. On signal, the first player of each team takes the chair, umbrella, and picnic basket to the goal. As soon as he crosses the line, he sets up the chair, sits on it, opens the umbrella, holds it above him, and puts the picnic basket on his lap. Then he puts the basket on the ground, folds the umbrella, stands, folds the chair, carries the three items to the starting line, gives them to the second player, and goes to the end of his line. The second player takes the items and heads for the goal, where he repeats the antics.

Each player in turn performs. When the last player completes the action and stands in place at the end of the team, he places the basket and chair on the ground and opens the umbrella, holding it up to indicate his team has finished. The first team to indicate in this way that it has finished wins the game.

Bulky Load

Players are in teams in shuttle-relay formation (see page 23). Mark the two goal lines for each team, 20 feet apart. In front of player Number 1 of each team place a folded chair, a carton or bushel basket, an old broom, and an automobile tire (same size for each group).

On signal, the first player of each team gathers up his unwieldy load and carries the items to player Number 2 of his team and goes to the end of that group. If he drops anything, he must stop and pick it up before proceeding. Number 2 takes the load and carries it to Number 3. The relay continues until the members of one team have finished. This team wins the game.

Rained Out

Players form teams and stand in single files behind the starting line, which is 50 feet from the goal line. Give the first player of each team a folded chair, an umbrella, and a picnic basket.

On signal the first player of each team rushes to the goal. Placing the umbrella and picnic basket on the ground he unfolds the chair and sits on it, facing the group. Then each player stands, folds the chair, and opens the umbrella. Since he is rained out, he carries the chair and picnic basket, and holds the open umbrella to protect himself from the imagined precipitation. Returning to the starting line he closes the umbrella, gives it, the chair, and the basket to the second player, and goes to the end of his line.

In turn each member of the team repeats the antics of the first player. The first team to complete the action wins the relay.

Through the Tire

Mark a starting line and 60 feet from it indicate a goal line. Players form teams and stand in single files behind the starting line. Give an automobile tire (same size for all teams) to the first player on each team. Tie a colored strip of cloth on one arm of the last player of every team.

On signal the first player of each team rolls the tire to the goal. If the tire falls, he must pick it up and continue rolling it. After crossing the goal line, the player holds the tire erect on the goal line with the hole facing his team. The second player then dashes to the goal, crawls through the tire, runs back to the starting line, touches the extended hand of the third player to start him toward the tire, and goes to the end of the line.

Dashing to the goal, crawling through the tire, and hustling back to the starting line continues until the last player, who is easily identified by the colored cloth on his arm, performs and returns to his place in line. As soon as he stands in place, the head player rolls the tire toward the starting line. The first team which crosses the starting line with its tire wins the relay.

Tire Crawl

Players form teams and stand in single files. Tie a colored cloth on one arm of the first player on each team and give him an automobile tire to hold erect.

On signal the second player crawls through the tire, and then stands and holds the tire in place. The player wearing the colored cloth goes to the end of the line while the third player crawls through the tire and goes to the end of the line. Play continues, each player crawling through the tire and then dashing to the end of the team. When the player with the colored cloth has crawled through the tire and returned to the end of the line, he shouts, "We are the deluxe tire crawlers." The first team to complete the action and make its claim wins the game.

Tire Roll

Draw a starting line; 100 feet from it indicate a goal line. Players form teams and stand in single files behind the starting line. Give a tire to the first player of each team.

On signal the first player of each group rolls the tire to the goal and back. As he crosses the starting line, he gives the tire to the second player and goes to the end of his line. The second player is off to the goal, and in turn each person on the team rolls the tire to the goal and back.

The first team to complete the action, with all members in their original positions, wins the game.

Necktie on and Off

Secure an old clean necktie for each team. Players form teams and stand in files facing the same direction. Give the first player of each team a necktie.

On signal, the first player places the tie around his neck and ties it. Then he turns and shakes hands with the second player. The second player unties the neck adornment, takes it off the first player, and ties it around his neck. Tying, shaking hands, and untying continues until the last player wears the tie. He rushes forward and shakes hands with the first player, who removes the tie. The head player raises his arm and waves the necktie to indicate that his team has finished. The first team to make this signal wins the game.

Washday Fun

Between two trees suspend a clothesline about 6 feet from the ground. Mark a starting line 30 feet from it. Players form teams

and stand in single files behind the starting line. Give the first player
on each team a bushel basket containing two men's socks, two
gloves, a pair of women's stockings, one old sheet, one towel, and
twelve clothespins.

On signal, the first player of each team hurries with his basket
to the clothesline. He must hang up each item separately and use
all twelve clothespins. If any item falls to the ground the player
must pick it up and hang it again.

As soon as everything is on the line to stay, the player rushes with
the basket back to the starting line. Giving the basket to the next
player on his team, he goes to the end of his line. The second player
rushes to the clothesline and takes the items off the line, one piece at
a time, placing the "wash" and the clothespins in the basket. Picking
up the basket he hurries to the starting line, gives the basket to the
third player, and goes to the end of his line. The third player hangs
the clothes again, and play continues in this way until all members of
one team have finished. The winners earn the title of "Speediest
Washday Funsters."

Hats On!

Players stand in single files facing the same direction. Give each
player a paper bag large enough to fit loosely on his head. Since
head sizes vary, have several sizes of bags on hand. A well-fitted
"hat" extends to the player's ears. Players may try on the hats for
size, but everyone removes his hat before the signal to begin.

On signal, the first player of each team puts his hat on his head.
As soon as the second player sees the first player wearing his hat,
he dons his own. Play continues with each player putting on his
hat in turn. The first team with all its members hatted wins the
game.

Passing the Cups

Players form teams and stand in single files. Give the last player
on each team six paper cups.

On signal, the last player on each team passes the cups, one at
a time, up the row ahead of him. When the first player receives the
cups, he stacks them on the ground, one inside the other. As soon
as he has the six cups, he picks them up, rushes to the rear of his
team, and passes the cups up the line. When the second player
finishes piling the six cups, he picks them up, hurries to the end of
the team, and starts to pass the cups up the line.

Passing continues until the last player has dashed to the rear with the cups and arrived at his original place at the end of the team. Holding the cups overhead he shouts, "We are the best cup stackers." The first team to complete the action wins the game.

Tin Can Roll

Draw a starting line and 60 feet from it indicate a goal line. Players form teams and stand in single files behind the starting line. Place a bushel basket on the goal line in front of each team. Give a No. 10 tin can with one end removed and a broom to the first player of each team. Be sure the can has no jagged edges.

Placing the tin can sideways at the starting line, the first player of each team holds his broom directly behind the can. On signal, the player rolls the can with his broom toward the goal. At the goal he must circle the bushel basket with the can and then head for the starting line. Crossing the line, he picks up the can, hands it and the broom to the second player, and goes to the end of the line.

Rolling the can to the goal and back to the starting line continues until the head player of one team returns to his place, puts the tin can on the handle of the broom, and waves it to indicate his team is victorious.

Foot and Hand Push

Mark a starting line and 60 feet from it indicate a goal line. Players are in teams and stand in single files behind the starting line. Give the first player of each team a No. 10 tin can with one end removed. Be sure the can has no jagged edges.

The first player of each team places the tin can sideways at the starting line. On signal, he rolls the tin can toward the goal with the inside of one foot. After crossing the goal he turns around and places the tin can at the goal line. Then he gets down on all fours and begins rolling the can with his hands to the starting line. As soon as he crosses it, he picks up the can, gives it to the second player who stands ready to start, and goes to the end of the line. Play continues until one team is first to finish, winning the game.

Obstacle Relay

Mark a starting line and 120 feet from it indicate a goal line. Players form teams and stand in single files behind the starting line. Between the starting and goal lines place a series of obstacles for each team. Ten feet ahead of the team put three cartons (have extras for replacements) into which a person can get two feet; 10 feet ahead of the cartons place a picnic table; 30 feet ahead of it put a bushel basket. Twenty feet ahead of the basket place four wooden 12-inch square blocks, 12 inches apart and in a line with the team. On the goal lay a folding chair.

On signal, the first player on each team dashes to the three cartons, steps with both feet into each one, runs to the picnic table and crawls under it, jumps over the bushel basket, steps on each of the four wooden blocks, and continues to the goal, where he sets up the folding chair and sits on it. Then he stands, folds the chair, places it on the goal line, and hurries back to the starting line, repeating the same actions when he comes to an obstacle. He may not bypass any obstacle.

As he reaches the starting line he touches the extended hand of the second person and goes to the end of his line. In turn each member of the team proceeds in the same way. The first team to have all members conquer the obstacles wins the game.

Potatoes Are Ready!

Players form teams, which sit in circles. Give one person on each team (the starter) a potato, a paring knife, a small metal pan, and a paper bag.

On signal, the starter peels the potato, putting the peels in the paper bag. He then places the knife and the peeled potato in the pan and passes them to the player on his right. The second player cuts the potato in half, places the halves and the knife in the pan, and passes them to his right. The third player cuts a slice from one half of the potato and passes everything on. In turn, each player continues to slice and pass.

When the last player finishes cutting a slice from the potato, he hands the pan with the much-handled spud and the knife to the starter. The starter of the team which finishes first stands and shouts, "Potatoes are ready!" and his team wins the game.

Basket Pass

Place the following items in each of two picnic baskets: paper plate, paper cup, fork, spoon, can opener, small pan, small can of pork and beans, and a napkin. The players form a circle, facing alternately in and out. Those facing in are Team 1; those facing out, Team 2. Select a starter for each team and give him an empty basket and one of the full baskets. He holds the empty basket and places the full one on the ground in front of him.

On signal, the starter passes the empty basket to his teammate on the right, who passes it on around the circle. Then the starter begins passing the items from the other basket, one at a time, to his right. He may pass the items in any order, but the napkin must be last. He does not pass the basket which held the items.

The last player of the team, who has received the empty basket first, is putting the items into it as they come. The napkin is his cue to start passing the items one at a time to his left, back to the starter. After the last item has left his hands he passes the empty basket. The starter has been placing the items back in his basket. When all items are replaced and he receives the empty basket, he holds it aloft and shouts, "All is ready!" The first team to complete the action wins the relay.

Pan and Can Pass

Players stand in a circle, facing alternately in and out. Those facing in are Team 1; those facing out, Team 2. Select a starter on each team and give him a small pan and a can of pork and beans. The starter holds the pan upside down in his right hand and places the can on the pan.

On signal, the starter of each team passes the pan and can of beans to the right hand of the person on his right, who passes in the same way to his right. Players should not use their left hands to pass, but if the can falls off the pan, the player replaces it before continuing.

When the last person on the team holds the pan and can, he passes them to his own left hand and then to the left hand of the player on his left. This time right hands are not used. In turn, each person passes the items to the left until the starter has the pan and can of beans. He holds them aloft, one in each hand, to indicate that his team has finished. The first team to finish wins the game.

Strange Going

Draw a starting line and 60 feet from it indicate a goal line. Players form teams of six and stand in single files behind the starting line. Ask each team to number off consecutively until each player has a number. Each member of a team is to proceed to the goal line and back by a different form of locomotion. Players of all teams which have the same number use the same method of locomotion. Number 1's hop on one foot to and from the goal; 2's skip; 3's gallop; 4's walk placing the heel of one foot at the toe of the other foot; 5's use a skating motion; 6's walk quickly, but may not run, to and from the goal.

On signal, Number 1 of each team hops on one foot to the goal and returns to the starting line. (He may change feet en route but may not run or walk between changes.) As soon as he crosses the starting line, he touches the extended hand of Number 2 and goes to the end of his line. The second player immediately starts skipping for the goal. Play continues with each member of the team following his assigned method of locomotion, as he proceeds to and from the goal line. The first team to complete the action wins the relay.

Rubber Band Stretch

Players form teams and stand in single files. Give the first player of each team a 1-inch-wide rubber band (cut from an old inner tube).

On signal, the first player on each team goes through the rubber band by putting it over his head, passing it down his body, and stepping from it. As soon as he steps from the rubber band, he picks it up and hands it to the second player on his team. Passing through the band continues until the last player completes his turn. He runs to the head of the line and gives the rubber band to the first player, who twirls it to indicate his team has finished. The first team to finish wins the relay.

RACE EVENTERS

Long Potato Peel

Players stand abreast in a line. Give each one a potato and a dull paring knife.

On signal, each player starts paring his potato and tries to keep the peel in one continuous strip. The person who is first to complete the feat wins the title, "the best long potato peeler." If no one succeeds in achieving one continuous strip, the individual presenting the longest one wins the event.

Change on the Go

Mark a starting line and 60 feet from it indicate a goal line. Players line up abreast and toe the starting line.

Blow a whistle to start the players hopping to the goal. When the whistle blows again everyone sits on the ground, takes off both shoes, and puts them on again. When the whistle sounds again, the players continue to hop toward the goal. The first player to cross the goal line wins the race.

Snatch Race

Between two trees or benches tie a rope about 4 feet from the ground. On it hang strips of colored cloth 24 inches long and 2 inches wide, one for each participant. Spread the cloths along the entire rope so that they can be snatched readily. The length of the rope depends upon the number of participants. Mark a starting line 100 feet from the rope. Players toe the starting line and face the goal.

On signal, the players dash forward to the line of cloth strips; each player snatches one from the line and runs back to the starting line. First player to return to the line with a colored cloth wins the race.

Players may not snatch the cloths from other participants. Each person must secure his own cloth from the source of supply—the rope at the goal. Have assistants at the goal to replace fallen cloths so that everyone has a chance to get a cloth.

Tie and Button Hustle

Players are in couples. The men sit in a line facing the leader and each woman stands at the right side of her partner. Give each man a piece of 4×6-inch cloth, a threaded needle, and a large button. Also give each man a piece of colored cloth the length and width of a man's tie to put around his neck.

On signal, each man commences sewing the button on the cloth and his partner proceeds to add a bit of dash to his attire by tying a bow with the colored cloth. Buttons must be sewed on securely and bows neatly tied. The first couple to complete the action wins the race.

Spud and Spoon

Mark a starting line and 60 feet from it indicate a goal line. Players stand in a line along the starting line. Give everyone a tablespoon and potato. Each player places the potato on his spoon.

On signal, each player races to the goal, carrying the potato on his spoon with his right hand. At the goal line he transfers the spoon and potato to his left hand and heads back toward the starting line. The first player carrying the potato on his spoon across the starting line wins the race.

If a potato falls while a player is en route, he must stop, pick up the potato, replace it on the spoon, and proceed.

Potato Race

Mark a starting line and 60 feet from it indicate a goal line. Give each contestant a potato. The players toe the starting line and place the potatoes on their heads.

On signal, each player hurries to the goal, balancing the potato on his head. At the goal line he must kneel on both knees and then return to the starting line. The first player to cross it with the potato on his head wins the race.

If a potato falls from a player's head, he may stop, replace it, and continue. This is the only time he may touch the potato during the race.

Speedy Letter Formers

Have the players form groups of twelve. Assign an area to each group.

Call a letter—for example, A. The players of each team immediately try to arrange themselves in a standing position to form the capital letter A. Everyone on the team must form a part of the letter in order to score. The team first to form a recognizable A scores a point.

Continue by calling various letters of the alphabet. The team with the highest score at the end of a designated time wins

Potato Push and Carry

Mark a starting line and 20 feet from it indicate a goal line. Players stand abreast at the starting line. Give each player a tablespoon and a potato, which he places directly behind the starting line.

On signal, each player begins pushing his potato with the tablespoon toward the goal line. As soon as he crosses it, he picks up the potato, places it on the spoon, and races back to the starting line. If the potato tumbles on the return trip, the player must stop, pick it up, place it on the spoon, and continue. The first player to carry the potato across the starting line wins the race.

Watch the Spills

Mark a starting line and 15 feet from it indicate a goal line. Players stand abreast at the starting line. From a pail of water, fill paper cups to the brim and give one to each player.

On signal, each player, carrying his paper cup, hops on one foot to the goal line. As he crosses it, he may shift to the other foot to hop back to the starting line. The player with the smoothest hop— the one who has the most water remaining in his cup—wins the race.

Nail Drivers

Feminine contestants gather around designated tables. Give each contestant six 2-inch nails, a hammer, and a 1-foot length of 4 × 4 lumber.

On signal, each contestant drives the nails into her piece of wood. First person to drive the six nails into the wood wins the contest. Bent-over nails do not qualify, but the player may remove any bent nails, straighten them, and try driving them into the wood again.

Nail Driving on Time. Give each feminine contestant a handful of nails. On signal each person begins driving the nails into the wood and continues for three minutes. Call time and have each player count the number of nails she has driven. One point is scored for each nail completely driven into the wood. Two points are deducted for each nail that is not completely driven into the wood or is bent over. Before time is called a player may remove the bent nails. The contestant with the most points wins the event.

Clothespin Race

Between two trees suspend a clothesline and 60 feet from it mark a starting line. Adjust the height of the rope according to the height of the contestants. Players stand abreast and toe the starting line. Give each player a small box and a black crayon, and have the players print their first names on the boxes. Collect the crayons. Each person places his box, name facing the goal, on the ground ahead of him. Distribute six clothespins to every player to deposit in the boxes.

On signal, each player picks up one clothespin, runs to the clothesline, and fastens the pin to it with one hand, holding the other hand behind his back. If his clothespin falls off the line, he must pick it up and replace it with one hand. As soon as the pin is on the line, the player hurries back to the line, gets another pin, and repeats the performance until all six pins are on the line. The first person to place his six pins on the line and resume his place at the starting line wins the race.

Suggestion: Restrict the number of participants at one time to eight.

Have assistants to supervise the placement of the pins to see that a pin is on the line before the player returns to the starting line. Any pins that fall off the line because of the other players' activity should not be counted against the individual who placed them on the line.

Horsepower

Mark a starting line and 60 feet from it indicate a goal line. Have the players pair up—a man paired with a boy. Ask each man (horse) to get down on his hands and knees directly behind the starting line. Request each boy (jockey) to mount his horse.

On signal, the horse and jockey race for the goal line. As they proceed to the goal, the jockey encourages his four-legged steed to turn on the horsepower. The first horse and jockey to cross the goal wins the race. If at any time the jockey falls off, the horse must stop and let his rider re-mount before running on. The jockey must be on the horse when they cross the goal line.

Tent Pitch

Players form teams of four. Give each team a tent kit: an old sheet (single bed size), a ball of heavy twine, scissors, two broom handles, a dozen 3-inch nails, and a hammer. Assign an area to each group. Have a committee of judges.

On signal, each team takes its supplies to the assigned area and within a designated time attempts to pitch a tent. Players may use only the items that are included in their tent kits.

Call time and ask each group to sit beside its creation. Request the committee of judges to view each outdoor housing unit and decide which one most resembles a tent.

A simple version of a pup tent is readily achieved. Place the sheet on the ground to determine its length, pound a broom handle into the ground at each end of the sheet, suspend a length of twine between the two handles, place the sheet over the twine and center it; then secure the bottom of the sheet to the ground by driving six nails into each side of it.

Suggestion: To get the tents dismantled and supplies returned, follow this activity with Tent Down.

Tent Down

This is a follow-up race to conduct after Tent Pitch (see above). Ask each group to select a bearer of supplies. The committee of judges sits at tables placed in a line 20 feet from each group so that each bearer of supplies covers the same distance in taking his supplies to the judges.

On signal, each group dismantles its tent, neatly organizes the equipment, and gives every item used in constructing the tent to the bearer of supplies. He hurries to the committee and gives the tent kit to one of the judges who immediately takes inventory of the items. The first bearer of supplies to check in the sheet, twine (used and unused), scissors, two broom handles, a dozen 3-inch nails, and a hammer wins the race for his group.

Steady, Please!

Players form two teams which face each other in lines about 10 feet apart. Have a medium-size pan filled with water, a clear plastic container, and six tablespoons for each team. Give six tablespoons to the first player on each team and place the pan on the ground in front of him. Place the plastic container in front of the last person.

On signal, the first player of each team fills a spoon with water and passes it to the second, who passes it on. The first player continues to fill the spoons with water, one at a time, and pass them on.

When the last player receives a spoon, he pours what remains of the water into the plastic container and immediately starts the spoon back up the line. Spoons are going in both directions, for the spoons containing the water are sent down the line, while the empty ones are on their way back to the beginning to be filled again.

At the end of 3 minutes call a halt and ask each team to present its plastic container. The team with the most water in the container wins the game.

Shoppers' Scramble

On a large picnic table place the following items or a similar variety: old sweaters, pairs of gloves and men's colored socks (do not keep the pairs together), unwanted costume jewelry, towels, and sheets. Heap the items on the table. Draw a starting line 10 feet from the table. Have a committee of at least four judges to help in scoring. Each judge has a list of the items with their values and some 3×5-inch cards or pieces of paper.

On signal, the shoppers rush to the bargain table and attempt to get as many items as possible within a designated time. Since the items possess different values, madame shopper must use her best technique to get the most for her struggle. Players score points as follows:

Sweater	20 points
Sheet	10
Pair of gloves	50
Pair of socks	50
Single glove	30
Single sock	30
Piece of costume jewelry	40
Towel	20

Call time and ask each shopper to check her bargains with the committee of judges, who evaluate her haul and issue a card to verify her achievement. After all merchandise is checked, the player with the most points is the winner of the struggle.

OUTDOOR
FUN MAKERS

CONTENTS

Getting individuals to use their eyes and ears outdoors is an awakening to the beauty and wonders of nature. In the outdoors everyone has the potentiality of being a discoverer, for the thrill of finding a bird, plant, tree, or shrub that is new to an individual is always present.

While the wide open spaces are not as wide as they once were—and squatter rights are limited to enjoying for a short time a particular area provided for the public—feeling at home in the outdoors is part of an American's cherished heritage.

Learning to know friends in nature is similar to becoming acquainted with human friends. Just as one recognizes his friends by their faces, voices, clothes, habits, and various other characteristics, one can learn to identify birds. Some individuals speak readily and introduce themselves. In their social realm some birds happily announce their names; for instance, the Eastern Phoebe introduces himself without any formality with "Phoe–be." Likewise the black-capped chickadee, the Eastern whippoorwill, and the bobwhite clearly state their names. The cardinal, the only red bird with a crest, is a sociable bird, for before he is even acquainted he expects a good time and remarks from the top of a tree, "What–cheer, cheer, cheer." Besides the social beckoning of the cardinal there is his bright red attire which one never forgets, for the black patch at the base of his bill is the only part of his wardrobe that is not red.

Some humans are boisterous, and that is equally true in the bird realm. The crow in flight sometimes appears to be rowing through the air as he utters a husky, "Ca–ah, ca–ah, ca–ah"; and the blue jay, the Paul Revere of the forest, announces to the other creatures that human beings are approaching. In contrast one finds the modest Eastern bluebird, the only blue bird that dons a red breast. As many human friends, he has a habit of being round-shouldered when he rests, while the Eastern Phoebe is the opposite, being known for his erect posture and his distinguishing custom of persistently wagging his tail as he perches. The house wren has the habit of scolding and cocking his tail over his back—a help in identifying the small brown-clothed fellow. Nuthatches are like those individuals one often hears comments about who always appear to do things in an opposite way, for they are the only tree-climbing birds that go down the trunk of a tree headfirst. They are so agile at climbing that they do not even brace their tails against the tree. Unlike the nuthatches are the woodpeckers, who use their tails as braces as they move up the trunk of a tree in their search for insects.

323

Additional helps in identifying our feathered friends include size; silhouette in the sky; shape, size, and color of bill; shape of tail; actions in climbing and perching; nesting habits; choice of food; and the range in which to be found. Besides the basic color of the bird's wardrobe there are the wing bars he may wear—lines of contrasting color at midwing; also, his breast might be plain, spotted, or striped; and he may have a stripe over the eye or a ring around it. While one may remember a person by the color of his hair or the lack of it, in the bird realm the color of the bird's crown is significant in identification of him. He may have a patch of a different color on the crown of his head, and the crown might be striped or barred or it may match his basic wardrobe.

Animals as well as birds have identifying features. Some of the ways to learn to identify members of the animal kingdom are listening to their characteristic sounds; observing the color of their fur; noting distinguishing footprints or tracks; knowing their size; and discovering their habits of eating and housing and their other activities.

In becoming acquainted with furry friends one becomes aware that curiosity is not only a human trait: for example, while walking through a field one may see a perky little gopher sitting up near the opening of his underground home, observing the behavior of the human animal. The gray fellow with the bushy tail curled over his back is on the alert, but he is quite undisturbed as he tosses the shells of his nut at the human who gazes up at him.

As one glances at the squirrel sitting on a branch he may notice the dancing of the leaves and branches in the strong wind. It is interesting to observe how the trees dance differently. He may, also, notice the differences in the trees and on closer observation the variation in the leaves.

Some of the identifying characteristics of trees are given in the following list:

Identification	*Example*
Life of Leaf	
All or nearly all leaves new each year (deciduous)	maple, birch, oak
Extends through several years (evergreen trees and shrubs)	needle-leafed trees (spruce, pine, Japanese yew, Pfitzer's juniper) and non-deciduous broad-leafed trees

Identification	*Example*

Arrangement of Leaves on Stem

Alternate	Eastern white oak
Opposite	maple
Alternate and spiral	willow
Whorled or cyclic	catalpa

Types of Leaf

Simple (consisting of one simple blade)	maple
Compound (consisting of several leaflets)	locust
Palmately compound (leaflets joined at the end of the petiole—the leaf stalk or slender stem which supports the blade of a foliage leaf)	horsechestnut
Pinnately compound (leaflets joined to the sides of the central axis of the leaf)	bitternut hickory

Arrangement of Principal Veins

Resembling a feather	elm
Resembling the fingers of a hand	maple

Design of Leaf

Shape (usually characteristic of a species)	long, narrow leaves of the willow
Tip and bottom (help in identification)	uneven heart shape of the linden
Edges or margins (often characteristic)	fine-toothed edge of birch leaf

Other details to note in the identification of trees include the following:

Leaf Texture	*Leaf Color*
Satiny smooth	Vary from deep green to yellow green
Waxy	
Leathery	Silvery
Hairy	Hues of red
Velvety	Bright autumn colors
Rough	Brown in late autumn

Silhouette of Trees

With leaves or needles	Without leaves in winter

Other Items of Identification

Bark (varies in color and texture)	Flowers
	Fruits

During the dormant season of deciduous trees examine:
Buds (which differ in size and form)
Leaf scars (which differ in shape and pattern)

As one practices using his eyes and ears outdoors he will want to add wild and garden flowers to his host of nature friends. Some of the details to observe in gaining their acquaintance include:

Shape of plant	Height
Kind of petals	Fragrance
Shape of leaves	Habitat: sun, shade, kind of soil, type
Color	of climate

Getting to observe flowers, trees, birds, and animals is an opening to nature's vast treasures. Whether an individual looks forward, back, sideways, up, or down, he is bound to discover something of interest in the outdoors. He needs merely to listen to enjoy nature's multiple chorus which gives repeated performances.

In the following games which take the players to the outdoors, the most valuable equipment used in playing them are the eyes and ears of the participants. To help the leader in his selection of the kind of activity to use with his group the games are divided among these classifications: defrosters, socializers, wide awakers, sense alerters, and creative fun makers. For ready reference, games falling under these divisions, are listed at the beginning of the chapter.

With nature supplying its treasure chest of beauty and wonder, the additional items needed to play the games are easily secured. In most instances the supplies consist of guidebooks to flowers, birds, and trees; 4 × 6-inch cards, paper, scissors, and pencils. Some of the creative activities of the outdoors require finger paint, paper, crayons, water colors, brushes, clay, mounting stock, as well as paper and pencils. The most unusual items include several pairs of tin shears and some No. 10 tin cans.

DEFROSTERS

Outdoor Orientation

For each player prepare a 4 × 6-inch card with the following questions written on the left side of it:

Where is space or equipment provided for building fires?
Under which trees are picnic tables found?
Near what landmark can one obtain water?
What landmark is near the place provided for active activities?
Under what kind of trees is there space for quiet activities?
What posted signs do you observe in the area? List them.
How many wastebaskets do you see?

Give a card and pencil to each player.

On signal, each player starts the search for the answers to the queries on his card. He will find the answers to all of the questions in a designated area. After the allotted time, reassemble the group and allow the person finding all the answers to read his list. If the list is correct, he wins the title of being "readily oriented to his environment." Have all the players make the necessary additions or corrections to the answers to the questions on their lists. Ask the players to keep the cards and use the facilities in the places that are provided.

Suggestion: Contact the person or group in charge of the outdoor area to be used regarding the rules for the particular section, and modify the questions accordingly.

Tree Threesome

Using garden stakes, prepare in triplicate the name of a tree for each pair of players. Prior to the game, place one of the stakes in front of the tree whose name it bears. Place the remaining two sets of names in two piles. Distribute the stakes, and be sure that there are two stakes in circulation for each tree. On signal, each player seeks the person having the same name of a tree. When the two find one another, they are partners and must search for the third stake. When they find the tree, they remove the stake and hurry to the leader with the three stakes. The first couple thus to complete the Tree Threesome wins the game.

Triplicate Wild Flowers. Imprint the name of a wild flower on triplicate garden stakes. Play the same as Tree Threesome.

Trios of Garden Flowers. Imprint the name of a garden flower on triplicate garden stakes. Play the same as Tree Threesome.

Vegetable Triplets. Imprint the name of a vegetable or fruit on triplicate garden stakes. Play the same as Tree Threesome.

SOCIALIZERS

Leaf Selection

Secure ten different kinds of leaves (obtain permission to take them). Have enough leaves to give each group of six a leaf of each kind. Players group, and each group forms a circle and sits on the grass. Give a 4 × 6-inch card, a pencil, and ten leaves to each group. Have each group select a recorder.

Within a designated time, each group tries to identify the ten leaves. The recorder writes the names of the leaves which the group decides are correct. At the end of the allotted time, call a halt to the leaf identification. Ask the team that identified ten or the number closest to it to have the recorder read the list. He shows each leaf as he reads its name. If the identifications are correct, the team wins the game.

Suggestion: For a follow-up to the identification, have the players locate the trees bearing the leaves on the winning list.

Locate the Trees

On a list for each group of six players write:

Names of four deciduous trees (lose all or most of their leaves annually) having simple leaves (consisting of one continuous blade)
Names of four deciduous trees having compound leaves (consisting of several leaflets)
Names of four deciduous trees having leaves that grow on the stem opposite one another
Names of four trees having leaves that are alternately arranged on the stem
Names of four evergreen trees
Names of two trees having opposite leaves and branches

Prior to the game place a garden stake bearing the name of the tree in front of each tree to be located. Have the players form groups of six, and give each one a list of trees and a pencil. Ask each group to appoint a recorder.

Within a given time each group sets out to locate the trees whose names appear on the list by looking for the stakes bearing the names of the trees. As the members find a tree the recorder makes a check next to it to indicate they have located it. They must also remember its location.

After the allotted time, call a halt to the search, and ask the recorder for the group finding all or most of the trees to read the names of the trees they have checked. The group must prove its answers by showing the other players where each tree is located. If the group's findings are correct, the members are acclaimed the "best tree locaters."

Some of the trees which might be included in the list are the following:

Deciduous trees having simple leaves:

American beech	Common basswood
Eastern white oak	White basswood
Bur oak	Hawthorn (flat-topped)
Sugar maple	White elm
Silver maple	Rock elm
Red maple	Slippery elm

Deciduous trees having compound leaves:

Black walnut	Honey locust
Bitternut hickory	Black locust
Shagbark hickory	Box elder
Mountain ash	Blue ash
Kentucky coffeetree	Black ash
White ash	

Deciduous trees having leaves that grow opposite one another on the stem:

Sugar maple	Blue ash
Silver maple	Black ash
Red maple	White ash
Box elder	Bitternut hickory
Shagbark hickory	

(On both the hickory trees the leaflets are opposite on the twig, while the individual leaves are alternate.)

Deciduous trees having leaves that are alternately arranged on the stem:

Black walnut	Scarlet hawthorn
Aspen	Black willow
American beech	Paper birch
Eastern white oak	Sassafrass
White elm	Common basswood
Slippery elm	White basswood
Rock elm	Mountain ash
Sycamore	

Evergreens:

White pine	White spruce
Jack pine	Black spruce
Virginia scrub pine	Red spruce
Eastern hemlock	Bur pine
Carolina spruce	Northern balsam
Southern balsam	

Trees having opposite leaves and limbs:

Maple	Dogwood
Ash	Horsechestnut

Work Before Food

Players form groups of three. Give each group a pair of tin shears, a No. 10 tin can (with one end removed leaving no jagged edges), a paper towel, a hamburger turner, butter or other fat, three hamburgers, and matches (the number depends upon the fire-lighting skill of the players). Assign one member of each group to create a stove from the tin can; the second and third are fuel-gatherers and fire-builders; all three help in frying the hamburgers.

Build the fires in permitted areas only; do not allow the fire-builders to select the places.

On signal, the stove-designer starts cutting and fashioning the

No. 10 tin can into a stove by cutting a 2- to 3-inch opening at the bottom of the can. He creates a chimney by making a cut near the top of the tin can on the side that is opposite the opening. While he creates the stove, the second and third members of the group go in search of tinder—material which ignites quickly—with the thickness of a match and kindling twigs ranging in thickness from the size of a pencil to the size of one's thumb. Fuel-gatherers may take their material from the ground or use dead branches from trees if permission is secured. To be prepared for dampness have a bag of charcoal available.

As soon as the fuel-gatherers return, they light the fire and place the stove, which should be ready, in position. When the top of the can is hot, have one of the threesome grease the top of the cooking area, wipe it off thoroughly with a paper towel, and then add butter or other fat to be used in frying the hamburgers. One member places the burgers on the stove; the other prepares to turn them at the proper time.

The first group to complete the previous action and to have their hamburgers ready to eat wins the event.

Pancake Is Ready! Have the cook present a brown—not burned— pancake prepared on the top of his unique stove. The first team whose cook's pancake meets the requirements shouts, "Pancake is ready!" and wins the game. Play the same as Work Before Food, substituting pancake ingredients for the hamburgers.

First Fire! Instead of creating a stove as the players did in Work Before Food, each group of three uses a stove provided by the park or other service. Each member of the trio gathers wood and helps build and start the fire. The first threesome to have the wood burning shouts, "First fire!" and wins the activity. Charcoal can be substituted for wood.

Let's Eat! Play the same as First Fire with the addition of having the individuals prepare and cook an entire meal outdoors. The first trio to be ready to serve shouts, "Let's eat!"

Suggestion: The menu should depend upon the choice of the individuals in the group as well as upon their experience in outdoor cookery. In some instances an unburned marshmallow is a real achievement to the novice in outdoor cooking.

WIDE AWAKERS

What Is It?

Go through an area in advance and select a number of trees, shrubs, and flowers which the players are to identify. Place a stake containing a number in front of each object to be identified. Keep a list of the numbers and the correct names of the objects. Have the players form groups of six. Give each group a 4 × 6-inch card and a pencil. Ask each group to appoint a recorder.

On signal, everyone hastens to find the marked objects. If the members of a group are able to identify an object, the recorder writes the number of it on the left side of the card and the name on the right side.

After a designated time, reassemble the players and have them sit on the grass. Have the recorder of each group read the identifications. For each object named with its general title, for example, "oak," or "ash," the group scores one point and the recorder marks it on the group's card. If the group lists specifically, "red oak," or "black ash," the players score three points. A "trillium" scores one point while a "nodding trillium" scores three points. The team with the most points wins the activity.

Colors to Remember

Take the group to a large garden containing an array of different kinds of flowers of various colors. Note in advance the various colors of the flowers and the names of them and keep a list. Have a 4 × 6-inch card and a pencil for each player.

Allow the group five minutes to observe the flowers in the garden. After the allotted time, reassemble the players and ask them to sit a short distance from the garden so that they cannot see the flowers. Distribute a card and a pencil to each person. Request the players to list the colors of the flowers they recall. The players do not need to know the names of the flowers.

Call a halt to the activity and request the player with the longest list to read the colors. Have the group return to the garden, and ask the player to point out the flowers whose colors he listed. If the colors actually exist in the garden, he wins the color-listing game.

The following lists give a few colors the players might mention for several kinds of flowers.

Flower	Color
Aster, Giants of California	Dark blue, light blue, lavender
Calendula, Sunshine	Buttercup yellow
Cardinal climber	Cardinal
Chrysanthemum, Eldorado	Yellow with dark center
Marigold, African	Orange
Butterfly flower	Pink, rose, white
Hollyhock	Maroon
Gaillardia	Bronze
Mourning Bride	Salmon

Plant Recognition. Have the players list the colors and give the names of the plants. Play the same as Colors To Remember.

SENSE ALERTERS

Senses Outdoors

Ask the players to sit on the grass. Give each a 4 × 6-inch card and a pencil.

Within a designated time, each player lists the objects or creatures he sees, hears, or smells. He does not have to list specific names unless he knows them (see suggestions below). After the allotted time, call the listing to a halt and ask the person with the longest list to read it. If the list is correct, the player is complimented for having the best "tools" for enjoying the outdoors.

Some of the objects and creatures the players might see, hear, or smell include:

See	Hear	Smell
Colorful birds	Chorus of birds	Fragrant flowers
Beautiful flowers	Solo of a bird	Grass freshly cut
Shrubs in bloom	Thundering waves	Aroma of a flowering shrub
Varied greens in the leaves and grass	Call of a pheasant	Scent of the evergreens
Different shapes of the trees	Rustle of leaves	Wood or charcoal from a nearby grill
Variation in bark	Chirping cricket	Meat being grilled
Busy ants	Croaking of a frog	Leaf mold
Clouds in the sky	Laughter of picnickers	Decayed wood
Gopher sitting up	Buzzing bee	Wet earth
Squirrel using a branch for a trapeze	Bark of a dog	Sweet clover
Toad hopping gaily	Waves breaking on a beach	Air before rain
Dancing leaves of the trees	Splash of a diving bird	Breeze off the lake

Open Ears. Have the players list only the creatures or objects that they hear. Play the same as Senses Outdoors.

Eyes on the Alert. Have the players list only the creatures or objects that they see. Play the same as Senses Outdoors.

Nose Knows. Have the players list only the objects that they smell. Play the same as Senses Outdoors.

Woodland Map

Players form groups of four. Give each group a piece of 8½ × 11-inch cardboard and a pencil.

Within a designated time, each group takes a certain area, out of view of the other players, and proceeds to make a map of the section by drawing in the silhouettes of trees, shrubs, plants, giving the names of the ones the members know and indicating paths or any items that are significant.

After the allotted time, call the map making to a halt and re-assemble the players. Since the test of a good map is its usefulness and accuracy, use it for a guide in checking the area with the players. Allow the players to decide which map is both useful and accurate. The group producing the map meeting these requirements wins the game. Ask the group whose map is being checked to offer no assistance in locating items.

Seeing Nature

Players sit in a wooded area. Select one player to be "it."

"It" initiates the activity by saying, for example, "I see a tree whose name begins with *B*." As soon as a player thinks he knows the tree, he offers his answer, for instance, "basswood." If the answer is correct, the player scores two points and is "it." When the answer is incorrect, any other player may give an answer. If he gives the correct name, the individual scores two points.

When the players are unable to guess the name of the object, "it" reveals the name. If his observation is correct, he scores two points for stumping the group. He selects someone to take his role.

The players are not restricted to the names of trees. They may use the initial of any object or creature which everyone may observe from the place at which he is sitting. While the players may use the same initial as often as they wish, they may not give the name of an object or creature more than once.

Find the Trees

Players are in groups of six. Give each group the pictures, but not the names, of ten trees that are in the immediate area. Have a balance of common and less-known trees in each set, so that every group will have an equal chance to locate them.

On signal, each group carefully examines the pictures and then sets out to find the corresponding trees in the wooded area. If the players do not know the name of a tree but can identify the tree as the same one for which they have a picture, reward their powers of observation by accepting it for an answer.

After a designated time, call the search to an end. Reassemble the players. Ask the group finding the assigned ten trees or most of them to prove their answers by showing the other players the location of each tree for which the members have a picture. If the trees are there, the group wins the game.

Seek the Wild Flowers

Give each group of six a wild flower guidebook that has colored illustrations, a 4 × 6-inch card, and a pencil. On each card write the names of six wild flowers which each group is to locate.

Armed with the guidebook each group sets out to find the specimens. They must note carefully where each flower is located. Flowers may not be handled.

At the end of a designated time, call a halt to the search and reassemble the players. Ask the group finding the six flowers or the closest number to guide the players to the locations so that they can check to see if the flower is an actuality or a hopeful wish. For actual flowers identified correctly the group scores five points. The team with the highest score wins the wild flower search.

Name the Garden Flowers. Give each group the names of ten garden flowers to identify and a book or catalog containing illustrations of the flowers. Play the same as Seek the Wild Flowers.

Head the File

While hiking on a path in the woods or in a park, the players walk in a double file.

Upon seeing a tree, flower, bird, or animal of particular interest, ask the first couple to identify it. Both players may offer an answer. If the couple successfully identifies the object or creature of nature, the twosome remains at the head of the file.

Request the second couple to identify the next creature or object. Continue by calling on each couple in turn.

Any couple that fails to identify an object or creature goes to the end of the file, and every other couple moves forward one place. The couple remaining at the head of the file the longest wins the game.

Roadside Cribbage

Request each player to gather twenty pebbles. The players hike along a path or in a park.

Everyone is on the alert to see and identify as many trees, flowers, animals, birds, insects, reptiles, and other creatures or objects of nature as possible, since each one has the following scoring value:

Each domestic animal or flock seen and identified	1 point
Each common tree or flower seen and identified (specify list of common trees)	1 point
Each bird or flock seen and identified	1 point

Each uncommon tree seen and identified (any tree not specified
    on the common list)   2 points
Each wild animal or reptile seen and identified   2 points
Each insect seen and identified   2 points

Whenever a player sees an object or creature, he points it out to the group and states its name. If he is the first individual to identify the object or creature correctly, he throws away the specified number of pebbles determined by the scoring value listed for each identification. No one is permitted to leave the group to seek objects or creatures. The player who is first to dispose of his pebbles through correct identifications wins the game.

Tree Friends

Have the players form two teams, and ask each to select a captain. Give each captain twenty stones.

As the group hikes along a path or roadside or in a park, the member of any team may exclaim when he sees a tree that he recognizes, "I see a tree friend." Stop at the tree and ask the others to help in deciding if the player really knows his tree friend. If he does, the captain of his team may throw a stone away. The first team to dispose of its stones by identifying twenty trees wins the game.

Suggestion: Whenever a player finds a tree he knows, add some information about the tree which helps other individuals to make some additional tree friends. An illustrated tree guide proves useful.

Flight of Seeds

Players form groups of six. Give each group a 3 × 5-inch card containing the names of ten plants and trees having seeds that are provided with parachutes or wings. Secure permission in advance to take the seeds and caution the players to be careful not to damage any branches of trees or plants. Label any trees or plants with which the players are unfamiliar. If a cattail is one of the items on the list, secure one or more in advance, since they are usually difficult to reach unless one has boots. Cut the cattail in segments and place on a table or carton that is available to the players.

On signal, each group is off to find the ten specimens. The first team to return with the correct items wins the "seedy search." Ask the other players to sit on the grass while the winning team presents the items and names them.

If the groups are unable to find the ten items within a reasonable time, call the search to a halt. Ask the group finding most of the items to present and name them. If they are correct, the group wins the search. Some of the seeds which might be used in the game include:

Parachutes	*Wings*
Dandelion	Maple
Milkweed	Elm
Cottonwood tree	Box elder
Cattail	Ash
Sycamore	Basswood

CREATIVE FUN MAKERS

Landscape

Provide for each participant a piece of 14 × 10-inch mounting board to substitute for an easel, a sheet of drawing paper the same size, thumbtacks, and crayons. Create an informal atmosphere by having each player obtain his drawing supplies from a table, move about, and sit anywhere he feels affords the angle of the landscape which he wishes to draw. Discourage loud conversation so that each person can enter the sanctuary of nature, listen and observe, and receive a message to express in his drawing.

Each player expresses how he feels about the landscape, or he may select a section of the landscape to interpret in crayon. After an allotted time, reassemble the players, and have each creator tell one thing he likes about his drawing. After everyone has a chance to make a positive comment about his own drawing, request each player to hold up his drawing while the members of the group in turn offer a positive remark about the landscape drawing. Negative comments are not allowed, for the sole purpose of the activity is encouraging creativity and expression through elements of the out-doors.

Suggestion: Each player may keep his drawing, or the creations may be used in a display of nature activities at a future date.

Waterscape. Provide water color paints, brushes, water, and paper, which the players will use in painting a water scene. Play the same as Landscape.

Suggestion: Waterscapes or water scenes may be created with crayons or finger paints as well as with water colors.

Cloudscape. Provide finger paints in various colors, paper, a pan of water to wet the paper, and picnic tables on which to place the wet paper. Cover the tables with a plastic or newspaper covering before finger painters go into action.

Each painter may stand or sit as he uses his fingers to depict the curly, light, feathery clouds or the massive cottony heaps which stimulate the imagination in seeing forms of birds and animals. The finger painter might also use his elbows to create bold effects which might in some cases symbolize the rain clouds that appear heavily ladened.

Play the same as Landscape.

Suggestion: Cloudscapes may, also, be painted with water colors or drawn with crayons.

Composite Arts

In addition to the supplies used in Landscape, Waterscape, and Cloudscape, have a supply of 8½ × 11-inch paper, lined music paper, clay, and pencils.

Allow the players ten minutes to wander quietly about a designated area and observe, hear, and absorb any of the beauty or wonders of the natural setting. After the allotted time, ask the group to assemble at the supply center—one or more picnic tables containing the creative tools of expression. Allow each player to select his medium of expression: painting, drawing, modeling, writing (prose or poetry), or do a variation of a bird song or other bit of song he heard. Everyone selects the materials he needs and finds his perfect spot for creating.

Within a designated time, reassemble the players and have everyone sit in a circle on the grass. Each artist presents his creation in turn, and every player makes one positive comment about his creative endeavor. When everyone has had a turn, the artist tells what he tried to express in his creation. No one may make any negative remarks about any creation, since encouragement in artistic attempts and an appreciation of the outdoors are the objectives of the activity.

Suggestion: Allow the individuals to keep their creative modes of expression or collect them and exhibit them in a display of nature activities at a future date.

Sturdy Mascot

Players are in teams of six.

On signal, each group searches in a designated area and selects a tree to be the group's mascot. After an allotted time, reassemble the groups. In turn have each group pantomime the name of the tree the members chose for a mascot. The team first to guess the mascot scores five points and gains the right to present the next mascot or to select the next group when the correct guessers already had a turn. If no one guesses the mascot, the actors announce the name of the chosen tree and have the honor of selecting the next actors. After all the groups have had a turn, the team with the highest score wins the activity.

Have the teams keep their mascots for new friends in nature.

Flower Chum. Have each group find a flower chum. Play the same as Sturdy Mascot.

Feathered Friend. Have each group find a feathered friend. Play the same as Sturdy Mascot.

Four-Legged Pal. Have each group adopt a four-legged creature for its pal. Play the same as Sturdy Mascot.

Tree Silhouettes

Players form groups of eight. Give each player scissors and a sheet of 8½ × 11-inch dark green drawing paper. Have a carton to collect waste paper.

Allow the players about five minutes to walk around a designated wooded area and to observe the silhouettes of the trees. Each person selects one tree whose silhouette he will create by cutting it from the drawing paper. Reassemble the players, and ask each group to sit together on the grass.

Within a specified time, each player cuts the silhouette of his selected tree from the drawing paper. After the allotted time, call a halt to the activity and ask the members of each group in turn to present their drawings to the others, who attempt to identify the silhouettes of the trees.

The first player to call the correct name scores five points for his team, and the player presenting the silhouette scores three points for his team for creating an identifiable silhouette. If the players are unable to identify a silhouette, the creator announces the name of the tree. His team, as well as the others, score one point for trying. At the conclusion of the presentations the team having the most points wins the silhouette-recognizing activity.

Have one individual pass the carton in which the players can put the waste paper. The players may keep the silhouettes which might motivate them in learning the identity of trees through this method. Have another player collect the scissors.

BIBLIOGRAPHY

BORST, EVELYNE. *The Book of Games for Boys and Girls: How to Lead and Play Them.* New York: The Ronald Press Co., 1953.

    Presents the psychology and value of play for elementary school boys and girls. Also, suggests techniques for developing leadership. Includes a wide selection of indoor and outdoor games requiring little or no equipment and many activities for picnics and special days: Columbus Day, Hallowe'en, Thanksgiving Day, Christmas, Lincoln's Birthday, Washington's Birthday, St. Patrick's Day, Easter, Arbor Day, and Bird Day.

DONNELLY, RICHARD J., HELMS, WILLIAM G., AND MITCHELL, ELMER D. *Active Games and Contests.* 2d ed.; New York: The Ronald Press Co., 1958.

    Acquaints the leader with all types of play activities of an active nature and offers games to fit almost any occasion which might arise. Two thousand odd games classified as Contests between Individuals; Contests between Groups; Games Resembling Contests; Goal, Tag, and Combat Games; Team Games; Water and Winter Activities. A companion volume to *Social Games for Recreation.*

HUNT, SARAH E., AND CAIN, ETHEL. *Games the World Around.* 2d ed.; New York: The Ronald Press Co., 1950.

    Contains four hundred folk games, contests, relays, and stunts for children from the ages six to sixteen. Representative of the following places: Africa, Alaska, Armenia, Belgium, Borneo, Burma, China, Cuba, Denmark, England, France, Germany, Greece, Hawaii, Holland, India, Ireland, Italy, Japan, Korea, Mexico, North American Indian, Norway, Palestine, Persia, Philippine Islands, Polynesia, Puerto Rico, Russia, Scotland, South and Central America, Spain, Sweden, Syria, Turkey.

KRAUS, RICHARD G. *Square Dances of Today and How to Teach and Call Them.* New York: The Ronald Press Co., 1950.

    A collection of square, circle, and longways dances, ice breakers, and mixers. Provides help in planning a lively program: lists dances for particular age groups, suggests square dance records with and without calls, offers methods for getting individuals into the swing, and includes musical scores within the nonprofessional pianist's range.

LEONHARD, CHARLES. *Recreation Through Music.* New York: The Ronald Press Co., 1952.

    Gives the recreational leader a background for presenting music as a medium of recreation. For a "sing" session it offers methods for planning, conducting, and interpreting songs, as well as including a long selective list of songs, many of which the recreational leader will wish to include in his repertoire.

INDEX